4

READING
EXPLORER

THIRD EDITION

PAUL MACINTYRE

DAVID BOHLKE

**NATIONAL
GEOGRAPHIC**
L E A R N I N G

Australia · Brazil · Mexico · Singapore · United Kingdom · United States

National Geographic Learning,
a Cengage Company

Reading Explorer 4
Third Edition

Paul MacIntyre and David Bohlke

Publisher: Andrew Robinson

Executive Editor: Sean Bermingham

Associate Development Editor: Yvonne Tan

Director of Global Marketing: Ian Martin

Heads of Regional Marketing:

Charlotte Ellis (Europe, Middle East and Africa)

Kiel Hamm (Asia)

Irina Pereyra (Latin America)

Product Marketing Manager: Tracy Bailie

Senior Production Controller: Tan Jin Hock

Associate Media Researcher: Jeffrey Millies

Art Director: Brenda Carmichael

Operations Support: Hayley Chwazik-Gee

Manufacturing Planner: Mary Beth Hennebury

Composition: MPS North America LLC

For permission to use material from this text or product, submit all requests online at **cengage.com/permissions** Further permissions questions can be emailed to **permissionrequest@cengage.com**

Student Book with Online Workbook:
ISBN-13: 978-0-357-12473-4

Student Book:
ISBN-13: 978-0-357-11629-6

National Geographic Learning
200 Pier Four Blvd
Boston, MA 02210
USA

Locate your local office at **international.cengage.com/region**

Visit National Geographic Learning online at **ELTNGL.com**
Visit our corporate website at **www.cengage.com**

Printed in China
Print Number: 01 Print Year: 2019

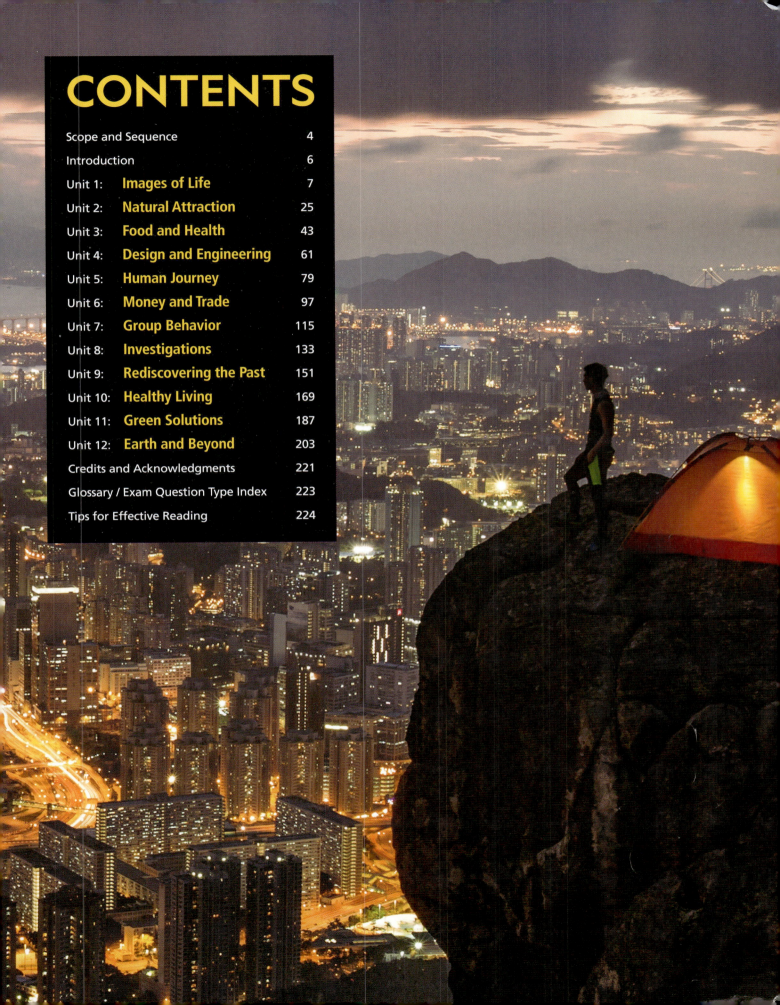

CONTENTS

Scope and Sequence   4

Introduction   6

Unit 1:   **Images of Life**   7

Unit 2:   **Natural Attraction**   25

Unit 3:   **Food and Health**   43

Unit 4:   **Design and Engineering**   61

Unit 5:   **Human Journey**   79

Unit 6:   **Money and Trade**   97

Unit 7:   **Group Behavior**   115

Unit 8:   **Investigations**   133

Unit 9:   **Rediscovering the Past**   151

Unit 10:   **Healthy Living**   169

Unit 11:   **Green Solutions**   187

Unit 12:   **Earth and Beyond**   203

Credits and Acknowledgments   221

Glossary / Exam Question Type Index   223

Tips for Effective Reading   224

SCOPE AND SEQUENCE

UNIT	THEME	READING	VIDEO
1	Images of Life	A: The Visual Village B: My Journey in Photographs	A Photographer's Life
2	Natural Attraction	A: Living Light B: Feathers of Love	Jellyfish
3	Food and Health	A: How Safe Is Our Food? B: The Battle for Biotech	Is Our Food Safe?
4	Design and Engineering	A: Design by Nature: Biomimetics B: Weaving the Future	Robotic Hands
5	Human Journey	A: The DNA Trail B: Fantastic Voyage	Cave Artists
6	Money and Trade	A: How Money Made Us Modern B: The Rise of Virtual Money	Take the Money … and Run?
7	Group Behavior	A: A Crowd in Harmony B: Our Online Behavior	Social Conformity
8	Investigations	A: Who Killed the Emperor? B: In the Crime Lab	Beating a Lie Detector
9	Rediscovering the Past	A: Virtually Immortal B: Lure of the Lost City	Archeology from Space
10	Healthy Living	A: Living Longer B: In Search of Longevity	You Are What You Eat
11	Green Solutions	A: Saving Water B: Technology as Trash	Your Water Footprint
12	Earth and Beyond	A: Planet Hunters B: The Threat from Space	Shooting Stars

READING SKILL	VOCABULARY BUILDING	CRITICAL THINKING
A: Understanding Words with Multiple Meanings B: Scanning for Information (1)—Short Answer Questions	A: Suffix -tic B: Synonyms of thus	A: Evaluating Pros and Cons B: Interpreting; Reflecting
A: Summarizing (1)—Using a Concept Map B: Identifying Figurative Language	A: Word root scend B: Suffix -ility	A: Speculating B: Interpreting/Applying; Speculating
A: Recognizing Cause and Effect Relationships (1) B: Evaluating Arguments	A: Suffix -wide B: Synonyms of diminish	A: Analyzing Solutions B: Evaluating Arguments and Ideas
A: Scanning for Information (2)—Matching Information to Paragraphs B: Recognizing Lexical Cohesion	A: Collocations with vital B: Prefix fore-	A: Applying Ideas B: Applying Ideas
A: Synthesizing Information B: Distinguishing Fact from Speculation	A: Collocations with rate B: Suffix -ous	A: Reflecting/Evaluating B: Reflecting
A: Understanding the Function of Sentences B: Summarizing (2)—Creating an Outline	A: Collocations with policy B: Word usage: principle vs. principal	A: Evaluating Pros and Cons B: Reflecting
A: Understanding Words from Context B: Understanding Word Roots and Affixes	A: Suffix -ant B: Collocations with pressure	A: Analyzing Information B: Applying Ideas; Reflecting
A: Evaluating Evidence B: Understanding Idiomatic Expressions	A: Collocations with dispute B: Word root leg	A: Interpreting/Reflecting B: Interpreting/Reflecting; Evaluating Reliability
A: Recognizing Ellipsis B: Scanning for Information (3)—Summary Completion	A: Collocations with virtual B: Word usage: legend vs. myth vs. folktale	A: Evaluating/Justifying B: Evaluating Pros and Cons; Reflecting
A: Recognizing Cause and Effect Relationships (2) B: Understanding Quantitative and Qualitative Data	A: Compound words with life B: Collocations with relief	A: Applying Ideas B: Relating to Personal Experience; Reflecting
A: Identifying Sources of Information B: Understanding a Writer's Attitude	A: Collocations with extent B: Collocations with substance	A: Evaluating Sources B: Inferring Attitude; Evaluating Solutions
A: Recognizing Cause and Effect Relationships (3) B: Interpreting Analogies	A: Prefix com- B: Prefix di-	A: Justifying an Opinion B: Evaluating Pros and Cons; Ranking Projects

READING EXPLORER brings the world to your classroom.

With *Reading Explorer* you learn about real people and places, experience the world, and explore topics that matter.

What you'll see in the Third Edition:

Real-world stories give you a better understanding of the world and your place in it.

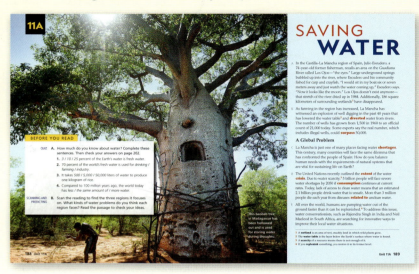

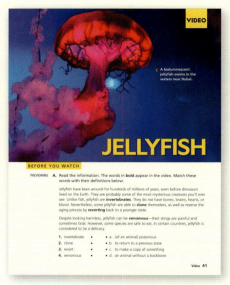

National Geographic Videos expand on the unit topic and give you a chance to apply your language skills.

Reading Skill and **Reading Comprehension** sections provide the tools you need to become an effective reader.

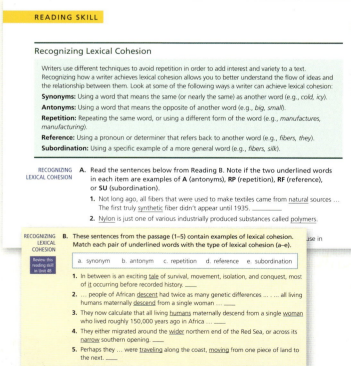

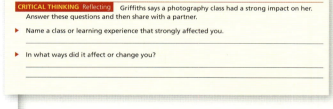

Expanded Vocabulary Practice sections teach you the most useful words and phrases needed for academic reading.

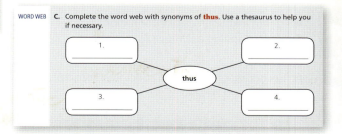

IMAGES
OF LIFE

A father and son share a quiet moment at a mosque in New Delhi, India.

WARM UP

Discuss these questions with a partner.

1. What kinds of things do you usually photograph?

2. What can a photograph do that words cannot?

Amateur photographer Haig Gilchrist captures the moment a giant wave hits a ferry near Sydney Harbour, Australia. This dramatic photo was viewed by thousands online.

BEFORE YOU READ

DEFINITIONS

A. Read the sentence below. Match the correct form of each word in **bold** with its definition (1–3).

In addition to using professional **photojournalists**, many magazines and newspapers today rely on **amateur** photographers to **document** important events.

1. _____ : to record in written or photographic form
2. _____ : working without being paid; not professional
3. _____ : a reporter who shares news using images

SKIMMING

B. Skim paragraphs A and B. Which of these statements would the author most likely agree with? Circle a, b, or c. Check your answer as you read the passage.

a. The quality of smartphone photos is usually not very good.
b. Smartphones and apps have allowed anyone to be a photographer.
c. Many photojournalists don't approve of amateur photography.

THE VISUAL VILLAGE

A Before the age of the smartphone, aspiring photographers had to learn how to use high-tech cameras and photographic techniques. Not everyone had cameras, and it took skill and a good eye to capture and create a great photograph. Today, with the huge range of camera apps on our smartphones, we are all amateur photographers. And pretty good ones, too: The quality of smartphone images now nearly equals that of digital cameras.

B The new ease of photography has given us a **tremendous** appetite for capturing the magical and the ordinary. We are **obsessed** with documenting everyday moments, whether it's a shot of our breakfast, our cat—or our cat's breakfast. And rather than collect pictures in scrapbooks, we share, like, and comment on them with friends and strangers around the globe.

C Even photojournalists are experimenting with cell phones because their near invisibility makes it easier to capture unguarded moments.[1] The Internet also allows photojournalists to avoid traditional media. They can now act as their own publishers—reaching huge audiences via social media sites such as Instagram. A photograph taken in New York can get a response from someone in Lagos within a second of being uploaded.

D In the past, magazines published unforgettable photos of important people and global events that captured our imaginations. These photos had the power to change public opinion—even the course of history. But if there are fewer memorable images today, it's not because there are fewer good images: It's because there are so many. No one image gets to be special for long.

E Cameras are everywhere—a situation that is transforming the way we experience **dramatic** events. When there are major political events or natural disasters, it is ordinary citizens with cell phones—not photojournalists— who often provide the first news images. Quality still matters, but it's less important than what's **instantly** shared.

F As people everywhere **embrace** photography and the media make use of citizen journalists, professional standards appear to be shifting. In the past, most people trusted photojournalists to accurately **represent** reality. Today, however, digital images can be altered in ways the naked eye might

---

1 Something done in an **unguarded moment** is done when you think no one is watching.

never notice. Any image can be altered to create an "improved" picture of reality. The average viewer is left with no way to assess the accuracy of an image except through trust in a news organization or photographer.

G The question of the accuracy of images gets even trickier when photojournalists start experimenting with camera apps—like Flickr or Instagram—which encourage the use of

filters. Images can be colored, brightened, faded, and scratched to make photographs more artistic, or to give them an antique look. Photojournalists using camera apps to cover wars and conflicts have created powerful images—but also **controversy**. Critics worry that antique-looking photographs romanticize war, while distancing us from those who fight in them.

A taxi driver in Kolkata, India, catches up on the news before starting his day (photographed by Annapurna Mellor).

H Yet, photography has always been more subjective than we assume. Each picture is a result of a series of decisions—where to stand, what lens[2] to use, and what to leave in or out of the frame. Does altering photographs with camera app filters make them less true?

---

2 A **lens** is a thin, curved piece of glass or plastic used in things such as cameras.

I There's something powerful and exciting about the experiment that the digital age has forced upon us. These new tools make it easier to tell our own stories, and they give others the power to do the same. Many members of the media get stuck on the same stories, focusing on elections, governments, wars, and disasters. In the process, they miss out on the less dramatic images of daily life that can be just as revealing and **relevant**.

J The increase in the number of photographs and photographers might even be good for **democracy** itself. Hundreds of millions of potential citizen journalists make the world smaller and help keep leaders honest. People can now show what they are up against, making it increasingly difficult for governments to hide their actions. If everyone has a camera, Big Brother[3] isn't the only one watching.

K Who knows? Our obsession with documentation and constantly being connected could lead to a radical change in our way of being. Perhaps we are witnessing the development of a universal visual language. It's one that could change the way we relate to each other and the world. Of course, as with any language, there will be those who produce poetry and those who make shopping lists.

L It's not clear whether this flowering of image-making will lead to a public that better appreciates and understands images. Or will it simply numb[4] us to the **profound** effects a well-made image can have? Regardless, the change is irreversible. Let's hope the millions of new photographs made today help us see what we all have in common, rather than what sets us apart.

---

3 **Big Brother** refers to a person or organization exercising total control over people's lives; the phrase originates from George Orwell's novel *1984*.

4 If an event or experience **numbs** you, you are not able to feel any emotions or think clearly.

READING COMPREHENSION

A. Choose the best answer for each question.

MAIN IDEA

1. According to the author, why are there fewer memorable photographs today?

    a. because the quality of many images is very poor
    b. because most images are not interesting to a global audience
    c. because traditional media refuse to publish amateur photos
    d. because there are so many good images these days

DETAIL

2. What kinds of images does the author think matter most these days?

    a. images that are important to people and can be shared quickly
    b. high-quality images that help show dramatic events
    c. images presented in a traditional way that reflect reality
    d. images that can be altered to improve one's sense of reality

PURPOSE

3. Why does the author put the word *improved* in quotation marks in paragraph F?

    a. The writer is using the exact word from another source.
    b. The writer wants to stress that the picture of reality is greatly improved.
    c. The writer feels it is questionable whether the picture is truly improved.
    d. The writer is not sure the reader understands the word, so draws attention to it.

INFERENCE

4. Who does the author criticize in paragraph J?

    a. citizen journalists   c. Big Brother
    b. government leaders   d. people who alter photos

PARAPHRASE

5. When referring to visual language, what does the author mean by *as with any language, there will be those who produce poetry and those who make shopping lists* (paragraph K)?

    a. It will be most useful for shopping and for writing beautiful poetry.
    b. It will be better because it can be used for a variety of things.
    c. Visual language has certain limitations compared to written language.
    d. Some people will use it for everyday things, and others for more creative things.

MAIN IDEA   **B. Match each paragraph with its main idea (a–e).**

1. Paragraph A •

    • a. More photojournalists are taking smartphone images now and uploading them to social media sites.

2. Paragraph C •

    • b. The effect on us of the increasing number of photographs is still uncertain.

3. Paragraph E •

    • c. When there are big or dramatic news stories, amateur photographers often share the first images with the public.

4. Paragraph G •

    • d. Altering photos with camera apps can give viewers a misleading impression about serious events such as wars.

5. Paragraph L •

    • e. Anyone can be an amateur photographer now because photos taken on smartphones are almost as good as photos taken on digital cameras.

Understanding Words with Multiple Meanings

Many words have more than one meaning. In some cases, the words may be different parts of speech; for example, a noun and a verb. They may be different in meaning (e.g., a **slip** of paper, to **slip** on the ice), or similar (e.g., to score a **goal**, my **goal** in life). In each case, you may need to use a dictionary to understand a word's exact meaning.

IDENTIFYING
MEANING

A. Scan paragraphs A–D in Reading A to find the words in **bold** below (1–6). Then choose the correct meaning (a or b) for each.

1. **age**   a. a period in history   b. how old someone is *1*
2. **pretty**   a. quite   b. attractive *2*
3. **appetite** a. physical hunger *3*   b. a strong desire
4. **act**   a. an action *4*   b. to behave
5. **second**   a. a 60th of a minute *5*   b. number two in a series
6. **course**   a. a class   b. the direction *6*

ANALYZING

B. Read each of these excerpts from Reading A (1–4). Choose the sentence in which the underlined word has the same meaning as the **bold** word.

1. … makes it easier to **capture** unguarded moments. (paragraph C)
   a. NASA is using space telescopes to help capture images of distant planets.
   b. The capture of the gang's leader should lead to less crime in the city.

2. Photojournalists using camera apps to **cover** wars … (paragraph G)
   a. The local media will cover the results of the election.
   b. His photo appeared on the cover of a magazine.

3. … a result of a **series** of decisions … (paragraph H)
   a. There has been an unusual series of events.
   b. What is the most popular comic book series?

4. … and what to leave in or out of the **frame**. (paragraph H)
   a. It looked like somebody was trying to frame him for the theft.
   b. Look in the camera frame and tell me what you see.

CRITICAL THINKING Evaluating Pros and Cons   Do you think news photographers should be allowed to use filters when publishing images of serious subjects (e.g., wars)? What are the pros and cons of doing so? Discuss with a partner and note your ideas.

Pros: *It could make the pictures clearer*

Cons: *It could make the photo look demeaning*

Your opinion: _____

COMPLETION **A.** Circle the correct words to complete the paragraph below.

Recent years have seen some ¹**relevant** / **dramatic** changes in photography. The availability of cell phones has allowed millions of people to ²**embrace** / **represent** photography as a hobby. Image-sharing apps allow anyone to share photos ³**instantly** / **profoundly** with friends and followers online; some people become ⁴**tremendous** / **obsessed** with capturing and documenting every detail of their lives. However, the popularity of image-sharing sites has also raised some ⁵**obsessive** / **controversial** issues—for example, when images of an individual are widely shared without the person's knowledge.

WORDS IN CONTEXT **B.** Complete each sentence with the correct answer (a or b).

1. A **controversy** involves _____ among people.
   a. agreement   b. disagreement

2. If a photo **represents** a place, it _____ what the place is like.
   a. shows   b. doesn't show

3. In a **democracy**, citizens _____ the right to vote.
   a. have   b. don't have

4. If the ideas in an old book are **relevant** today, they _____ matter.
   a. no longer   b. still

5. If you feel a **tremendous** amount of pressure, you feel _____ of pressure.
   a. a lot   b. a little bit

6. Something that is **profound** is felt or experienced very _____.
   a. briefly   b. strongly

WORD FORMS **C.** We can add *-tic* to some nouns to form adjectives (e.g., *drama* + *-tic* = **dramatic**). Complete the sentences below using the adjectives in the box.

athletic	democratic	dramatic	genetic

1. A person's _athletic_ ability—for example, their speed and strength—may be partly affected by _genetic_ factors.

2. In the 20th century, many countries held their first _democratic_ elections.

3. In 2011, Amy Weston took a(n) _dramatic_ photo of a woman leaping to safety from a burning building.

BEFORE YOU READ

DEFINITIONS **A.** You are going to read about photographer Annie Griffiths. Below are some expressions she uses (1–5). What do you think they mean? Match each one with its definition (a–e).

1. small talk   a. light conversation
2. put at ease   b. addicted; obsessed
3. hooked   c. make people feel comfortable
4. by some miracle   d. extremely good; excellent
5. top-notch   e. amazingly; surprisingly

PREDICTING **B.** What could be some challenges of being a professional photographer? Discuss with a partner. Then check your ideas as you read the passage.

< Annie Griffiths has photographed in nearly 150 countries during her career.

MY JOURNEY IN PHOTOGRAPHS

BY ANNIE GRIFFITHS

> An Omani fisherman casts his net at dawn.

A I got my first real job at age 12, as a waitress. I am convinced that I learned more as a waitress than I ever did in a classroom. When I went on to college, it also paid for **tuition** and housing and—eventually—a camera. But best of all, being a waitress taught me to quickly assess and understand all kinds of people. I learned how to make small talk and how to quickly put people at ease—great training for a journalist. Waiting tables also taught me **teamwork** and service and humor.

B From the moment I picked up a camera, I was hooked. I lost interest in other studies, and all I wanted to do was take pictures for the university newspaper, the *Minnesota Daily*. In six months, I was able to get a lot of great experience. The week I finished college, I was contacted by the *Worthington Daily Globe*, a regional daily newspaper in southern Minnesota with a history of excellence in photography. By some miracle I was hired, and the two-year experience that followed was like a master class in photojournalism.

C Jim Vance was the top-notch publisher of the *Globe*. He had very high **expectations** of all the staff. With little or no instruction from him, writers and photographers were expected to fill the paper with stories that were important to our readers. I didn't know it at the time, but this independent reporting was perfect training for my future career.

D Among the most important things I learned at the *Globe* was that if you can make friends with a shy Norwegian farmer and be invited to his kitchen table, you can probably do well in any culture on Earth. I worked with a wonderful writer named Paul Gruchow. Together we would search the farming communities for stories. Paul had grown up on a farm himself and lived through personal tragedy, so he was able to **project** warmth and understanding to anyone he met. Farmers would invite us into their homes and willingly share their personal thoughts with us. From Paul I learned how to be a patient listener, as well as the importance of giving each subject time and **sincere** attention.

A portrait of an Indian woman from a poor background who became a solar engineer

E It was while I was working at the *Globe* that I happened to answer the phone one morning. A man's voice asked, "You a photographer?" When I replied that indeed I was, the voice responded, "This is Bob Gilka. *National Geographic*. I need a hail[1] damage picture. You guys get a big hailstorm last night?" I **overcame** my nervousness and said, "Yes, sir." When he asked if I could take the picture for him, I again said, "Yes, sir."

F My little picture of hail damage in southern Minnesota was well received, and a year later, I was working for Bob—*National Geographic*'s legendary director of photography. **Thus** began one of the most important relationships of my life.

Lessons on the Road

G I was the youngest photographer working for *National Geographic* when I arrived in 1978, and I spent at least a decade just trying not to make mistakes. With each new assignment came the fear that this was going to be the one where they figured out that I couldn't do the job.

H On many assignments, the most challenging part **turned out** to be the transportation. Over the years, I traveled by horse, car, train, truck, and all sorts of old vehicles. I traveled by mule[2] in Mexico, by ship along the Indian Ocean, by fishing boat in the Sea of Galilee, by moped[3] in Bermuda, by sailboat in Sydney. I flew in helicopters chasing bears in the Arctic. Twice, while flying in light planes, pilots have had to make emergency landings far from any airport. But there were also wonderful experiences. In Africa I traveled by balloon, ultralight aircraft, and elephant. In a rubber raft off the west coast of Mexico, I was suddenly lifted out of the water on the back of a friendly whale.

I Wherever I traveled in the world, taking beautiful pictures was always my goal. However, later in my career, I also wanted my pictures to make a real difference in people's lives. That is why each spring I tour two or three developing countries, shooting **portraits** of people whose lives are better because of the dedicated workers who care about them. The photos are used in a variety of fund-raising products. The other issue that stole my heart was the environment. With support from the National Geographic Expeditions Council, I have traveled all over the United States to photograph the last one percent of wilderness left here.

J I am deeply grateful for my life in photography and the amazing lessons it has taught me. I have learned that women really do hold up half the sky; that language isn't always necessary, but touch usually is; that all people are not alike, but they do mostly have the same hopes and fears; that judging others does great harm, but listening to them **enriches**; and that it is impossible to hate a group of people once you get to know one of them as an individual.

---

1 **Hail** is small balls of ice that fall from the sky like rain.
2 A **mule** is a hybrid between a horse and a donkey.
3 A **moped** is a type of lightweight motorcycle.

A. Choose the best answer for each question.

PURPOSE

1. What is the purpose of paragraph A?

    a. to show how working as a waitress is similar to life as a photographer
    b. to explain how Griffiths' first job helped prepare her for her future career
    c. to compare Griffiths' life before and after being a waitress
    d. to describe how Griffiths became interested in photography at college

SEQUENCE

2. What happened after Griffiths graduated from college?

    a. She picked up a camera for the first time.
    b. She began working at the *Minnesota Daily*.
    c. She got a job at the *Worthington Daily Globe*.
    d. She started teaching photography.

DETAIL

3. Which sentence does NOT describe Griffiths' job at the *Globe*?

    a. She received detailed instructions from her publisher.
    b. She learned how to be a patient listener.
    c. The experience prepared her well for a job at *National Geographic*.
    d. She was expected to fill the paper with stories that readers wanted.

DETAIL

4. What kind of transportation challenge does Griffiths mention?

    a. having an accident in a fishing boat
    b. getting attacked by an elephant
    c. being forced to land in a remote place
    d. getting lost in the ocean in a rubber raft

MAIN IDEA

5. According to Griffiths, what has life as a photographer taught her?

    a. that language is essential for communication
    b. that most people have very different hopes and fears
    c. that expressing an opinion is as important as listening
    d. that it is important to get to know people as individuals

IDENTIFYING MEANING

Review this reading skill in Unit 1A

B. Scan the section "Lessons on the Road" to find the words in bold below (1–6). Then choose the correct meaning (a or b) for each.

1. spent   a. paid money for something   b. passed time in a specific way

2. light   a. not heavy   b. pale; not dark

3. back   a. rear surface of a body   b. in the opposite direction

4. spring   a. to suddenly jump forward   b. the season after winter

5. left   a. went away   b. remaining

6. once   a. one time only   b. as soon as; when

Scanning for Information (1)—Short Answer Questions

Scanning is an important skill for taking exams, but how you approach scanning should depend on the question type. With **short answer questions**, for example, read each question carefully first to determine the information you need. Check if there is a word limit for each answer. Identify key words in the questions, and think about what synonyms might be in the text. Then scan to find the relevant parts of the text. Note that answers normally follow the order they appear in the text.

ANALYZING **A.** Read the questions below. What kind of answer will you need to scan for? Circle a, b, or c.

1. What kind of photographic equipment did Griffiths' waitress job help pay for?
   a. an object   b. a number   c. a reason

2. For how long was Griffiths employed at the *Worthington Daily Globe*?
   a. a place   b. a specific date   c. a time period

3. What was Bob Gilka's role at *National Geographic*?
   a. a person's name   b. a place   c. a job title

4. Where did Griffiths travel by moped?
   a. a reason   b. a place   c. a number

5. Why did Griffiths' goals change later in her career?
   a. an example   b. an activity   c. a reason

SCANNING **B.** Scan Reading B and write short answers to the questions above.
1. I can't _____
2. _____
3. _____
4. _____
5. _____

CRITICAL THINKING Interpreting

▶ Griffiths says she has learned that "women really do hold up half the sky." What do you think she means by this? Discuss with a partner.

▶ What examples can you think of that support her statement? Note some ideas below. Then share them with a partner.

_____
_____
_____

COMPLETION   **A.** Circle the correct words to complete the paragraph below.

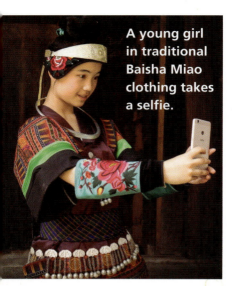

A young girl in traditional Baisha Miao clothing takes a selfie.

There are a few things to keep in mind when taking a selfie. First, think about what emotion you want to convey. For example, do you want the photo to ¹**turn out** / **project** love, sadness, or joy? Do you want it to look natural or perhaps more formal and posed? Decide on your location, and try different angles and distances. Experiment with different camera features. Remember, though, that while new technologies may ²**enrich** / **overcome** your photo, you might prefer a simpler ³**portrait** / **tuition**, even one in black and white. How your final selfie ⁴**overcomes** / **turns out** will ⁵**thus** / **portrait** depend on a number of factors.

DEFINITIONS   **B.** Match the words in the box with the definitions below.

enrich	expectation	overcome
sincere	teamwork	tuition

1. _____ : to successfully deal with a problem

2. _____ : a belief that someone will or should achieve something

3. _____ : honest; not pretending or lying

4. _____ : payment for instruction, especially in a college or university

5. _____ : the effort of people working together to get something done

6. _____ : to improve or make better

WORD WEB   **C.** Complete the word web with synonyms of **thus**. Use a thesaurus to help you if necessary.

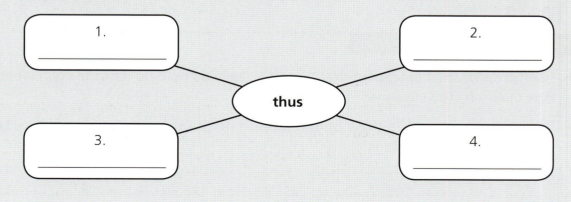

1. _____

2. _____

thus

3. _____

4. _____

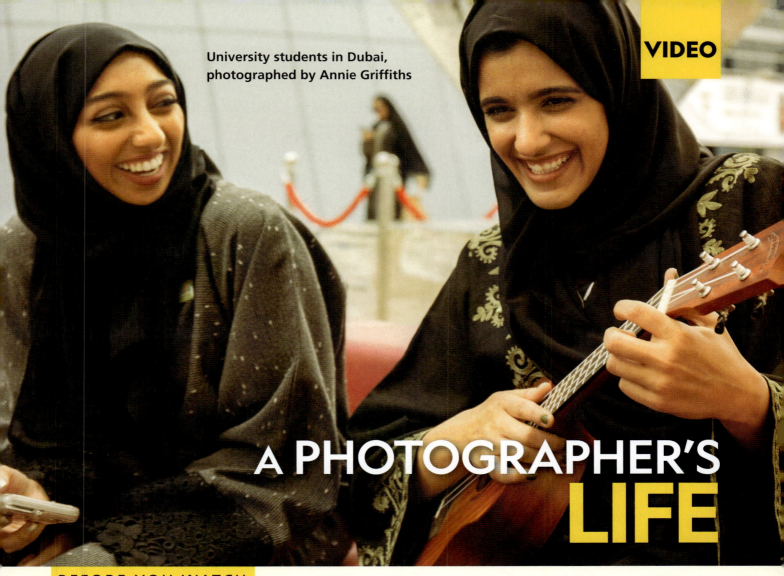

University students in Dubai, photographed by Annie Griffiths

VIDEO

A PHOTOGRAPHER'S LIFE

DISCUSSION **A.** You are going to watch an interview with Annie Griffiths. Discuss these questions with a partner.

1. Based on the information in Reading B and the photo above, what kinds of photos do you think Griffiths likes to take?

2. What do you think Griffiths hopes to achieve with her photography?

PREDICTING **B.** Read these extracts from the video. What words do you think are missing? Discuss with a partner and complete the sentences with your guesses. Use one word for each blank.

"I think our kids also understand that people all over the world are ¹_____ — that you don't assume that they are going to be the same as we are. But then if you go into each culture open, and look ²_____ in the eye, and observe and ³_____, you're going to make ⁴_____ ..."

"[Photography is] a wonderful, terrible job because you get this ⁵_____ to go out and do it, but then you're supposed to do it ⁶_____ than it's ever been done before."

GIST **A.** Watch the video. Check your guesses in Before You Watch B. Are they correct or similar to what Annie Griffiths says in the video?

MULTIPLE CHOICE **B.** Watch the video again. Choose the correct answer for each question.

1. What did Griffiths want to be before she got interested in photography?

   a. a writer   b. a painter

2. What benefit did Griffiths' daughter gain from the family's travels?

   a. She can speak several languages.   b. She is now a confident traveler.

3. What tip does Griffiths give for immersing yourself in a different culture?

   a. staying away from tourist hotspots   b. respecting the local way of life

4. According to Griffiths, what is one of the most inspirational parts about photography?

   a. It gives you the opportunity to be creative and grow artistically.

   b. A good photo can help shape or change public opinion.

CRITICAL THINKING Reflecting   Griffiths says a photography class had a strong impact on her. Answer these questions and then share with a partner.

▶ Name a class or learning experience that strongly affected you.

_____

▶ In what ways did it affect or change you?

_____

_____

VOCABULARY REVIEW

Do you remember the meanings of these words? Check (✓) the ones you know. Look back at the unit and review any words you're not sure of.

Reading A

☐ controversy*   ☐ democracy   ☐ dramatic*   ☐ embrace   ☐ instantly

☐ obsessed   ☐ profound   ☐ relevant*   ☐ represent   ☐ tremendous

Reading B

☐ enrich   ☐ expectation   ☐ overcome   ☐ portrait   ☐ project*

☐ sincere   ☐ teamwork   ☐ thus   ☐ tuition   ☐ turn out

* Academic Word List

NATURAL
ATTRACTION

WARM UP

Discuss these questions with a partner.

1. Which animals are known for their bright colors or spectacular appearance?

2. In what ways do you think those characteristics help the animals?

^ The Victoria crowned pigeon is known for its large head crest of lacy feathers.

2A

DISCUSSION **A.** Read the information below. What types of animals do you know that are bioluminescent? Make a list.

Bioluminescence is the production and emission of light by living organisms, through chemical reactions occurring inside their bodies. Simply put, creatures that are bioluminescent can glow in the dark. Examples of bioluminescent creatures can be found in the ocean, on land, and in the air.

PREDICTING **B.** Why might it be useful for an organism to be bioluminescent? Brainstorm some purposes with a partner. Check your ideas as you read the passage.

> **The bioluminescent bay on the Puerto Rican island of Vieques**

LIVING LIGHT

A The ability of some species to create light—known as bioluminescence—is both magical and commonplace. Magical, because of its glimmering beauty. Commonplace, because many life forms can do it. On land the most familiar examples are fireflies, **flashing** to attract mates on a warm summer night. But there are other luminous land organisms, including glow-worms, millipedes, and some 90 species of fungus. Even some birds, such as the Atlantic puffin, have beaks that glow in the dark.

B But the real biological light show takes place in the sea. Here, an **astonishing** number of beings can make light. Some, such as ostracods, are like ocean fireflies, using flashes of light to attract a mate. There are also glowing bacteria, and light-making fish, squid, and jellyfish. Indeed, of all the groups of organisms known to make light, more than four-fifths live in the ocean.

C As a place to live, the ocean has a couple of peculiarities. Firstly, there is almost nowhere to hide, so being **invisible** is very important. Secondly, as you **descend**, sunlight disappears. At first, red light is absorbed. Then the yellow and green parts of the spectrum disappear, leaving just the blue. At 200 meters below the surface, the ocean becomes a kind of perpetual twilight,[1] and at 600 meters the blue fades out too. In fact, most of the ocean is as black as the night sky. These **factors** make light uniquely useful as a weapon or a veil.

Hiding with Light

D In the ocean's upper **layers**, where light penetrates, creatures need to blend in to survive. Any life form that stands out is in danger of being spotted by **predators**—especially those swimming below, looking up. Many life forms solve this problem by avoiding the light zone during the day. Others—such as jellyfish and swimming snails—are **transparent**, ghostlike creatures, almost impossible to see.

E Other sea species use light to survive in the upper layers—but how? Some, such as certain shrimp and squid, illuminate their bellies to match the light coming from above. This allows them to become invisible to predators below. Their light can be turned on and off at will—some even have a dimmer switch.[2] For example, certain types of shrimp can alter how much light they give off, depending on the brightness of the water around them. If a cloud passes overhead and briefly blocks the light, the shrimp will dim itself accordingly.

F But if the aim is to remain invisible, why do some creatures light up when they are touched, or when the water nearby is **disturbed**? A couple of reasons. First, a sudden burst of light may startle[3] a predator, giving the prey a chance to escape. Some kinds of deep-sea squid, for example, give a big squirt of light before darting off into the gloom.

G Second, there is the principle of "the enemy of my enemy is my friend." Giving off light can help summon the predator of your predator. Known as the "burglar alarm" effect, this is especially useful for tiny life forms, such as dinoflagellates, that cannot swim fast. For such small beings, water is too viscous[4] to allow a quick getaway—it would be like trying to swim through syrup. Instead, when threatened by a shrimp, for example, these organisms light up. The flashes attract larger fish that are better able to spot—and eat—the shrimp. The chief defense for these tiny organisms is therefore not fight or flight—but light.

---

1 **Twilight** is the time of day after the sun sets but before it becomes completely dark.

2 A **dimmer switch** is a device—such as those found on lamps—that can control the brightness of a light.

3 If something **startles** you, it causes you to feel surprised or shocked.

4 A liquid that is **viscous** is thick and not easy to move through.

5 **Flagella** are thin, threadlike structures that enable tiny organisms such as bacteria or protozoa to swim.

STARS OF THE SEA

One of the best places in the world to see a natural light show is Vieques, a small island that belongs to Puerto Rico. The island is famous for its *bahía bioluminiscente,* or "bio bay"—home to **countless** dinoflagellates. These dust-size beings are named for their two flagella[5] and the whirling motion they make (*dinos* means "whirling" in Greek). Dinoflagellates light up whenever the water around them moves; they are the organisms typically responsible for the flashes of light you sometimes see when swimming or boating on a dark night.

Visitors to Vieques can join an evening tour group and set out across the bay in transparent canoes. The island has only a few streetlights, so when the moon is not yet risen, the sea is dark and the sky is full of stars. Fish dart through the water, looking like meteors. Eventually, the movement of the canoes disturbs the dinoflagellates, and they light up in a bright, flickering stream. Watching them through the canoe's transparent floor can give a powerful impression that the water is part of the sky, and you are paddling through the stars.

Examples of bioluminescence in the natural world include (1) the comb jelly, (2) the firefly, (3) squid, and (4) some species of mushroom.

DEFENSE

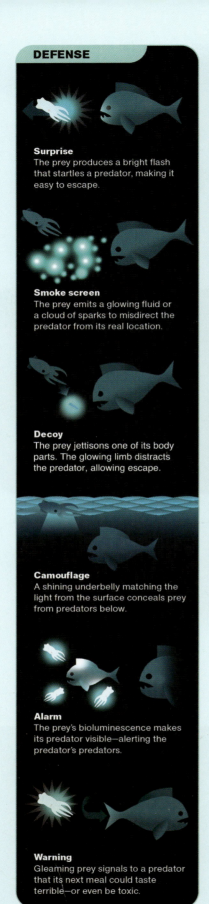

Surprise
The prey produces a bright flash that startles a predator, making it easy to escape.

Smoke screen
The prey emits a glowing fluid or a cloud of sparks to misdirect the predator from its real location.

Decoy
The prey jettisons one of its body parts. The glowing limb distracts the predator, allowing escape.

Camouflage
A shining underbelly matching the light from the surface conceals prey from predators below.

Alarm
The prey's bioluminescence makes its predator visible—alerting the predator's predators.

Warning
Gleaming prey signals to a predator that its next meal could taste terrible—or even be toxic.

OFFENSE

Shock
A burst of bright light from a bioluminescent predator stuns prey and leaves it open to attack.

Lure
Prey is attracted to the glow produced by a predator.

Beacon
Predators seek out the glimmer that tells them that bioluminescent creatures are gathering.

Searchlight
A predator turns on its natural spotlight to locate prey in a dark ocean.

REPRODUCTION

Attraction
Flickers of light signal that a bioluminescent insect is ready to meet new mates.

Invitation
Mushrooms may spread their spores by using luminescence to attract insects to land on them.

Lightness of Being

Glow-in-the-dark light may seem mysterious, but organisms use it for practical purposes. Bioluminescence warns off predators, lures prey, and attracts mates. Making light is such a useful trait that it has evolved independently at least 40 times, for three main reasons.

JASON TREAT, NGM STAFF. ART: ELEANOR LUTZ
SOURCE: STEVEN HADDOCK, MONTEREY BAY AQUARIUM RESEARCH INSTITUTE

A. Choose the best answer for each question.

MAIN IDEA

1. All life forms with bioluminescence _____ .

    a. live in or near water
    b. are able to create light
    c. use light to attract mates
    d. use light to protect themselves

DETAIL

2. Which of these is NOT explained in the passage?

    a. why some bioluminescent creatures produce light
    b. why invisibility is important to many sea creatures
    c. why some birds have beaks that glow in the dark
    d. how various creatures near the ocean's surface hide themselves

COHESION

3. In which position should this sentence be added to paragraph D?
These creatures only rise toward the surface at night.

    a. after the first sentence
    b. after the second sentence
    c. after the third sentence
    d. after the fourth sentence

DETAIL / SYNTHESIZING

4. According to paragraph E, how do certain shrimp in the ocean's upper layers use bioluminescence?

    a. as a decoy   c. as an alarm
    b. as camouflage   d. as a warning

INFERENCE

5. What is meant by the "burglar alarm" effect?

    a. Light allows predators to spot their prey in total darkness.
    b. A sudden flash of light startles predators, allowing their prey to escape.
    c. When lit up, tiny organisms such as dinoflagellates can swim faster.
    d. Organisms produce light, which attracts the predators of their predators.

EVALUATING STATEMENTS

B. Are the following statements true or false according to the reading passage, or is the information not given? Circle **T** (true), **F** (false), or **NG** (not given).

1. Most bioluminescent creatures in the sea live near the surface.   T F **NG**

2. Six hundred meters below the surface, sunlight stops penetrating the ocean.   **T** F NG

3. Dinoflagellates use light to help them find and eat shrimp.   T **F** NG

4. Human activity in the Vieques "bio bay" stops dinoflagellates from lighting up.   T **F** NG

5. Visitors to the Vieques "bio bay" can only see dinoflagellates in the summer.   T F **NG**

Summarizing (1)—Using a Concept Map

To help you identify and remember a passage's key ideas, it can be useful to take notes using a concept map. This allows you to see the relationships and connections between the writer's main and supporting ideas. To create a concept map, start with the main topic in the middle, add subtopics around it, and then list supporting details and examples for each subtopic.

SUMMARIZING **A.** Complete the concept map below with words from Reading A.

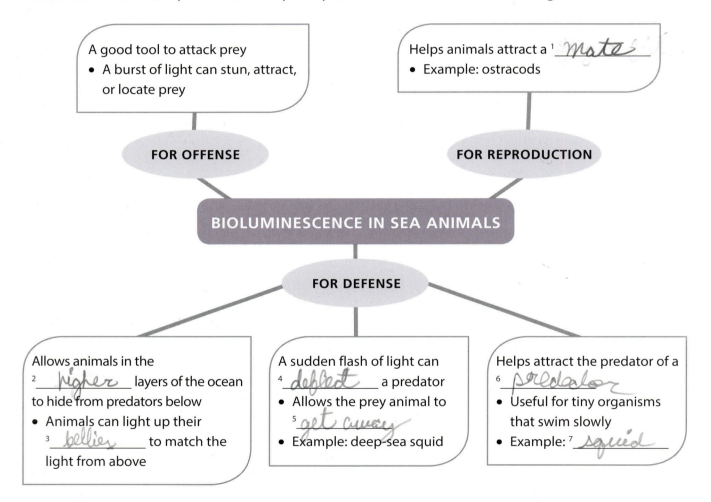

A good tool to attack prey
- A burst of light can stun, attract, or locate prey

Helps animals attract a ¹ _mate_
- Example: ostracods

FOR OFFENSE

FOR REPRODUCTION

BIOLUMINESCENCE IN SEA ANIMALS

FOR DEFENSE

Allows animals in the ² _higher_ layers of the ocean to hide from predators below
- Animals can light up their ³ _bellies_ to match the light from above

A sudden flash of light can ⁴ _deflect_ a predator
- Allows the prey animal to ⁵ _get away_
- Example: deep-sea squid

Helps attract the predator of a ⁶ _predator_
- Useful for tiny organisms that swim slowly
- Example: ⁷ _squid_

CRITICAL THINKING Speculating   The reading passage mentions that Atlantic puffins have beaks that glow in the dark. What do you think is the purpose of the glowing beak? Discuss with a partner.

> **A puffin beak glows under a black light.**

VOCABULARY PRACTICE

COMPLETION

A. Circle the correct words to complete the information below.

A(n) [1]**astonishing** / **disturbed** variety of sea creatures use bioluminescence. Brittle stars, for example, can [2]**flash** / **descend** a green light when they are threatened by [3]**layers** / **predators**. Some brittle stars can even detach their arms. Predators are attracted to the detached, glowing arm of the brittle star, giving the animal a chance to escape. It later regrows its arm.

Some species of sea cucumber can attach their body parts onto other animals. When frightened or [4]**transparent** / **disturbed**, these sea cucumbers break off the bioluminescent parts of their bodies onto nearby fish. The predator will follow the glow on the fish, while the sea cucumber simply crawls away.

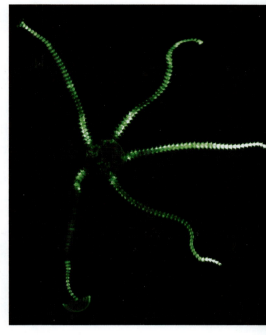

∧ **Brittle stars are closely related to starfish.**

WORDS IN CONTEXT

B. Complete the sentences. Circle the correct words.

1. When you **descend** a staircase, you go *up* / *down.*

2. If something is **transparent**, *you can* / *cannot* see through it.

3. Something described as **countless** has a very *low* / *high* number.

4. A **factor** is something that *is unlikely* / *affects* a result.

5. The purpose of adding a **layer** of clothing would likely be to get *warmer* / *wetter.*

6. If something is **invisible**, it *can* / *cannot* be seen.

WORD ROOTS

C. The word **descend** contains the word root *scend*, which means "move toward." Complete the sentences with the correct words from the box.

ascend	crescendo	~~descend~~	transcend

1. The plane began to _descend_ as it approached its destination.
2. Divers must not _ascend_ too quickly to the water's surface.
3. Musical symphonies often include a series of softer melodies that build toward a powerful _crescendo_
4. Some types of music are able to _transcend_ cultural boundaries and become popular worldwide.

BEFORE YOU READ

DISCUSSION **A.** Look at the photo below. In what way(s) is this bird unusual? Discuss your ideas with a partner.

SKIMMING **B.** Look at the reading title and headings on the next three pages. Check (✓) the information about birds of paradise you think will be covered in the passage. Then read the passage to check your answers.

☐ a. why they have colorful feathers ☐ c. their migration patterns
☐ b. how they show off their feathers ☐ d. threats to their survival

^ A male Wilson's bird of paradise

FEATHERS OF LOVE

A Covered in soft, black feathers, the **noble** performer bows deeply to his audience. From the top of his head grow several long feathers that tap the ground as he begins his dance. This dancing bird is Carola's parotia, just one of the many birds of paradise that live on the island of New Guinea. This male bird is attempting to impress a row of females that are watching him from a branch above.

B Keeping the females' attention isn't easy. He pauses for dramatic effect, then **commences** his dance again. His neck sinks and his head goes up and down, head feathers **bouncing**. He jumps and shakes his feathers until his performance finally attracts the attention of one of the females.

An Amazing Performance

C In the dense jungle of New Guinea is nature's most **absurd** theater, the special mating game of the birds of paradise. To attract females, males' feathers resemble costumes worthy of the stage. The bright reds, yellows, and blues stand out sharply against the green of the forest. It seems that the more extreme the male's costume and colors, the better his chance of attracting a mate.

D In addition to having extremely beautiful feathers, each species has its own type of display behavior. Some dance on the ground, in areas that they have cleared and prepared like their own version of a dance floor. Others perform high in the trees.

E The male red bird of paradise shows off his red and yellow feathers in a display called a "butterfly dance." He spreads and moves his wings intensely, like a giant butterfly. The male Carola's parotia, however, is the dance king of the birds of paradise; he has serious dance moves! These include one in which he spreads out his feathers like a dress, in a move called the "ballerina[1] dance." While some birds of paradise perform alone, others perform in groups, creating an eye-catching performance that female birds find impossible to resist. Hanging from nearby branches, male Goldie's birds **prominently** display the soft red feathers that rise from their backs as they flap[2] their wings. Excited females soon choose the one that pleased them the most.

The Evolution of Color

F These brilliantly colored birds of paradise have developed over millions of years from ancient birds whose feathers were dark and boring in comparison. Of today's 45 brightly colored birds of paradise species, most live only on New Guinea. These birds of paradise invite us to solve a mystery of nature. It seems to be a contradiction[3] that such extreme feathers and colors could have been favored by the process of **evolution**. After all, these same brightly colored feathers that attract mates also make the birds much more noticeable to predators. The answer lies in the safe environment in which the birds live, and a process of evolution known as sexual selection.

---

1 A **ballerina** is a female ballet dancer.

2 If a bird or an insect **flaps** its wings, the wings move quickly up and down.

3 If an aspect of a situation is a **contradiction**, it is completely different from other aspects and makes the situation confusing.

G "Life here is pretty comfortable for birds of paradise. The island's unique environment has allowed them to go to extremes unheard of elsewhere," says biologist Ed Scholes. Under **harsher** conditions, he says, "evolution simply wouldn't have come up with these birds." Fruit and insects are abundant all year round, and predators are few. The result is a perfect environment for birds.

H Sexual selection has thus been the driving force in the evolution of birds of paradise. Freed of other pressures, birds of paradise began to specialize in attracting mates. Over millions of years, they have slowly **undergone** changes in their colors, feathers, and other talents. Characteristics that made one bird more attractive than another were passed on and enhanced over time. "The usual rules of survival aren't as important here as the rules of successful mating," Scholes adds.

I The diversity of New Guinea's birds also springs from its varied environments: from coastal plains to cloud forests, from swamps[4] to mountains rising as high as 5,000 meters. The landscape has many physical barriers that isolate animal populations, allowing them to develop into distinct species.

4 A **swamp** is an area of very wet land with wild plants growing in it.

> The island of New Guinea is home to nearly 40 species of birds of paradise, more than anywhere else in the world. Most live within a single mountain range and altitude. This isolation allows the birds to evolve separately into their wonderful varieties.

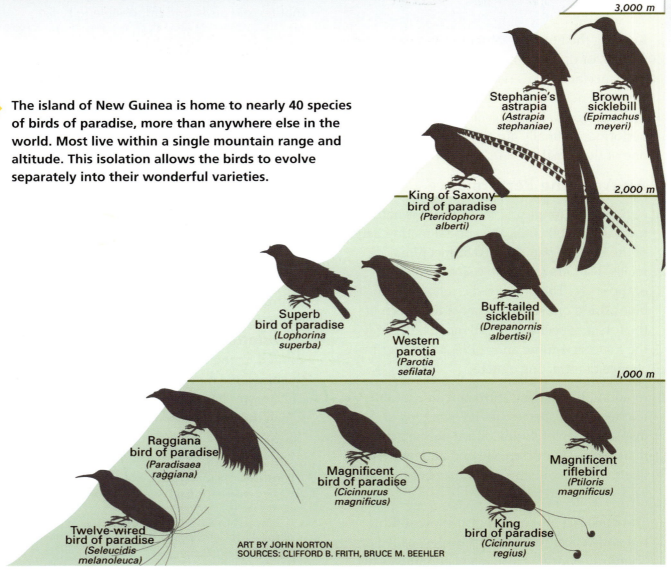

3,000 m

Stephanie's astrapia (*Astrapia stephaniae*)

Brown sicklebill (*Epimachus meyeri*)

King of Saxony bird of paradise (*Pteridophora alberti*)

2,000 m

Superb bird of paradise (*Lophorina superba*)

Western parotia (*Parotia sefilata*)

Buff-tailed sicklebill (*Drepanornis albertisi*)

1,000 m

Raggiana bird of paradise (*Paradisaea raggiana*)

Magnificent bird of paradise (*Cicinnurus magnificus*)

Magnificent riflebird (*Ptiloris magnificus*)

Twelve-wired bird of paradise (*Seleucidis melanoleuca*)

King bird of paradise (*Cicinnurus regius*)

ART BY JOHN NORTON
SOURCES: CLIFFORD B. FRITH, BRUCE M. BEEHLER

Trouble in Paradise

J The people of New Guinea have been watching the displays of the birds of paradise for centuries. "Locals will tell you they went into the forest and copied their **rituals** from the birds," says anthropologist Gillian Gillison. At local dance performances, the painted dancers still evoke the birds with their movements and beautiful costumes. "By wearing the feathers," Gillison says, "... you capture the animal's life force."

K In the past, demand for the birds' feathers resulted in a huge amount of hunting. At the peak of the trade in the early 1900s, 80,000 skins a year were exported from New Guinea for European ladies' hats. Nowadays, few birds die for fashion or for traditional costumes: Ceremonial feathers are passed down from generation to generation. Although local people are still permitted to hunt the birds for traditional uses, they usually target older male birds, leaving younger males to continue **breeding**.

L There are more serious threats to the birds, however. An illegal market in feathers still exists. Large farms use up thousands of hectares of forest where birds of paradise once lived. Logging,[5] oil prospecting, and mining also present dangers to New Guinea's forests. Meanwhile, human populations continue to grow.

M David Mitchell, a conservationist, is relying on the help of local villagers to record where the birds display and what they eat. He hopes to not only gather data, but also encourage protection of the birds' habitat. The strategy seems to be working. "I had come to cut down some trees and plant yam[6] vines," says Ambrose Joseph, one of Mitchell's farmers. "Then I saw the birds land there, so I left the trees alone." For millions of years, these impressive birds have danced to find their mates. They'll keep dancing for as long as the forest offers them a stage.

5 **Logging** is the business of cutting down trees for use as wood.
6 A **yam** is a root vegetable, like a potato, that grows in tropical areas.

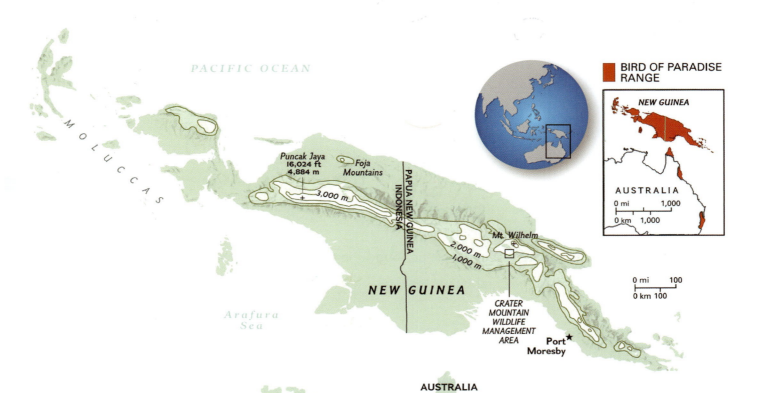

A. Choose the best answer for each question.

MAIN IDEA

1. Why do birds of paradise dance and display their feathers?

   a. to frighten away predators   c. to exercise and clean their bodies

   b. to attract a mate   d. to show possession of an area

DETAIL

2. Which factor is NOT mentioned as a reason for the birds' unusual characteristics?

   a. the widespread availability of fruit and insects

   b. the wide variety of environments

   c. the wide variety of breeding systems

   d. the lack of predators

CAUSE AND EFFECT

3. Why did so many birds of paradise die in the early 1900s?

   a. There was a high demand for feathers to use in European hats.

   b. The birds got sick after early interactions with humans.

   c. Industrial development destroyed the birds' habitat.

   d. Logging drastically reduced the birds' habitat.

INFERENCE

4. Why do local people continue to hunt birds of paradise?

   a. to eat them   c. to make traditional costumes

   b. to protect smaller birds   d. to keep their numbers down

COHESION

5. The following sentence would best be placed at the beginning of which paragraph?
   However, there may be some good news for the birds.

   a. paragraph E   c. paragraph L

   b. paragraph I   d. paragraph M

IDENTIFYING MEANING

Review this reading skill in Unit 1A

B. Scan the reading passage to find the words in bold below. Then choose the correct meaning (a or b) for each.

1. bows (paragraph A)

   a. loops or knots   b. bends body forward

2. row (paragraph A)

   a. a number of things in a line   b. a noisy argument or fight

3. stage (paragraph C)

   a. a place where people perform   b. a period or part of an activity

4. display (paragraph D)

   a. to make visible   b. an event or performance meant to entertain

5. present (paragraph L)

   a. a gift   b. to cause something

Identifying Figurative Language

Writers use figurative language—similes, metaphors, and personification—to create an image of someone or something in the reader's mind.

A **simile** compares two different things using *like* or *as*: *Her skin was as cold as ice.*
A **metaphor** says one thing *is* another thing: *During rush hour, the road is a parking lot.*
Sometimes the comparison in a metaphor is implied: *He has a heart of stone.*
Personification gives humanlike qualities to something nonhuman: *Lightning danced across the sky.*

IDENTIFYING FIGURATIVE LANGUAGE

A. Look at these sentences from Reading B. Mark each one as an example of a simile (**S**), a metaphor (**M**), or personification (**P**). Some may have more than one answer.

1. _____ Covered in soft, black feathers, the noble performer bows deeply to his audience. (paragraph A)

2. _____ He spreads and moves his wings intensely, like a giant butterfly. (paragraph E)

3. _____ The male Carola's parotia, however, is the dance king of the birds of paradise. (paragraph E)

4. _____ These include one in which he spreads out his feathers like a dress. (paragraph E)

5. _____ They'll keep dancing for as long as the forest offers them a stage. (paragraph M)

IDENTIFYING FIGURATIVE LANGUAGE

B. Look back at Reading A ("Living Light"). Underline these examples of figurative language (1–5) in the passage.

1. A simile in paragraph C
2. A metaphor in paragraph E
3. A simile in paragraph G
4. A simile in the sidebar "Stars of the Sea" (second paragraph)
5. A metaphor in the sidebar "Stars of the Sea" (second paragraph)

CRITICAL THINKING Interpreting / Applying

▶ What does each example of figurative language in activity B mean? What is the writer emphasizing? Discuss with a partner.

▶ Think of some similes or metaphors you could use to describe someone you know. Note your ideas below and then share with a partner.

_____

_____

VOCABULARY PRACTICE

COMPLETION **A.** Complete the paragraph using the correct form of words from the box.

> **absurd   bounce   prominent   ritual**

Over the years, the male Carola's parotia bird of paradise has developed a special mating ¹_____ that involves a lot of bowing and flapping. On its head, the bird has several long and ²_____ quills, which it ³_____ up and down in hopes of attracting a female. "Its mating dance is so ⁴_____," says researcher Jennifer Holland, "that I could hardly keep from laughing."

▲ **A male parotia dances to attract a female companion.**

DEFINITIONS **B.** Match the words in the box with the definitions below.

> **evolution   breed   commence   noble   harsh   undergo**

1. _____ : (for animals) to mate and have babies

2. _____ : to begin

3. _____ : to experience something necessary or unpleasant

4. _____ : cruel or severe

5. _____ : having fine personal qualities or appearance

6. _____ : the way in which living things change and develop over millions of years

WORD FORMS **C.** We can add *-ility* to some adjectives to form nouns (e.g., **noble** + *-ility* = *nobility*). Complete the sentences below with the correct form of words from the box. One word is extra.

> **hostile   mobile   noble   reliable   stable**

1. Economic development is more likely to occur during periods of political _____.

2. Oil is not a _____ energy source in the long term, as supplies are limited.

3. Communication breakdowns can produce a _____ environment in the workplace.

4. The widespread availability of cars in the 20th century led to an increase in personal _____.

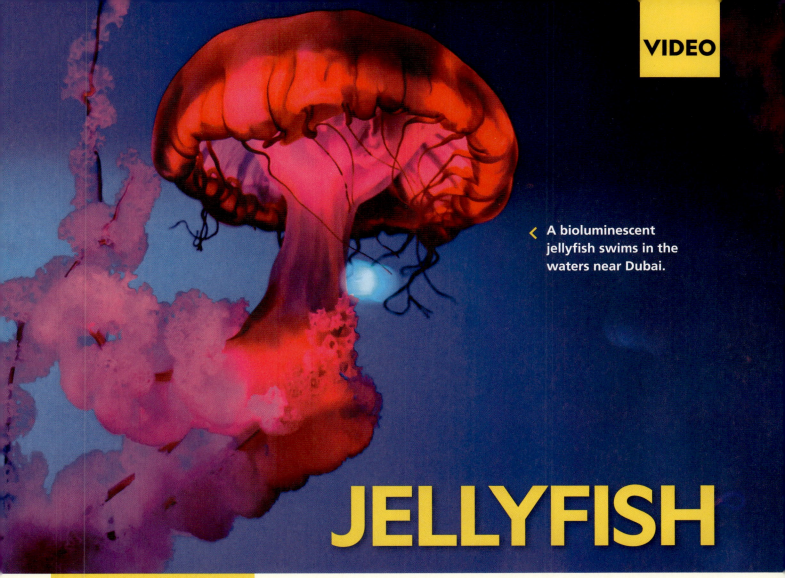

A bioluminescent jellyfish swims in the waters near Dubai.

JELLYFISH

BEFORE YOU WATCH

PREVIEWING   **A.** Read the information. The words in **bold** appear in the video. Match these words with their definitions below.

Jellyfish have been around for hundreds of millions of years, even before dinosaurs lived on the Earth. They are probably some of the most mysterious creatures you'll ever see. Unlike fish, jellyfish are **invertebrates**. They do not have bones, brains, hearts, or blood. Nevertheless, some jellyfish are able to **clone** themselves, as well as reverse the aging process by **reverting** back to a younger state.

Despite looking harmless, jellyfish can be **venomous**—their stings are painful and sometimes fatal. However, some species are safe to eat. In certain countries, jellyfish is considered to be a delicacy.

1. invertebrate   •   • a. (of an animal) poisonous

2. clone   •   • b. to return to a previous state

3. revert   •   • c. to make a copy of something

4. venomous   •   • d. an animal without a backbone

GIST **A.** Watch the video. Check (✓) the topics that are covered in the video.

☐ a. how the jellyfish got its name

☐ b. the diet of a jellyfish

☐ c. how jellyfish reproduce

☐ d. what jellyfish taste like

☐ e. problems that large groups of jellyfish can cause

COMPLETION **B.** Watch the video again and complete the notes below. Use up to two words for each blank.

Interesting facts about jellyfish

• Since jellyfish aren't actually fish, some scientists have started using the umbrella term [1]"_____" instead.

• By undergoing transdifferentiation, the "immortal jellyfish" can revert back to a [2]_____ and start its life cycle all over again.

• The Australian box jellyfish is considered to be the most [3]_____ marine animal in the world.

• Jellyfish are mostly made of [4]_____; if a jellyfish washes ashore, it will mostly [5]_____.

• Jellyfish blooms have clogged fishing gear, destroyed ships, and closed [6]_____.

CRITICAL THINKING Speculating   Some jellyfish are bioluminescent. How might this ability be useful to them? Refer to the infographic on page 30 for ideas and discuss with a partner.

VOCABULARY REVIEW

Do you remember the meanings of these words? Check (✓) the ones you know. Look back at the unit and review any words you're not sure of.

Reading A

☐ astonishing ☐ countless ☐ descend ☐ disturb ☐ factor*

☐ flash ☐ invisible* ☐ layer* ☐ predator ☐ transparent

Reading B

☐ absurd ☐ bounce ☐ breed ☐ commence* ☐ evolution*

☐ harsh ☐ noble ☐ prominently ☐ ritual ☐ undergo*

* Academic Word List

3

FOOD AND HEALTH

A woman collects tomatoes in a greenhouse in the Netherlands.

Discuss these questions with a partner.

1. What kinds of foods can be dangerous to your health?

2. In what ways could the world increase its supply of food?

BEFORE YOU READ

DEFINITIONS **A.** Read this information and match each word or phrase in **bold** with its definition (1–4).

In recent years, **bacteria** found in foods are posing increased health risks—particularly to people with weakened **immune systems**. While improvements in **sanitary** practices have reduced some **foodborne** threats, new hazards have arisen because of changes in our lifestyle and in food production methods.

1. _____ : clean and not dangerous for your health

2. _____ : very small organisms that can cause disease

3. _____ : parts and processes of the body that fight illness

4. _____ : carried into our bodies through the things we eat

PREDICTING **B.** What causes food poisoning, and how can we avoid it? Discuss with a partner. Then check your ideas as you read the passage.

HOW SAFE IS OUR FOOD?

A The everyday activity of eating involves more risk than you might think. It is estimated that each year in the United States, 48 million people suffer from foodborne diseases; 128,000 of them are hospitalized, and 3,000 die. In the developing world, **contaminated** food and water kill over half a million children a year. In most cases, virulent[1] types of bacteria are to blame.

B Bacteria are an **integral** part of a healthy life. There are 200 times as many bacteria in the intestines[2] of a single human as there are human beings who have ever lived. Most of these bacteria help with **digestion**, making vitamins, shaping the immune system, and keeping us healthy. Nearly all raw food has bacteria in it as well. But the bacteria that produce foodborne illnesses are of a different, more dangerous kind.

Bad Bacteria

C Many of the bacteria that produce foodborne illnesses are present in the intestines of the animals we raise for food. When a food animal containing dangerous bacteria is cut open during processing, bacteria inside can contaminate the meat. Fruits and vegetables can pick up dangerous bacteria if washed or watered with contaminated water. A single bacterium, given the right conditions, divides rapidly enough to produce billions over the course of a day. This means that even only lightly contaminated food can be dangerous. Bacteria can also hide and multiply on dishtowels, cutting boards, sinks, knives, and kitchen counters, where they're easily transferred to food or hands.

D Changes in the way in which farm animals are raised also affect the rate at which dangerous bacteria can spread. In the name of efficiency and economy, fish, cattle, and chickens are raised in giant "factory" farms, which **confine** large numbers of animals in tight spaces. Cattle, for example, are crowded together under such conditions that if only one animal is contaminated with the virulent bacteria *E. coli* O157:H7, it will likely spread to others.

Tracking the Source

E Disease investigators, like Patricia Griffin, are working to find the sources of these outbreaks[3] and prevent them in the future. Griffin, of the Centers for Disease Control and Prevention (CDC) in the United States, has worked in

▲ Students study new techniques of food production at Wageningen University & Research, Netherlands.

---

1 Something that is **virulent** is dangerous or poisonous.
2 Your **intestines** are the tubes in your body through which food passes when it has left your stomach.
3 If there is an **outbreak** of something unpleasant, such as violence or a disease, it happens suddenly.

∧ A medical researcher examines a sample of *E. coli*.

the foodborne-disease business for 15 years. Periodic *E. coli* outbreaks turned her attention to the public food safety threat that exists in restaurants and in the food production system. Food safety is no longer just a question of handling food properly in the domestic kitchen. "Now," Griffin says, "we are more aware that the responsibility does not rest solely with the cook. We know that contamination often occurs early in the production process—at steps on the way from farm or field or fishing ground to market."

F Griffin's job is to look for trends in food-related illness through the analysis of outbreaks. Her team tries to identify both the food source of an outbreak and the contaminating bacteria. To link cases together, the scientists use a powerful tool called PulseNet, a national computer network of health laboratories that matches types of bacteria using DNA[4] analysis. PulseNet allows scientists to associate an illness in California, say, with one in Texas, tying together what might otherwise appear as unrelated cases. Then it's the job of the investigators to **determine** what went wrong in the food's journey to the table. This helps them decide whether to recall[5] a particular food or to change the process by which it's produced.

G In January 2000, public health officials in the state of Virginia noted an unusual group of patients sick with food poisoning from salmonella.[6] Using PulseNet, the CDC identified 79 patients in 13 states who were **infected** with the same type of salmonella bacteria. Fifteen had been hospitalized; two had died. What was the common factor? All had eaten mangoes during the previous November and December. The investigation led to a single large mango farm in Brazil, where it was discovered that mangoes were being washed

in contaminated water containing a type of salmonella bacteria. Salmonella contamination is a widespread problem; salmonella cases involving contaminated chicken, melons, coconut, and cereals were reported in 2018.

H The mango outbreak had a larger lesson: We no longer eat only food that is in season or that is grown locally. Instead, we demand our strawberries, peaches, mangoes, and lettuce year-round. As a result, we are depending more and more on imports. Eating food grown elsewhere in the world means depending on the soil, water, and sanitary conditions in those places, and on the way in which their workers farm, harvest, process, and transport the food.

Reducing the Risk

I There are a number of success stories that provide hope and show us how international food production need not mean increased risk of contamination. Costa Rica has made sanitary production of fruits and vegetables a **nationwide** priority. Fresh fruits and vegetables are packed carefully in sanitary conditions; frequent hand washing is **compulsory**; and proper toilets are provided for workers in the fields. Such changes have made Carmela Velazquez, a food scientist from the University of Costa Rica, **optimistic** about the future. "The farmers we've trained," she says, "will become models for all our growers."

J In Sweden, too, progress has been made in reducing the number of foodborne disease at an early stage. Swedish chicken farmers have eliminated salmonella from their farms by thoroughly cleaning the area where their chickens are kept, and by using chicken feed that has been heated to rid it of dangerous bacteria. Consequently, the chickens that Swedes buy are now salmonella-free. These successes suggest that it is indeed **feasible** for companies and farms to produce safe and sanitary food, while still making a profit.

---

4 **DNA** is a material in living things that contains the code for their structure and many of their functions.

5 When sellers **recall** a product, they ask customers to return it to them.

6 **Salmonella** is a group of bacteria that cause food poisoning.

A. Choose the best answer for each question.

GIST

1. What is the reading mainly about?

   a. new research regarding the effects of foodborne bacteria

   b. the decline in sanitary conditions in restaurants and farms around the world

   c. sources of dangerous foodborne bacteria, their detection, and control

   d. the importance of advanced technology in the fight against foodborne bacteria

DETAIL

2. Why is even a single disease-causing bacterium dangerous?

   a. It can mix with other bacteria.

   b. It is often hard to detect.

   c. Just one can kill a small child.

   d. It can multiply very quickly.

PURPOSE

3. What is PulseNet used for?

   a. to match cases of foodborne illness that have the same source

   b. to identify restaurants with poor sanitary conditions

   c. to connect patients who have foodborne illnesses with doctors

   d. to record best practices in food production methods

DETAIL

4. According to the passage, why are people eating more imported food now?

   a. People want to have certain foods year-round.

   b. Imported foods are usually cheaper.

   c. Imported foods are usually safer.

   d. Consumers have more sophisticated tastes.

PARAPHRASE

5. What does Carmela Velazquez mean in paragraph I when she says, "The farmers we've trained will become models for all our growers"?

   a. The farmers will go on TV to talk about what they learned from her.

   b. More farmers will adopt the habits that were taught to the trained farmers.

   c. Both farmers and growers will now work together to assure food safety.

   d. Farmers need to listen to the growers to learn and decide what works for them.

EVALUATING STATEMENTS

B. Are the following statements true or false according to paragraph G, or is the information not given? Circle T (true), F (false), or NG (not given).

1. The salmonella outbreak in 2000 first affected people in Virginia.		**T F NG**
2. Everyone affected by that outbreak had eaten mangoes in the previous months.		**T F NG**
3. The outbreak was investigated by the Centers for Disease Control and Prevention.		**T F NG**
4. The salmonella outbreak was caused by farmers not washing their mangoes.		**T F NG**
5. Salmonella can contaminate several different kinds of food.		**T F NG**

Recognizing Cause and Effect Relationships (1)

A cause is an action or a condition that makes something happen. An effect is a result of that action. Some texts use words that indicate cause and effect relationships, such as *caused*, *as a result*, *because (of)*, *so*, *due to*, *consequently*, *thus*, and *the reason*. In other cases, a writer may imply a cause-effect relationship without using these words. As you read, try to make connections between events by asking *What caused …?* and *What was the result of …?* questions.

ANALYZING

A. Read the sentences below. In each sentence, underline the cause.

1. I didn't go to the doctor because I forgot about the appointment.
2. The medicine in our cabinet was old, so we threw it out.
3. The reason I didn't go to school was that I had a stomachache.
4. Due to new health guidelines, all food will be removed from the staff fridge on weekends.
5. Investigators believe improper hand washing caused the disease outbreak at the school.

CAUSE AND EFFECT

B. Match each cause below with its effect according to information from Reading A.

Causes

1. cutting open a food animal during processing •
2. the use of "factory" farms •
3. a salmonella outbreak linked to mangoes •
4. all-year demand for fresh fruits and vegetables •
5. improving sanitary conditions on farms •

Effects

• a. fewer cases of contaminated produce
• b. the death of two people
• c. meat can be contaminated by the bacteria inside
• d. greater dependence on imports
• e. bacteria will likely spread from animal to animal

CRITICAL THINKING Analyzing Solutions   Discuss these questions with a partner.

▶ How have Costa Rica and Sweden reduced the occurrence of foodborne diseases? Complete these notes with information from the reading passage.

Costa Rica: focus on safer farming of _____

Sweden: focus on safer farming of _____

▶ What might be some of the challenges of each approach? Note your ideas below.

_____

_____

DEFINITIONS **A.** Read the information below. Match each word in **red** with its definition (1–6).

In 2008, **contaminated** food caused a scare in the United States. Nine people died and 700 people **nationwide** suffered **infection** from salmonella poisoning. Authorities **determined** that the cause of the salmonella outbreak was peanut products.

Peanuts are used in a wide variety of products and are an **integral** part of health bars, cookies, ice cream varieties, and even dog biscuits. Although officials couldn't order a **compulsory** recall, stores voluntarily removed peanut products from their shelves.

▲ The average American consumes 1.5 kilograms of peanut butter every year.

1. _____ : required by law or a rule

2. _____ : being an essential part of something

3. _____ : happening or existing in all parts of a country

4. _____ : discovered the facts or truth about something

5. _____ : dirty or harmful because of dirt, chemicals, or radiation

6. _____ : the process of bacteria or viruses invading the body and making someone ill

WORDS IN CONTEXT **B.** Complete each sentence with the correct answer (a or b).

1. If contamination is **confined**, it _____ .
   a. occurs within a certain area
   b. has spread to many areas

2. **Digestion** is the body's system of _____ .
   a. fighting disease
   b. breaking down food

3. If a project is **feasible**, it _____ be done.
   a. can
   b. cannot

4. An **optimistic** person believes that the future will be _____ than today.
   a. worse
   b. better

WORD PARTS **C.** The suffix -*wide* in **nationwide** means "extending throughout." Complete the sentences using the words in the box. One word is extra.

city	company	nation	world

1. The outbreak was confined to the U.S.; it affected 12 states _____**wide**.

2. Shanghai has implemented a _____**wide** smoking ban in all its public parks.

3. Affecting millions of people _____**wide**, malaria is particularly prevalent in tropical countries.

BEFORE YOU READ

DISCUSSION **A.** Read the information below. What risks might be associated with biotech foods? Discuss with a partner.

In recent years, scientists have discovered ways of altering the genes of foods. For example, corn can be changed genetically so it's more resistant to insects, diseases, and droughts. While these biotech foods seem to offer clear benefits, critics say there are risks of genetically altering our food.

PREDICTING **B.** Read the questions below. Discuss your answers with a partner. Then read the passage to check your ideas.

1. Are biotech foods safe for humans?

2. Can biotech foods harm the environment?

3. Can biotech foods help feed the world?

The eggplants on the right have been genetically altered to increase insect resistance.

THE BATTLE FOR BIOTECH

A Genetic engineering (GE) of crops and animals through the manipulation of DNA is producing a **revolution** in food production. The potential to improve the quality and **nutritional** value of the food we eat seems unlimited. Such potential benefits **notwithstanding**, critics fear that genetically engineered products— so-called biotech foods—are being rushed to market before their effects are fully understood.

Q: What exactly are biotech foods?

B Biotech foods are produced from animals and plants that have been genetically altered. Genetic alteration is nothing new. Humans have been altering the genetic **traits** of plants for thousands of years by keeping seeds from the best crops and planting them the following years, and by breeding varieties to

Two 18-month-old coho salmon show the difference genetic engineering can make. The top fish has been given a modified gene that allows it to grow at a faster pace.

similar. In so doing, they transferred tens of thousands of genes. In contrast, today's genetic engineers can transfer just a few genes at a time between species that are distantly related, or not related at all. There are surprising examples: Rat genes have been inserted into lettuce plants to make a plant that produces vitamin C. Moth genes have been inserted into apple trees to add disease resistance. The purpose of conventional and modern techniques is the same—to insert genes from an organism that carries a desired trait into one that does not. Several dozen biotech food crops are currently on the market, among them varieties of corn, soybeans, and cotton. Most of these crops are engineered to help farmers deal with common farming problems such as weeds,[1] insects, and disease.

Q: Are biotech foods safe for humans?

D As far as we know. So far, problems have been few. In fact, according to a 2016 report from the National Academy of Sciences in the United States, "No differences have been found that indicate a higher risk to human health and safety from these GE foods than from their non-GE counterparts." Some GE foods might even be safer than non-GE foods. Corn damaged by insects often contains high levels of fumonisins—toxins[2] that grow in the wounds of the damaged corn. Lab tests have linked fumonisins with cancer in animals. Studies show that most corn **modified** for insect resistance has lower levels of fumonisins than conventional corn damaged by insects.

E However, biotech foods have had problems in the past. One such problem occurred in the mid-1990s, when soybeans were modified using genes from a nut. The

make them taste sweeter, grow bigger, or last longer. In this way, we've transformed the wild tomato from a fruit the size of a small stone to the giant ones we have today.

C On the other hand, the techniques of genetic engineering are new and different. **Conventional** breeders always used plants or animals that were related, or genetically

---

1 A **weed** is a wild plant that prevents other plants from growing properly.
2 A **toxin** is any poisonous substance produced by bacteria, animals, or plants.

TYPE AND LOCATION OF GE CROPS, 2015

U.S.

CANADA

UNITED STATES

MEXICO

HONDURAS

COSTA RICA

COLOMBIA

BRAZIL

BOLIVIA

PARAGUAY

CHILE   URUGUAY

ARGENTINA

CZECH REP   SLOVAKIA
ROMANIA

PORTUGAL   SPAIN

BURKINA FASO   SUDAN

SOUTH AFRICA

| CORN | SOYBEAN | COTTON | CANOLA | SUGAR BEET | ALFALFA | PAPAYA | SQUASH | POPLAR | BRINJAL/ EGGPLANT | POTATO | APPLE |

---

modified soybeans contained a protein[3] that causes reactions in humans who are **allergic** to nuts. While this protein was discovered before any damage was done, critics fear that other harmful proteins created through genetic modification may slip by unnoticed. Moving genes across dramatically different species—such as rats and lettuce—also makes critics nervous. They fear something could go wrong either in the function of the inserted gene or in the function of the host[4] DNA, with the possibility of unexpected health effects.

---

3 **Protein** is a substance found in food like meat and eggs.

4 A **host** is an animal or plant in which a foreign organism lives.

5 **Pesticides** are chemicals used to kill harmful insects.

Q: Can biotech foods harm the environment?

F Most scientists agree that the main safety issues of GE crops involve not people but the environment. Allison Snow, a plant ecologist at Ohio State University, worries that GE crops are being developed too quickly and released before they've been adequately tested.

G On the other hand, advocates of GE crops argue that some genetically modified plants may actually be good for the land, by offering an environmentally friendly **alternative** to pesticides,[5] which can pollute water and harm animals. Far fewer pesticides need to

and many other scientists argue that genetic modification can help address the urgent problems of food shortage and hunger by increasing crop quantities. Crops can be engineered to grow in areas with harsh, dry climates or in soils not usually suitable for farming.

I According to the World Health Organization, an estimated 250 million children in the world suffer from vitamin A **deficiency**. Between 250,000 and 500,000 go blind every year as a result, with half of those children dying within a year of losing their sight. "Golden rice"—a biotech variety named for its yellow color—is thought by some to be a potential solution to the suffering and illness caused by vitamin A deficiency.

J Other experts, however, claim that the biotechnology industry has exaggerated the benefits of golden rice. "Golden rice alone won't greatly **diminish** vitamin A deficiency," says Professor Marion Nestle of New York University. "Beta-carotene,[7] which is already widely available in fruit and vegetables, isn't converted to vitamin A when people are malnourished. Golden rice does not contain much beta-carotene, and whether it will improve vitamin A levels remains to be seen."

Q: What's next?

K Whether biotech foods will deliver on their promise of eliminating world hunger and improving the lives of all remains to be seen. Their potential is enormous, yet they carry risks. If science proceeds with caution, testing new products thoroughly and using sound judgment, the world may avoid the dangers of genetic modification while enjoying its benefits.

be applied to cotton plants that have been genetically modified to produce their own natural pesticides. While applied chemical pesticides kill nearly all the insects in a field, biotech crops with natural pesticides only harm insects that actually try to eat those crops.

Q: Can biotech foods help feed the world?

H "Eight hundred million people on this planet are malnourished,"[6] says Channapatna Prakash, a native of India and a scientist at Tuskegee University's Center for Plant Biotechnology Research in the U.S.A., "and the number continues to grow." Prakash

---

6 Someone who is **malnourished** is weakened from not eating enough food.

7 **Beta-carotene**, a natural substance found in red or orange fruit and vegetables, is used in the body to create vitamin A.

A. Choose the best answer for each question.

PURPOSE

1. What is the author's purpose in writing the passage?

    a. to make biotech foods seem as attractive as possible

    b. to show both sides of the biotech foods issue

    c. to convince the reader that biotech foods are dangerous

    d. to explain why biotech foods will probably not be successful

DETAIL

2. Which of the following is NOT practiced by conventional breeders?

    a. using related organisms to breed

    b. altering the genetic traits of organisms

    c. creating organisms with desired traits

    d. transferring just a few genes at a time from one organism to another

▲ **A genetically modified variety of cherry tomato**

INFERENCE

3. What is the danger of fumonisins?

    a. They might cause cancer in humans.

    b. They could reduce insect resistance in modified corn.

    c. They might cause insects to damage corn plants.

    d. They could kill insects.

DETAIL

4. Which of these concerns about GE crops is NOT mentioned?

    a. Some GE crops are being developed too quickly.

    b. Something could go wrong when moving genes across dramatically different species.

    c. GE crops are being released before they've been adequately tested.

    d. GE species will pollute water and harm animals.

MAIN IDEA

5. What is the main idea of the final paragraph?

    a. With care, the potential of biotech foods could possibly be realized.

    b. The risks of biotech foods seem to outweigh any possible benefits.

    c. The world has already seen great advances due to biotech foods.

    d. Biotech food development has been slowed by the many risks involved.

MATCHING

B. What are some of the effects of genetic alterations on crop production? Match an effect (a–d) with each crop (1–3) according to information from the reading passage. One effect is extra.

1. corn ___b___   **2.** soybean ___d___   **3.** cotton ___c___

a. It is more nutritious because it contains higher amounts of vitamin C.

b. It has lower levels of a particular group of toxins.

c. It requires fewer chemical pesticides, so it is better for the environment.

d. Since it contains nut proteins, people could have allergic reactions.

Evaluating Arguments

Writers sometimes present two sides of an argument—giving reasons for and against an idea. Understanding both sides is a useful way to consider an issue. It can also help you decide on your own opinion. To evaluate a writer's arguments, it can be useful to list the reasons for and against in a T-chart.

ANALYZING **A.** Look back at Reading B. Find arguments for and against biotech foods in the text.

COMPLETION **B.** Complete the chart below with words or phrases from Reading B.

Arguments for biotech foods	Arguments against biotech foods
Good history People have been changing plants genetically for [1] _thousands_ of years with no problems.	**Unexpected consequences** Something could go wrong when genes are moved across different species, with the possibility of [5] _health affects_ .
Safe for humans Studies indicate GE foods do not pose a [2] _higher risk_ to human health than non-GE foods.	**Environmental risks** GE crops are sometimes released into the environment before they have been [6] _tested_ .
Environmental benefits GE crops can produce their own [3] _Natural_ pesticides, so farmers can apply fewer [4] _Chemical_ pesticides.	**Unproven benefits** The health benefits of some GE foods may have been exaggerated.
Increased crops Farmers can grow more crops in areas that are usually not suitable for farming.	

CRITICAL THINKING Evaluating Arguments

▶ Look at the arguments in the chart above. Underline any evidence from the reading passage (e.g., examples, statistics, expert opinions) that supports each argument. I)

▶ Based on the information from the reading passage, would you eat genetically modified foods? Why or why not? Note your answers below. Then share with a partner.

_no_

COMPLETION   **A.** Complete the information using the correct form of words from the box. Two words are extra.

> allergic   conventional   diminish
> modify   notwithstanding   revolution

According to a recent study, Chinese farmers growing rice that has been genetically [1]_____ successfully reduced pesticide use by 80 percent. The GE rice seed also boosted crop production by almost 10 percent. Some think this could signal a(n) [2]_____ in food and agriculture.

However, critics worry that some people may suffer unexpected [3]_____ reactions to GE foods. Such fears and concerns [4]_____, proven examples of problems with GE foods have been quite rare.

^ Genetically modified produce

WORDS IN CONTEXT   **B.** Complete the sentences. Circle the correct words.

1. **Nutritional** food is food that is *bad / good* for you.

2. If you have an **alternative**, there is *a choice / no choice*.

3. A diet **deficient** in protein includes too *much / little* protein.

4. A **conventional** way of doing something is *a new / the usual* way.

5. An example of a plant's **traits** might be its *price / size*.

6. When something **diminishes**, it becomes *smaller / bigger* in size or importance.

WORD USAGE   **C.** The words in **bold** below are near synonyms of **diminish**. Circle the correct word to complete each sentence. Use a dictionary or thesaurus to help you.

1. In the United States, crop yields are expected to **fade** / decline because of droughts.

2. Increases in oil production in the United States will lessen / **drop** the need to import oil.

3. Many countries think it's a good idea to **contract** / reduce the amount of pesticides used in agriculture.

4. Some consumers were initially reluctant to buy GE foods—but this resistance has started to **contract** / fade.

Workers check the quality of tomatoes at a food processing plant.

IS OUR FOOD SAFE?

BEFORE YOU WATCH

DISCUSSION **A.** Think of the process food goes through from farm to table. At what stages can health risks occur? What are some ways food can make us sick? List some ideas with a partner.

PREVIEWING **B.** Read this extract from the video. Match the words and phrases in **bold** with their definitions (1–3).

> "How often does food make us sick? It's **hard to tell** since so many cases go **unreported**. And **globalization** of food production makes it harder and harder to track. But we do know this: At least one in six Americans gets sick from food poisoning every year."

1. _____ : expansion throughout the world

2. _____ : difficult to detect or understand

3. _____ : kept private or hidden

MAIN IDEAS   **A. Watch the video. Check (✓) the ideas that are mentioned.**

☐ a. Contaminated water, animals, or equipment can taint food.

☐ b. Symptoms of food poisoning may start within hours after eating contaminated food.

☐ c. The majority of foodborne illnesses in the U.S. is caused by unknown pathogens.

COMPLETION   **B. Watch the video again and complete the notes below.**

Annual food poisoning statistics in the U.S.

• number of people who end up hospitalized: [1]_____

• number of people killed: [2]_____

2011 E. coli outbreak in Germany

• nearly [3]_____ people became sick with diarrhea, fever, and vomiting

• officials determined that [4]_____ were the real cause

• number of deaths reported: [5]_____; number of countries affected: [6]_____

CRITICAL THINKING Evaluating Ideas   How strongly do you agree with the following statements
(1 = strongly disagree; 5 = strongly agree)? Circle your answers. Then discuss with a partner.

1. The government should ban all chemical pesticides.   1   2   3   4   5

2. Restaurants involved in food poisoning cases should face criminal prosecution.   1   2   3   4   5

3. Eating home-cooked meals is safer than dining out.   1   2   3   4   5

VOCABULARY REVIEW

Do you remember the meanings of these words? Check (✓) the ones you know. Look back at the
unit and review any words you're not sure of.

Reading A

☐ compulsory   ☐ confine*   ☐ contaminate   ☐ determine   ☐ digestion

☐ feasible   ☐ infect   ☐ integral*   ☐ nationwide   ☐ optimistic

Reading B

☐ allergic   ☐ alternative*   ☐ conventional*   ☐ deficiency   ☐ diminish*

☐ modify*   ☐ notwithstanding*   ☐ nutritional   ☐ revolution*   ☐ trait

* Academic Word List

4

DESIGN AND ENGINEERING

The Lotus Temple in Delhi, India, is noted for its half-open lotus flower design.

Discuss these questions with a partner.

1. Think of some famous or innovative buildings. What do you think influenced or inspired their design?

2. Can you think of any man-made objects or machines that were inspired by nature?

61

BEFORE YOU READ

DEFINITIONS **A.** Read the information below and match each phrase in **bold** with its definition (1–4).

Biomimetic engineers have a **specific purpose** in mind: to create designs that **have the potential** to change our everyday lives. These engineers **draw inspiration** from designs found in nature, many of which are **incredibly complex**. They then apply the design principles in order to improve existing technologies or to create entirely new ones.

1. _____ : to get ideas

2. _____ : extremely difficult to understand

3. _____ : to possess the capability

4. _____ : a definite goal or aim

SKIMMING **B.** Skim paragraph A and answer these questions.

1. Who is Andrew Parker?

2. What special ability does the thorny devil have?

3. What does Parker want to do with the knowledge he has obtained?

DESIGN BY NATURE:
BIOMIMETICS

A One cloudless midsummer day, biologist Andrew Parker knelt in the baking red sand of an Australian desert and gently placed the right back leg of a thorny devil into a dish of water. The thorny devil—a small lizard that has learned to survive in the extreme heat of the Australian desert—has a secret that fascinated Parker. "Look, look!" he exclaimed. "Its back is completely drenched!"[1] Sure enough, in less than a minute, water from the dish had traveled up the lizard's leg, across its skin, and into its mouth. It was, in essence, drinking through its foot. The thorny devil can also do this when standing on wet sand—a **vital** competitive advantage in the desert. Parker had come here to solve the riddle of how it does this, not from purely **biological** interest, but with a specific purpose in mind: to make a **device** to help people collect water in the desert.

From Natural Wonder to Useful Tool

B Parker is a leading scientist in the field of biomimetics—applying designs from nature to solve problems in engineering, materials science, medicine, and other fields. His studies of the body coverings of butterflies and beetles have led to brighter screens for cell phones. He has even drawn inspiration from nature's past: While visiting a museum in Poland, he noticed a 45-million-year-old fly trapped in amber[2] and observed how the shape of its eye's surface reduced light reflection. This shape is now being used in solar panels to make them more efficient.

---

1 If something is **drenched**, it is completely wet.
2 **Amber** is a hard yellowish-brown substance used for making jewelry.

❮ **A thorny devil lizard**

Cockleburs have hooked spines that attach to clothing and animal fur. This design inspired the creation of Velcro (right).

C As part of the next **phase** in his plan to create a water-collection device inspired by the lizard, Parker sent his observations to Michael Rubner and Robert Cohen, two colleagues at the Massachusetts Institute of Technology. Parker is full of enthusiasm about the many possibilities of biomimetics. Rubner and Cohen, on the other hand, are much more practical; they focus on the ideas that have a chance of being applied successfully. This combination of biological **insight** and engineering pragmatism[3] is vital to success in biomimetics. And it has led to several promising technologies.

D Though Rubner and Cohen are certainly impressed by biological structures, they consider nature just a starting point for innovation. Cohen says, "The natural structure provides a clue to what is useful … But maybe you can do it better." They consider a biomimetics project a success only if it has the potential to make a useful tool for people. "Looking at pretty structures in nature is not sufficient," says Cohen. "What I want to know is can we actually transform these structures into [something] with true utility[4] in the real world?"

Unlocking Nature's Secrets

E The work of Parker, Rubner, and Cohen is only one part of a growing global biomimetics movement. Scientists around the world are studying and trying to copy a wide variety of nature's design secrets. In the United States, researchers are looking at the shape of humpback whale fins in order to help wind turbines

3 **Pragmatism** means dealing with problems in a practical way.
4 The **utility** of something is its usefulness.

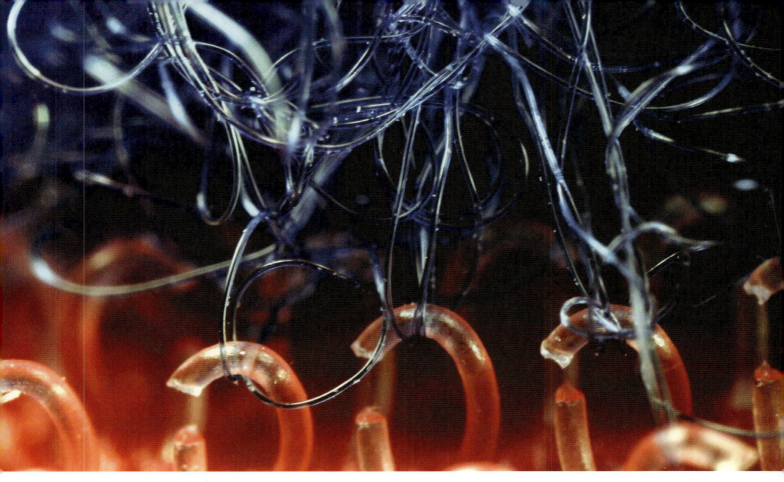

▲ **A close-up look at Velcro**

generate more electric energy. The shape of the body of a certain fish has inspired designers at Mercedes-Benz to develop a more efficient car design. By analyzing how termites[5] keep their large mounds at the right temperature and humidity, architects in Zimbabwe have built more comfortable buildings. And in Japan, medical researchers have developed a painless needle that is similar in shape to the proboscis[6] of a mosquito.

The Bio-Inspired Robot

F   Potentially, one of the most useful applications of biomimetics is the robot. Robots can perform tasks that might be too boring or dangerous for humans, but they can be extremely difficult to build. Professor Ronald Fearing of the University of California is creating a tiny robot fly that can be used in surveillance[7] or rescue operations. Fearing's fly is a simplified copy of the real thing. "Some things are just too mysterious and complicated to be able to replicate,"[8] he says. It will still be years before his robot fly can perform anything like an actual fly, but Fearing is confident that over time he will close the **gap** between nature and human engineering.

G   At Stanford University in California, Mark Cutkosky is working on a robot gecko. Cutkosky studied the extremely small structures on the tiny lizard's feet that allow it to run up and down **vertical** walls. He applied what he learned to create

---

5   **Termites** are small insects that eat wood.
6   A **proboscis** is a long mouth part, usually of an insect.
7   **Surveillance** is the close observation of a person or place, especially by the police or army.
8   If you **replicate** something, you make a copy of it.

Stickybot, a robot that can walk up and down smooth vertical surfaces. The U.S. military, which **funds** the project, hopes that one day Stickybot will be able to climb up a building and stay there for days, monitoring the area below. Cutkosky believes there will be a range of nonmilitary uses as well. "I'm trying to get robots to go places where they've never gone before," he says. For now, Stickybot can only climb extremely smooth surfaces—unlike a real gecko, which can run up just about any surface very quickly.

H Despite the promise of the field and the brilliant people who work in it, biomimetics has led to surprisingly few business successes. Perhaps only one product has become truly famous—Velcro. The material was invented in 1948 by Swiss engineer George de Mestral, who copied the way seeds called cockleburs stuck to his dog's fur. Some blame industry, whose short-term expectations about how soon a project should be completed and become profitable conflict with the time-consuming nature of biomimetics research. But the main reason biomimetics hasn't yet been a business success is that nature is incredibly complex.

I **Nonetheless**, the gap with nature is **gradually** closing. Researchers are using more powerful microscopes, high-speed computers, and other new technologies to learn more from nature. A growing number of biomimetic materials are being produced. And although the field of biomimetics has yet to become a very successful commercial industry, it has already developed into a powerful tool for understanding nature's secrets.

⌃ **Gecko toes have adaptations that enable them to adhere to most surfaces.**

MORE NATURE-INSPIRED INNOVATIONS

- A type of glass has been created that draws inspiration from spider webs. Birds can see the ultraviolet reflective strands in the glass, and thus avoid flying into it.

- Water does not stick to a lotus leaf because of its surface structure. Copying this process, one company has developed a water-repelling sealant that can be sprayed on surfaces.

- Swimmers can now swim faster because of new suits that mimic the design of sharkskin. This design is also used to reduce friction on ships, submarines, and airplanes.

- High-speed trains have long beak-shaped noses, modeled after the kingfisher bird. This reduces noise and allows the train to travel much faster.

- A new fan on the market is based on the spiral shape seen in tornadoes and whirlpools. The fan cools the air more efficiently than traditional fans.

⌃ **A swimmer tests a new swimsuit designed to increase speed.**

A. Choose the best answer for each question.

DETAIL   **1.** Why did Andrew Parker go to the Australian desert?

     a. to capture and bring back a thorny devil
     b. to learn how the thorny devil collects water
     c. to study the diet of the thorny devil
     d. to prove that thorny devils don't need water

DETAIL   **2.** What has the study of termite mounds inspired?

     a. a more efficient car design   c. more comfortable buildings
     b. improved wind turbines   d. a painless needle

REFERENCE   **3.** What does *things* in Ronald Fearing's quote "Some things are just too mysterious and complicated …" (paragraph F) refer to?

     a. abilities   c. copies
     b. robot flies   d. rescue operations

DETAIL   **4.** According to the passage, what is a limitation of Stickybot?

     a. It can't climb up rough, uneven surfaces.
     b. It can move forward but not backward.
     c. It is too heavy to stay on a wall for long.
     d. The military won't let others use the technology.

DETAIL   **5.** Which of these statements about biomimetics is NOT true?

     a. Parker hopes to create a water-collection device inspired by the thorny devil.
     b. Studying humpback whale fins may be useful for improving wind turbines.
     c. The body of a certain fish has inspired a car design.
     d. Stickybot is perhaps the most famous biomimetic creation so far.

MATCHING   **B.** **What are some applications of biomimetics? Match each application (1–4) with the animal trait that inspired it (a–d).**

     a. butterfly body coverings
     b. spider webs
     c. sharkskin
     d. kingfisher beaks

     _b_ **1.** make rail travel quieter and faster
     _a_ **2.** develop brighter cell phone screens
     _D_ **3.** create a type of glass that is more bird-friendly
     _c_ **4.** design new swimwear that can make swimmers move faster

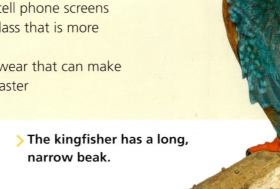

> **The kingfisher has a long, narrow beak.**

Scanning for Information (2)—Matching Information to Paragraphs

Scanning is an important skill for taking exams, but how you approach scanning should depend on the question type. With **matching information questions**, you have to match statements about reasons, descriptions, examples, and so forth from a text to particular paragraphs. First, read each statement carefully and identify key words or phrases. These exact words may not appear in the passage, so you will need to think of synonyms or antonyms that might. For example, if you are asked to find a prediction, you might want to scan for "will" in the text.

MATCHING **A.** Read the sentences below (1–3) from Reading A. Match each sentence with the type of information it contains (a–c).

1. Cutkosky believes there will be a range of nonmilitary uses as well. •

• a. a reason

2. For now, Stickybot can only climb extremely smooth surfaces—unlike a real gecko, which can run up just about any surface very quickly. •

• b. a prediction

3. The main reason biomimetics hasn't yet been a business success is that nature is incredibly complex. •

• c. a contrast

SCANNING **B.** Find the following information in Reading A and note which paragraph (A–I) each item appears in.

_____ 1. a definition of biomimetics

_____ 2. a prediction about the future of robot flies

_____ 3. the reason the U.S. military is financing a biomimetic project

_____ 4. an example of a biomimetic product that has become truly famous

CRITICAL THINKING Applying Ideas Work in a group. Imagine you are tasked with inventing a new biomimetic application. Look at the animal attributes below. Choose one and come up with a biomimetic application for it.

- worms that glow in the dark
- snakes that shed their skin
- beavers that have waterproof fur
- octopuses that can change color

< **A bioluminescent European glow-worm**

VOCABULARY PRACTICE

COMPLETION **A.** Circle the correct words to complete the paragraph.

One of the earliest examples of biomimicry is the Eastgate Centre in Harare, Zimbabwe. Designed by the architect Mick Pearce, this large office building doesn't use conventional heating or air conditioning, but is [1]**nonetheless** / **vital** regulated such that it is never too hot or too cold. Pearce noticed that African termites keep their mounds cool inside by using a clever system of air vents that open and close, regulating temperature. This [2]**phase** / **insight** inspired him to design the Eastgate Centre to work in a similar way. A series of [3]**funds** / **gaps**, vents, and [4]**vertical** / **gradual** chimneys move air through the building—using less than 10 percent of the energy of a conventional building its size. As the temperature [5]**gradually** / **biologically** rises and falls outside, it stays comfortable inside.

∧ **Eastgate Centre, Harare, Zimbabwe**

WORDS IN CONTEXT **B.** Complete each sentence with the correct answer (a or b).

1. If an organization **funds** a project, they _____ it.
   a. are inspired by   b. pay for

2. **Biological** processes are those that describe _____.
   a. living organisms   b. mechanical objects

3. A **device** is an object created _____.
   a. by natural processes   b. for a particular purpose

4. A **phase** of an engineering project refers to _____.
   a. its overall cost   b. a particular stage

5. Something that is **vital** is _____.
   a. necessary   b. disproved by others

COLLOCATIONS **C.** The words in the box are often used with the word **vital**. Complete the sentences with the correct words from the box. One word is extra.

absolutely	importance	link	role

1. The tourism industry is of vital _____ to the national economy.

2. Biomimetic research is _____ vital if we wish to develop more sustainable solutions to human challenges in design and engineering.

3. Mick Pearce has played a vital _____ in designing eco-friendly buildings in Africa.

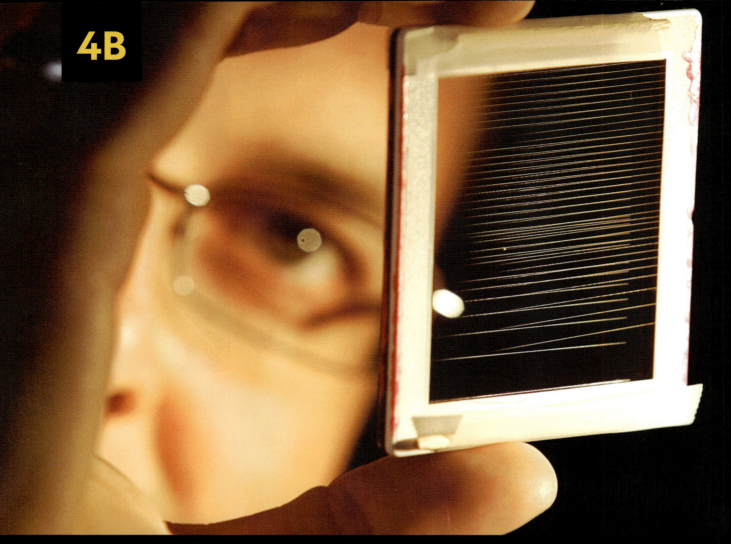

4B

∧ Biochemist Thomas Scheibel holds a frame containing **synthetic** spider's thread. This artificial **fiber**—stronger than real silk—could be used to create **textiles** for clothing and other products.

BEFORE YOU READ

DEFINITIONS **A.** Read the caption above. Use the words in **bold** to complete these definitions (1–3).

  1. _____ are types of woven cloth.

  2. A _____ is a thin thread of a natural or artificial substance.

  3. _____ products are made from chemicals or artificial substances.

PREDICTING **B.** What are some recent innovations in textiles and clothing? Discuss with a partner and note some ideas. Then read the passage and check if any of your ideas are mentioned.

_____

_____

WEAVING THE FUTURE

A Alex Soza is a young Danish fashion designer. He says his ideas come to him in dreams: "I daydream. That's how I get ideas." One of his inventions, a jacket that stays **suspended** in the air like a balloon after it is taken off, arose from such a daydream. "I was on the subway," he explained, "and this picture of a floating jacket popped into my mind." Soza is one of many dreamers and pioneers who are turning textile **fantasies** into realities.

High-Tech Textiles

B Not long ago, all fibers that were used to make textiles came from natural sources: wool from the hair of sheep, cotton from the cotton plant, silk from silk worms. The first truly synthetic fiber didn't appear until 1935, when scientists at the DuPont Company invented nylon. Nylon is just one of various industrially produced substances called polymers. Polymers can be pulled into a thread, which makes them well suited for use in textile **manufacturing**.

C Synthetic textiles have come a long way since nylon. Kevlar, a textile that is stronger than steel, is used in bulletproof vests and in ropes used by astronauts. Coiled fibers are used in clothing that contracts in cold weather to keep someone warm, and expands in hot weather, creating small holes to keep someone cool. Other high-tech fibers can resist very high temperatures—perfect for firefighters and race-car drivers.

D Not all companies are **forthcoming** about their products for fear of having their ideas stolen. However, Hugues Vinchon, a manager at Dubar Warneton—a manufacturer of high-tech textiles in France—is happy to display some of his company's amazing synthetic fibers. There is an oil-eating textile that absorbs five times its weight in oil, and is perfect for cleaning up oil spills. Another absorbs vibrations;[1] "Can you imagine a motorboat you

---

1 A **vibration** is a small, fast, and continuous shaking movement.

Sensors on this smart shirt can monitor the wearer's breathing and transmit the data to a cell phone.

can't hear?" he says. There is also an ordinary-looking cloth bag that is completely water soluble,[2] according to Vinchon. "It's strong enough to carry heavy objects. But if I dip it in boiling water, it disappears."

E Some high-tech textiles draw their inspiration from nature. Spider silk is a natural fiber that is five times as strong as steel. Unfortunately, spiders cannot be farmed as they will eat each other. The biotechnology firm Nexia has come up with a possible alternative to spider farming: They have inserted a spider gene into goats, **thereby** causing the goats to produce a milk that contains a protein required for spider silk. Nexia's head, Jeff Turner, is already dreaming of applications for the new fiber, named BioSteel. "Why use rockets to lift objects into orbit?[3] ... Why not have a [big] satellite and dangle a rope down to Earth and pull them up? ... [There's] not a rope that will hold its weight at that length—but spider silk with its high strength-to-weight ratio could."

Wearable Electronics

F Textiles have always been used in clothing. Modern, high-tech textiles may redefine what clothes are all about. "In the past, clothing protected us from the elements," says Ian Scott, head of technology for women's wear at department store Marks & Spencer. "Then clothing became about fashion. The future is about clothing that can do something for you. It's no longer passive. It's active." One example of this active clothing that he hopes to sell in the next few years is an "intelligent bra," a sports bra that can sense stress and adjust its dimensions to give perfect support. Another sports product is Komodo Technologies' smart sleeve for athletes. It has built-in sensors[4] that measure your fitness

---

2 If something is water **soluble**, it will dissolve in water.

3 An **orbit** is the curved path in space that an object follows as it moves around a planet, moon, or star.

4 A **sensor** is an instrument that reacts to certain physical conditions, such as heat or light.

and stress levels. The data can then be viewed on a smartphone app. The company is also researching ways the sleeve can help detect heart disease.

G Other wearable electronics are being pioneered at a design laboratory in London run by the European manufacturer Philips Electronics. They are in the planning stages for various high-tech products, including an "intelligent" electronic apron. This smart apron acts as a kind of remote-control device. It has a built-in microphone that allows the wearer to operate kitchen **appliances** using voice commands.

H While there are many interesting clothing innovations in the pipeline, few have hit the market. One that did was marketed a few years ago as the first wearable electronics jacket. The jacket, called the ICD+, sold for about a thousand dollars. It had an MP3 player and cell phone. Headphones were built into the hood, and it had a microphone in the collar. Clive

van Heerden, director of the Intelligent Fibres group of Philips Design, pointed out that it was an early first step, and a conservative one: "We want to make the jacket that makes the coffee and picks up the kids and keeps track of the shopping list, but it's not going to happen overnight."

Future Warriors

I One of the most important areas of clothing innovation is for the military. High-tech textiles are everywhere at the U.S. Army Soldier Systems Center in Natick, Massachusetts. As part of their Future Warrior program, researchers are developing uniforms that will make a soldier difficult or impossible to see. Fibers in the uniform would take on the same color, brightness, and patterns of the wearer's surroundings. A soldier dressed in such a uniform would become nearly invisible to the enemy.

J In addition to clothing innovations, the researchers at Natick are also working on **portable** buildings made of what are essentially large, high-strength textile balloons. This "airbeam" technology would allow a team to build a hangar[5] in a **fraction** of the time it would take to build one out of metal. The largest air-filled beams, about 0.75 meters in diameter and 24 meters long, are so **rigid** that you can hang a heavy truck from one. Whereas a conventional metal hangar takes ten people five days to set up, one made of airbeams can be set up by just six people in two days.

K Today's textile innovations are astonishing. From Alex Soza's artistic jacket to smart aprons to invisible military uniforms, high-tech textiles will soon be appearing in more and more places. Who can **foresee** what these textile innovators will dream up next? "It's about imagination!" says Soza, with a bright look in his eye. "It's a beautiful dream! It's turning science fiction into scientific fact!"

---

5 A **hangar** is a large building in which aircraft are kept.

A. Choose the best answer for each question.

PURPOSE

1. What is the main purpose of the passage?

    a. to provide a historical overview of innovative fashion styles

    b. to introduce the reader to developments in high-tech textiles

    c. to convince the reader to buy the latest synthetic fashions

    d. to explain how modern fashions are often inspired by nature

INFERENCE

2. Why does Hugues Vinchon mention a motorboat you can't hear?

    a. to explain one of the properties of an oil-absorbing fabric

    b. to give an example of how quietly his textile factory runs

    c. to evoke admiration for a fabric that can absorb vibrations

    d. to show that he is not afraid of having his ideas stolen

INFERENCE

3. Which person do you think would be most likely to design a coat made of paper with six sleeves that three people can wear together?

    a. Alex Soza

    b. Hugues Vinchon

    c. Jeff Turner

    d. Ian Scott

PARAPHRASE

4. What does Clive van Heerden mean, when talking about the jacket, that "it's not going to happen overnight" (paragraph H)?

    a. It's not going to happen until tomorrow.

    b. It's going to take a short time to happen.

    c. It's going to take a long time to happen.

    d. It's probably never going to happen.

COHESION

5. The following sentence would best be placed at the end of which paragraph?

    Thanks to them, the world of high-tech textiles is an exciting place to be these days.

    a. paragraph A

    b. paragraph B

    c. paragraph I

    d. paragraph K

SCANNING

Review this reading skill in Unit 4A

B. Find the following information in the passage. Note which paragraph (A–K) each item appears in.

    _C_ **1.** a reason why there are no spider farms

    _D_ **2.** three examples of fibers from natural sources

    _K_ **3.** a quote from someone who discusses science fiction

    _F_ **4.** the purpose of everyday clothing in the past

    _A_ **5.** an explanation of how a fashion designer gets his ideas

Recognizing Lexical Cohesion

Writers use different techniques to avoid repetition in order to add interest and variety to a text. Recognizing how a writer achieves lexical cohesion allows you to better understand the flow of ideas and the relationship between them. Look at some of the following ways a writer can achieve lexical cohesion:

Synonyms: Using a word that means the same (or nearly the same) as another word (e.g., *cold, icy*).

Antonyms: Using a word that means the opposite of another word (e.g., *big, small*).

Repetition: Repeating the same word, or using a different form of the word (e.g., *manufactures, manufacturing*).

Reference: Using a pronoun or determiner that refers back to another word (e.g., *fibers, they*).

Subordination: Using a specific example of a more general word (e.g., *fibers, silk*).

RECOGNIZING
LEXICAL COHESION

A. Read the sentences below from Reading B. Note if the two underlined words in each item are examples of **A** (antonyms), **RP** (repetition), **RF** (reference), or **SU** (subordination).

1. Not long ago, all fibers that were used to make textiles came from <u>natural</u> sources … The first truly <u>synthetic</u> fiber didn't appear until 1935. _*A*_

2. <u>Nylon</u> is just one of various industrially produced substances called <u>polymers</u>. _____

3. <u>Polymers</u> can be pulled into a thread, which makes <u>them</u> well suited for use in textile manufacturing. _____

4. Coiled fibers are used in clothing that contracts in cold weather to keep someone <u>warm</u>, and expands in hot weather, creating small holes to keep someone <u>cool</u>. _____

5. Textiles have always been used in <u>clothing</u>. Modern, high-tech textiles may redefine what <u>clothes</u> are all about. _____

RECOGNIZING
LEXICAL COHESION

B. Look back at Reading B to find these examples of lexical cohesion.

1. an antonym of *passive* in paragraph F   _____

2. a synonym of *intelligent* in paragraph G   _____

3. the word(s) referred to by *It* in paragraph G, line 7   _____

4. a synonym of *impossible to see* in paragraph I   _____

5. a different form of the word *innovations* in paragraph K   _____

CRITICAL THINKING Applying Ideas   Can you think of possible future applications of wearable electronics? Discuss with a partner and note your ideas below.

_____

_____

VOCABULARY PRACTICE

COMPLETION   **A.** Complete the paragraph with words from the box.

fantasy	rigid	suspended	thereby

∧ *The Mastaba*, **London**

The artist Christo uses colorful man-made materials to temporarily change how an outdoor place looks, ¹_____ allowing people to see the place in a new way. In *The Gates*, large sheets of orange fabric were ²_____ over 7,500 vinyl frames and placed around Central Park in New York. In *The Mastaba*, Christo used over 7,000 oil barrels painted pink and blue to construct a large, ³_____ sculpture that floated on a lake in London. It takes an incredible amount of time to construct these kinds of projects. Once Christo settles on an artistic idea, it takes time, work, and money to turn his ⁴_____ into reality.

DEFINITIONS   **B.** Match the words in the box with the definitions below.

appliance	foresee	forthcoming
fraction	**manufacturing**	**portable**

1. _____ : able to be easily carried or moved

2. _____ : a small part or amount of something

3. _____ : a device (often electrical) used at home

4. _____ : to realize something before it happens

5. _____ : willing to give information or to talk

6. _____ : the business of producing goods on a large scale

WORD PARTS   **C.** The prefix *fore-* in **foresee** means "before." Complete the sentences using the words in the box. One word is extra.

cast	front	ground	sight

1. Sales of smart clothing are **fore**_____ to rise in the future.

2. Steve Jobs had the **fore**_____ to reimagine the cell phone.

3. Companies like Philips Electronics are at the **fore**_____ of wearable technologies.

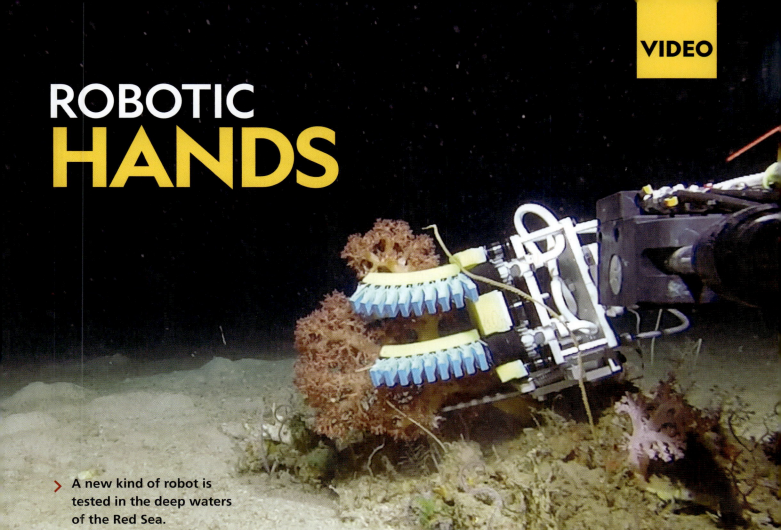

ROBOTIC HANDS

> **A new kind of robot is tested in the deep waters of the Red Sea.**

BEFORE YOU WATCH

PREVIEWING **A.** Read the information. The words in **bold** appear in the video. Match these words with their definitions below.

Marine biologists collect samples of deep-sea **corals** in order to analyze their **genomes** and other characteristics. They often use underwater robots to collect samples from the ocean. Unfortunately, these mechanical "hands" can destroy **fragile** marine life—their hard, metal fingers are unable to **grab** deep-sea organisms without damaging them. Marine biologist David Gruber and roboticist Robert Wood are now developing a new kind of robot to address this problem.

1. coral •
2. genome •
3. fragile •
4. grab •

• a. easily broken or damaged
• b. to hold tightly
• c. the complete set of genetic information in an organism
• d. a hard substance formed in the sea from the bones of very small sea animals

DISCUSSION **B.** Look at the photo above and read the caption. How might this robotic hand be better suited for collecting deep-sea organisms? Discuss with a partner.

GIST **A.** Watch the video. Check (✓) two things that are shown in the video.

    ☐ a. the development of the squishy robot fingers in a lab

    ☐ b. scientists testing the squishy robot fingers in a deep-sea environment

    ☐ c. above-water applications of the squishy robot fingers

EVALUATING STATEMENTS **B.** Watch the video again. Are the following statements true or false? Circle **T** (true) or **F** (false).

1.	The team is testing the squishy robot fingers in the Red Sea because it is a very rich coral environment.	T	F
2.	The squishy robot fingers are made of rubber.	T	F
3.	The squishy robot fingers were originally developed for oil exploration.	T	F
4.	The squishy robot fingers do not work well on land.	T	F
5.	The deep-sea test of the squishy robot fingers was successful.	T	F

CRITICAL THINKING Applying Ideas   Work in a small group and discuss these questions.

▶ Which trait or ability of an animal or a plant not mentioned in this unit do you think would be useful to replicate? Brainstorm a list of attributes and note your ideas below.

_____

_____

▶ Choose one of your ideas above. Can you think of a practical use for it?

_____

VOCABULARY REVIEW

Do you remember the meanings of these words? Check (✓) the ones you know. Look back at the unit and review any words you're not sure of.

Reading A

☐ biological	☐ device*	☐ fund*	☐ gap	☐ gradually
☐ insight*	☐ nonetheless	☐ phase*	☐ vertical	☐ vital

Reading B

☐ appliance	☐ fantasy	☐ foresee	☐ forthcoming*	☐ fraction
☐ manufacturing	☐ portable	☐ rigid*	☐ suspend*	☐ thereby

* Academic Word List

5

HUMAN JOURNEY

> ⌄ A reenactment of the migration of early human hunter-gatherers

WARM UP

Discuss these questions with a partner.

1. What do you know about the lives of early humans?

2. What kinds of evidence help us learn about our human ancestors?

5A

BEFORE YOU READ

UNDERSTANDING MAPS

A. The map on page 82 shows the likely migration routes of our human ancestors as they populated the world. Study the map and complete each of these sentences with the name of a continent.

1. The first modern humans originally came from ___Europe___.

2. The continent most recently populated by modern humans is ___USA___.

3. Modern humans crossed over to North America from

_____.

4. ___World___ was populated by modern humans 40,000–30,000 years ago.

SKIMMING

B. Skim the reading passage on the next three pages. What kinds of evidence are scientists looking for to understand the migrations of our human ancestors?

> As our human ancestors spread out across the continents, they gave rise to a variety of faces and races.

THE DNA TRAIL

A Everybody loves a good story, and when it's finished, this may be the greatest one ever told. It begins in Africa with a group of people. There are perhaps just a few hundred, surviving by hunting animals and gathering fruits, vegetables, and nuts. It ends about 200,000 years later, with their seven billion **descendants** spread across the Earth.

B In between is an exciting tale of survival, movement, isolation, and conquest, most of it occurring before recorded history. Who were those first modern people in Africa? What routes did they take when they left their home continent to expand into Europe and Asia? When and how did humans reach the Americas? For decades, the only proof was found in a small number of **scattered** bones and artifacts that our ancestors had left behind. In the past 20 years, however, DNA technologies have allowed scientists to find a record of ancient human migrations in the DNA of living people.

Tracing Ancestry in DNA

C "Every drop of human blood contains a history book written in the language of our genes," says population geneticist[1]

Spencer Wells. The human genetic code, or genome, is 99.9 percent **identical** throughout the world. The **bulk** of our DNA is the same. However, the remainder is responsible for our individual differences—in eye color or disease risk, for example. On very rare occasions, a small change—called a mutation—can occur. This can then be passed down to all of that person's descendants. Generations later, finding that same mutation in two people's DNA indicates that they share the same ancestor. By comparing mutations in many different populations, scientists can **trace** their ancestral connections.

D These ancient mutations are easiest to track in two places. One is in DNA that is passed from mother to child (called mitochondrial DNA, or mtDNA). The other is in DNA that travels from father to son (known as the Y chromosome, the part of DNA that determines a child will be a boy). By comparing the mtDNA and Y chromosomes of people from various populations, geneticists can get a rough idea of where and when those groups separated in the great migrations around the planet.

---

1 A **geneticist** is a scientist who studies DNA and genes.

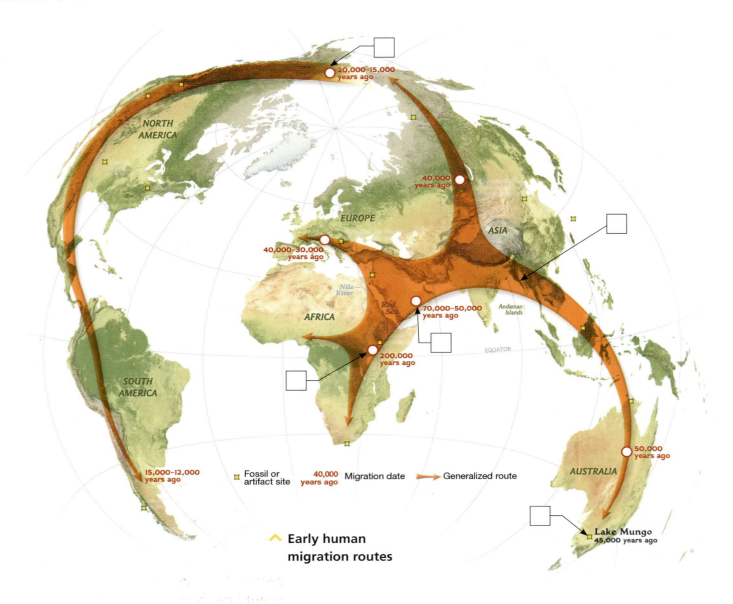

North America

20,000-15,000 years ago

40,000 years ago

Europe

Asia

40,000-30,000 years ago

Nile River

Red Sea

Africa

70,000-50,000 years ago

Andaman Islands

EQUATOR

200,000 years ago

South America

15,000-12,000 years ago

☒ Fossil or artifact site   **40,000 years ago** Migration date   ➤ Generalized route

50,000 years ago

AUSTRALIA

Lake Mungo 45,000 years ago

∧ Early human migration routes

Out of Africa

E   In the mid-1980s, a study compared mtDNA from people around the world. It found that people of African descent had twice as many genetic differences from each other than did others. Because mutations seem to occur at a steady **rate** over time, scientists concluded that modern humans must have lived in Africa at least twice as long as anywhere else. They now **calculate** that all living humans maternally descend from a single woman who lived **roughly** 150,000 years ago in Africa, a "mitochondrial Eve." If geneticists are right, all of humanity is linked to Eve through an unbroken chain of mothers. This Eve was soon joined by "Y-chromosome Adam," the possible genetic father of us all, also from Africa. DNA studies have confirmed that all the people on Earth can trace their ancestry to ancient Africans.

F   What seems certain is that at a remarkably recent date—probably between 50,000 and 70,000 years ago—one small group of people, the ancestors of modern humans outside of Africa, left Africa for western Asia. They either migrated around the wider northern end of the Red Sea, or across its narrow southern opening.

G Once in Asia, genetic evidence suggests, the population split. One group stayed temporarily in the Middle East, while the other began a journey that would last tens of thousands of years. Moving a little farther with each new generation, they followed the coast around the Arabian Peninsula, India, and Southeast Asia, all the way to Australia. "The movement was probably imperceptible," says Spencer Wells. "It was less of a journey and probably more like walking a little farther down the beach to get away from the crowd."

H Archeological evidence of this 13,000-kilometer migration from Africa to Australia has almost completely **vanished**. However, genetic traces of the group that made the trip do exist. They have been found in the DNA of indigenous[2] peoples in Malaysia, in Papua New Guinea, and in the DNA of nearly all Australian aborigines. Modern discoveries of 45,000-year-old bodies in Australia, buried at a site called Lake Mungo, provide physical evidence for the theories as well.

I People in the rest of Asia and Europe share different but equally ancient mtDNA and Y-chromosome mutations. These mutations show that most are descendants of the group that stayed in the Middle East for thousands of years before moving on. Perhaps about 40,000 years ago, modern humans first advanced into Europe.

Peopling the Americas

J About the same time as modern humans pushed into Europe, some of the same group that had paused in the Middle East spread east into Central Asia. They eventually reached as far as Siberia, the Korean peninsula, and Japan. Here begins one of the last chapters in the human story— the peopling of the Americas. Most scientists believe that today's Native Americans descend from ancient Asians who crossed from Siberia to Alaska in the last ice age. At that time, low sea levels would have exposed a land bridge between the continents. Perhaps they—only a few hundred people—were traveling along the coast, moving from one piece of land to the next, between a freezing ocean and a wall of ice. "A coastal route would have been the easiest way in," says Wells. "But it still would have been a hell of a trip." Once across, they followed the **immense** herds[3] of animals into the mainland. They spread to the tip of South America in as little as a thousand years.

ALTERNATIVE ROUTES?

Scientists have long believed that modern humans originated in Africa, because that's where they've found the oldest bones. Geneticists have come to the same conclusion based on analysis of human DNA. However, there is less consensus about the routes our ancestors took. For example, genetic data suggests that Europe might have been settled by an inland migration from India, rather than directly from the Middle East. "I think the broad human prehistoric framework is in place," says geneticist Peter Forster of the McDonald Institute for Archaeological Research, "and we are now fitting in the details."

K Genetic researchers can only tell us the basic outlines of a story of human migration that is more complex than any ever written. Many details of the movements of our ancestors and their countless individual lives can only be imagined. But thanks to genetic researchers—themselves descendants of mtDNA Eve and Y-chromosome Adam—we have begun to unlock important secrets about the origins and movements of our ancient ancestors.

---

2 **Indigenous** people or things belong to the country in which they are found, rather than coming there or being brought there from another country.

3 A **herd** is a large group of animals of the same type that live together.

A. Choose the best answer for each question.

GIST

1. What could be another title for this reading?

  a. Finding Y-Chromosome Adam   c. What DNA Teaches Us about Our Past
  b. Who Were the First Humans?   d. The Discovery of DNA in Africa

PARAPHRASE

2. Which of the following is closest in meaning to "Every drop of human blood contains a history book written in the language of our genes" (paragraph C)?

  a. A drop of blood contains information that can reveal a person's ancestral history.
  b. The organization of information in a history book is similar to the structure of DNA.
  c. Every drop of blood contains enough DNA information to fill many history books.
  d. Although people speak different languages, all human blood is similar.

DETAIL

3. What is true about the first group of humans that moved from Africa into Asia?

  a. Most of the migrants turned back into Africa.
  b. They divided into two groups.
  c. Most of the migrants moved quickly into Europe.
  d. They all stayed in the Middle East for thousands of years.

VOCABULARY

4. In paragraph G, the word *imperceptible* could be replaced with _____.

  a. unnoticeable   c. unpredictable
  b. illogical   d. unbelievable

FACT OR THEORY

5. Which statement is a theory, not a fact according to the passage?

  a. Mutations are easiest to find in mtDNA and in the Y chromosome.
  b. The majority of DNA is the same for humans across the world.
  c. The bodies found at Lake Mungo are tens of thousands of years old.
  d. Humans traveled along the coast of a land bridge between Siberia and Alaska.

RECOGNIZING LEXICAL COHESION

Review this reading skill in Unit 4B

B. These sentences from the passage (1–5) contain examples of lexical cohesion. Match each pair of underlined words with the type of lexical cohesion (a–e).

| a. synonym | b. antonym | c. repetition | d. reference | e. subordination |

1. In between is an exciting <u>tale</u> of survival, movement, isolation, and conquest, most of <u>it</u> occurring before recorded history. __d__

2. … people of African <u>descent</u> had twice as many genetic differences … . … all living humans maternally <u>descend</u> from a single woman … __a__

3. They now calculate that all living <u>humans</u> maternally descend from a single <u>woman</u> who lived roughly 150,000 years ago in Africa … __e__

4. They either migrated around the <u>wider</u> northern end of the Red Sea, or across its <u>narrow</u> southern opening. __b__

5. Perhaps they … were <u>traveling</u> along the coast, <u>moving</u> from one piece of land to the next. __D__

Synthesizing Information

Many reading passages contain visuals such as photos and maps that illustrate information from the passage; the ideas in the passage may also be supported by photo captions and sidebars. Synthesizing—connecting—information from the text with these other features will help you more fully comprehend the passage.

SYNTHESIZING   **A.** Read these paraphrased sentences from Reading A. Then label the parts of the map on page 82 that are being referenced (1–5).

1. Scientists have concluded that all living humans maternally descend from a single woman who lived a long time ago in Africa.

2. Probably between 50,000 and 70,000 years ago, one small group of people left Africa for western Asia.

3. Moving a little farther with each new generation, they followed the coast toward Southeast Asia.

4. Modern discoveries of 45,000-year-old bodies in Australia, buried at a site called Lake Mungo, provide physical evidence for the theories.

5. Most scientists believe that today's Native Americans descend from ancient Asians who crossed from Siberia to Alaska during the last ice age.

SYNTHESIZING   **B.** Read the sidebar "Alternative Routes?" on page 83 and answer the questions below with a partner.

1. How does the information about Europe expand on the reading passage?

2. Peter Forster says, "I think the broad human prehistoric framework is in place." Which idea in paragraph K does this expert opinion support?

3. What is one discovery from the reading passage that has helped "fit in the details"?

CRITICAL THINKING Reflecting/Evaluating   Discuss these questions with a partner.

▶ Humans continue to migrate around the world today. What are some possible reasons for the current migrations? Note your ideas below.

_____

_____

▶ What are the implications of current human migration? Consider both positive and negative effects.

Positive effects: _____

Negative effects: _____

COMPLETION   **A.** Complete the paragraph with words from the box. Four words are extra.

bulk	**calculate** 2	**descendant**	**identical**	**immense** 4
rate 5	**roughly** 1	**scattered** 3	**trace**	**vanished** 6

▲ **A sculpture of a Neanderthal draws attention from passersby in Dusseldorf, Germany.**

Before modern humans, or *Homo sapiens*, migrated out of Africa, Neanderthals had occupied parts of Europe and Asia for 1 _____ 200,000 years. Scientists 2 _____ that there were no more than 15,000 of them at their population's peak. They were, however, 3 _____ over a(n) 4 _____ area throughout Europe, the Middle East, and Asia. They were shorter than modern humans, but stronger. Their tools were rough and simple. Additionally, their food was not as varied; the 5 _____ of their diet was meat. At some point, the Neanderthals 6 _____ from Earth. The reason remains a mystery. Modern *Homo sapiens* may have killed them off, or they may have died from disease or climate change.

DEFINITIONS   **B.** Match the words in **red** in activity A with these definitions (1–5).
1. __immense__ : the main or largest part of something
2. __identically__ : similar in every detail; exactly alike
3. __trace__ : to follow something to its origin
4. __descendant__ : a person related to someone from an earlier generation
5. __rate__ : the speed at which something happens, or the number of times it happens in a particular period

COLLOCATIONS   **C.** The words in the box are often used with the word **rate**. Complete the sentences with the correct words from the box.

alarming 4	**steady** 3	**success** 2	**unemployment** 1

1. When new jobs are created, the __unem__ rate is lowered.
2. DNA-testing websites claim to have a good _____ rate for decoding people's genetic ancestry.
3. The economy is continuing to grow at a slow but _____ rate.
4. Arctic sea ice is melting at a(n) _____ rate, which is bad news for global sea levels.

BEFORE YOU READ

DISCUSSION **A.** Look at the picture below and read the caption. Discuss these questions with a partner.

1. Why do you think the Lapita decided to undertake such a risky adventure?

2. How did the Lapita locate hundreds of distant islands scattered across the largest ocean on Earth?

SCANNING **B.** Scan the reading passage on the next four pages to see if your predictions in activity A were correct.

Scientists believe many Polynesians are descendants of an earlier group of Pacific Islanders called the Lapita who—thousands of years ago—began exploring the Pacific Ocean.

FANTASTIC
VOYAGE

A It is mid-afternoon on the island of Bora Bora in French Polynesia. Thousands of cheering spectators crowd the shore to see the end of the Hawaiki Nui Va'a, a challenging 130-kilometer Polynesian canoe race that virtually stops the nation. "This is our heritage," says Manutea Owen, a former canoe champion and a hero on his home island of Huahine. "Our people came from over the sea by canoe. Sometimes when I'm out there competing, I try to imagine what they must have endured and the adventures they had crossing those huge distances."

Pioneers of the Pacific

B Manutea Owen's ancestors colonized nearly every island in the South Pacific. This was a remarkable feat[1] of human **navigation**—comparable with humans going to the moon. Only recently have scientists begun to understand where these amazing voyagers came from, and how—with simple canoes and no navigation equipment— they reached hundreds of islands scattered across an ocean that covers nearly a third of the globe. This expansion into the Pacific was accomplished by two extraordinary civilizations: the Lapita and the Polynesians.

C From about 1300 to 800 B.C., the Lapita people colonized islands that **stretch** over millions of square kilometers, including the Solomon Islands, Vanuatu, Fiji, New Caledonia, and Samoa. Then, for unknown reasons, they stopped. There was an

interval of around 1,000 years before the Polynesian civilization—descendants of the Lapita—launched a new period of exploration. They outdid the Lapita with unbelievable feats of navigation. They expanded the boundaries of their world until it was many times the size of that explored by their ancestors. Their colonies included the Cook Islands, French Polynesia, Hawaii, and Easter Island, eventually reaching South America around A.D. 1000.

How Did They Do It?

D   There is one **stubborn** question for which archeology has yet to provide any answers. How did the Lapita and early Polynesian pioneers accomplish a feat that is **analogous** to a moon landing? Little evidence remains to help us understand their remarkable sailing skills. Unfortunately, no one has found an **intact** Lapita or early Polynesian canoe that might reveal the sailing techniques used. Nor do the oral histories[2] and traditions of later Polynesians offer any insights as to how their ancestors navigated areas of open ocean thousands of kilometers wide without becoming lost. "All we can say for certain is that the Lapita had canoes that were capable of ocean voyages, and they had the ability to sail them," says Geoff Irwin, a professor of archeology at the University of Auckland. Nonetheless, scientists have some theories about the secrets of these explorers' successes.

E   Sailors have always relied upon the so-called trade winds, winds that blow steadily and in predictable directions over the ocean's surface. Irwin notes that the Lapita's expansion into the Pacific was eastward, against steady trade winds. Sailing against the wind, he argues, may have been the key to their success: "They could sail out for days into the unknown …, secure in the knowledge that if they didn't find anything,

---

1 If you refer to something as a **feat**, you admire it because it is an impressive and difficult achievement.
2 **Oral history** is the collection and study of spoken memories, stories, and songs.

∨ **Hawaiian canoeists race in the waters of Kauai island, using a modern version of an ancient design.**

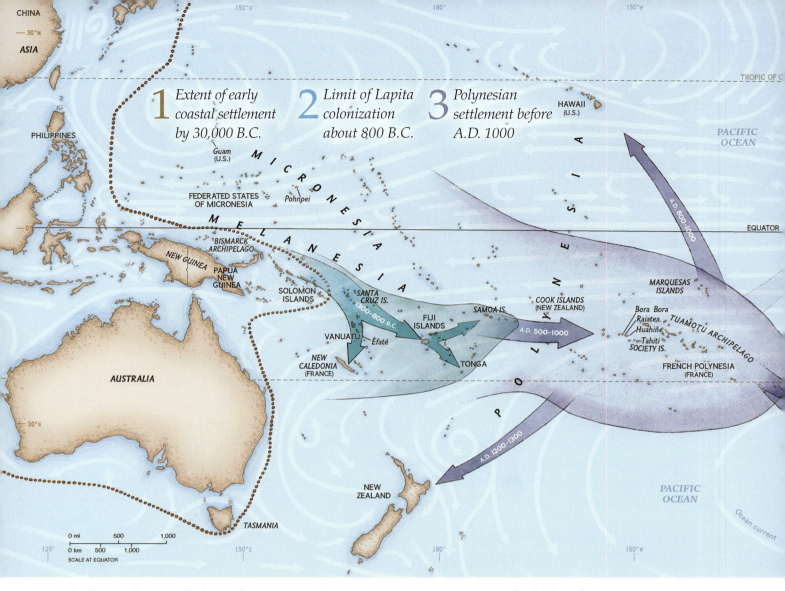

The Lapita traveled east from New Guinea some 3,000 years ago, and within a few centuries reached Tonga and Samoa. A thousand years later, their Polynesian descendants pushed farther, eventually reaching the most remote islands in the Pacific.

they could turn around and catch a swift ride home on the trade winds." For returning explorers, successful or not, the geography of their own archipelagos[3] provided a safety net. It ensured that sailors wouldn't sail too far and become lost in the open ocean. Vanuatu, for example, is a chain of islands 800 kilometers long with many islands within sight of each other. Once sailors hit that string of islands, they could find their way home.

F Irwin hypothesizes that once out in the open ocean, the explorers would detect a variety of **clues** to follow to land. This included seabirds and turtles that need islands on

which to build their nests, coconuts and twigs[4] carried out to sea, and the clouds that tend to form over some islands in the afternoon. It is also possible that Lapita sailors followed the smoke from distant volcanoes to new islands.

Helped by El Niño?

G These theories rely on one unproven point— that the Lapita and early Polynesians had mastered the skill of sailing against the wind

---

3 An **archipelago** is a large group or chain of islands.
4 A **twig** is a very small, thin branch.

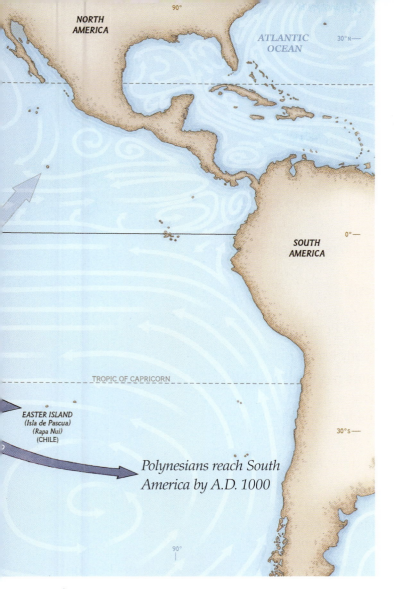

Polynesians reach South
America by A.D. 1000

distant voyages. Anderson believes that the Lapita may have taken advantage of trade winds blowing east instead of west, thereby voyaging far to the east without any knowledge of tacking techniques.

The success of the Lapita and their descendants may have been due to their own sailing skills, to reverse trade winds, or to a mixture of both. Or it may even have been due to facts still unknown. But it is certain that by the time Europeans came to the Pacific, nearly every piece of land—hundreds of islands in all—had already been discovered by the Lapita and the Polynesians. Exactly why these ancient peoples set out on such giant migrations remains a mystery. However, as Professor Irwin puts it, "Whatever you believe, the really fascinating part of this story isn't the methods they used, but their motives. The Lapita, for example, didn't need to pick up and go; there was nothing forcing them, no overcrowded homeland. They went because they wanted to go and see what was over the **horizon**."

using a technique called "tacking." Rather than give all the credit to their bravery and technique, Atholl Anderson of the Australian National University thinks that they might also have been lucky—helped by a weather **phenomenon** known as El Niño.

H El Niño occurs in the Pacific Ocean when the surface water temperature is unusually high. It **disrupts** world weather in a variety of ways. One of its effects is to cause trade winds in the South Pacific to weaken or to reverse direction and blow to the east. Scientists believe that El Niño phenomena were unusually frequent around the time of the Lapita expansion, and again between 1,200 and 1,600 years ago, when the early Polynesians began their even more

∧ **This Lapita pot was uncovered in a 3,000-year-old burial site on Efate Island, Vanuatu.**

A. Choose the best answer for each question.

GIST
1. What could be another title for this reading?

   a. How Ancient Peoples Explored the Pacific
   b. How El Niño Helped the Lapita
   c. The Race Between the Lapita and the Polynesians
   d. An Oral History of the Lapita

REFERENCE
2. The phrase *these amazing voyagers* in paragraph B refers to _____ .

   a. men who went to the moon
   b. the Lapita and the early Polynesians
   c. today's Polynesians
   d. Manutea Owen and the people of Bora Bora

DETAIL
3. How might El Niño have assisted early Pacific sailors?

   a. by making the water temperature more comfortable
   b. by creating calmer sea conditions
   c. by reversing the direction of the trade winds
   d. by making tacking easier

DETAIL
4. What is true for both the Lapita and the early Polynesians?

   a. They reached South America.
   b. They may have been helped by El Niño.
   c. They colonized New Caledonia and Samoa.
   d. Their navigational techniques are well understood.

PARAPHRASE
5. What does Irwin mean by "they wanted to go and see what was over the horizon" (paragraph I)?

   a. The Lapita were motivated by a curiosity about new places.
   b. The Lapita hoped for greater security in faraway places.
   c. The Lapita desired better living conditions on other islands.
   d. The Lapita needed to find food and fresh water overseas.

UNDERSTANDING MAPS
B. Look back at the map on pages 90–91. Are the following statements true or false, or is the information not given? Circle **T** (true), **F** (false), or **NG** (not given).

1. Australia was already populated by 30,000 B.C.   T F NG

2. The Lapita sailed as far as New Zealand.   T F NG

3. The Polynesians who sailed to the Hawaiian Islands came from the Marquesas Islands.   T F NG

4. Most of the islands of French Polynesia are of volcanic origin.   T F NG

5. The Polynesians did not reach South America.   T F NG

Distinguishing Fact from Speculation

Texts often contain a mix of facts and speculations. Facts are ideas that are known to be true, or that can be proven. A speculation is a person's guess about what they think happened; in these situations, there isn't enough information to be certain. *Speculation* and *theory* are often used as interchangeable terms. Words that usually indicate a speculation (or theory) include *believe, think, hypothesize, suggest, argue, may, might, possibly, likely,* and *perhaps*. By distinguishing fact from speculation, you will be better able to evaluate the information and ideas in a passage.

FACT OR
SPECULATION

A. Read these sentences from Reading B. For each, write F (fact) or S (speculation).

1. From about 1300 to 800 B.C., the Lapita people colonized islands that stretch over millions of square kilometers. _____

2. All we can say for certain is that the Lapita had canoes that were capable of ocean voyages, and they had the ability to sail them. _____

3. Sailing against the wind, [Irwin] argues, may have been the key to their success. _____

4. Irwin hypothesizes that once out in the open ocean, the explorers would detect a variety of clues to follow to land. _____

5. Anderson believes that the Lapita may have taken advantage of trade winds blowing east instead of west, thereby voyaging far to the east without any knowledge of tacking techniques. _____

FACT OR
SPECULATION

B. Find the information below (1–4) in Reading B. Is each presented as a fact or a speculation? Write F (fact) or S (speculation). Then circle the words in the passage that indicate the speculations.

1. Lapita sailors followed the smoke from distant volcanoes to new islands. (paragraph F) _____

2. One of El Niño's effects is to cause trade winds in the South Pacific to weaken or to reverse direction. (paragraph H) _____

3. El Niño phenomena were unusually frequent around the time of the Lapita expansion. (paragraph H) _____

4. By the time Europeans came to the Pacific, nearly every piece of land had already been discovered by the Lapita and the Polynesians. (paragraph I) _____

CRITICAL THINKING Reflecting   Discuss these questions with a partner.

▶ According to Professor Irwin, the Lapita didn't have to explore; they just wanted to "see what was over the horizon." Are there any expeditions or explorations today with similar motives? Note some ideas below.

_____

▶ Would you like to join these kinds of expeditions? Why or why not?

COMPLETION **A.** Circle the correct words to complete the information below.

It was once widely accepted that the first people in the Americas arrived by walking across a land bridge from Siberia. They then traveled south between great sheets of ice that [1]**navigated / stretched** across North America at that time. Today, this theory is being challenged. An alternative idea suggests that instead of a single first migration, groups came at separate [2]**intervals / clues**. Another theory suggests that they may have [3]**disrupted / navigated** their way along the shoreline using kayaks.

The debate over this migration path is one of many disputes in the field of archeology. Evidence from the distant past is hard to find, so theories are often based on very small [4]**clues / analogies**. As new evidence is uncovered that [5]**navigates / disrupts** existing ideas, experts often need to adjust their theories.

^ **Archeologists discovered a digging stick in Chile, estimated to be 12,500 years old.**

WORDS IN CONTEXT **B.** Complete the sentences. Circle the correct words.

1. A **phenomenon** is an event that *is observable / cannot be seen*.
2. Two things are **analogous** when they are *different / similar*.
3. If an ancient pot is found **intact**, it is *broken / complete*.
4. The **horizon** is the line where the *water and shore / earth and sky* seem to meet.
5. A **stubborn** problem is *difficult / easy* to fix or deal with.

WORD PARTS **C.** The word **analogous** contains the suffix **-ous**, which means "full of" or "possessing." Add this suffix to the words in the box to complete the sentences.

continue	courage	fame

1. Bora Bora is one of the most _____ islands in French Polynesia.
2. The _____ rowing of a canoe would tire anyone out quickly.
3. Early sailors were _____ to cross such large areas of unknown ocean.

CAVE
ARTISTS

Artwork on the walls of Chauvet Cave, France, is believed to be more than 30,000 years old.

BEFORE YOU WATCH

PREVIEWING   **A.** Read the information. The words in **bold** appear in the video. Match these words with their definitions below.

Cave paintings—or cave art—**depict** a variety of things, from animals **engraved** in the rock to hand stencils made by placing a hand on the wall and blowing **pigment** at it. At around 40,000 B.C., cave artists **predominantly** drew and painted large predator species, but by around 25,000 B.C., hunted animals became the favorite theme. Some of the animals depicted in cave art are now extinct.

1. depict   •
   • a. a colored powder used to make paint

2. engrave   •
   • b. mainly; for the most part

3. pigment   •
   • c. to represent in a drawing or painting

4. predominantly •
   • d. to cut or carve words or pictures into the surface of a hard object

DISCUSSION   **B.** Why do you think our ancient ancestors made these kinds of images on cave walls? Discuss with a partner and note some ideas.

_____

_____

WHILE YOU WATCH

GIST **A.** Watch the video. Check (✓) the questions that are answered in the video.

- ☐ a. Where are art-filled caves predominantly located?
- ☐ b. How old is cave art?
- ☐ c. Who discovered the first cave painting?
- ☐ d. How was cave art created?
- ☐ e. What steps are researchers taking to preserve cave paintings?
- ☐ f. What can we learn from cave art?

COMPLETION **B.** Watch the video again and complete the notes below.

Ancient cave art

- predominantly found in France and ¹_____
- scientific testing has revealed most art to be less than ²_____ years old
- mostly depicts animals that humans would have encountered during the ³_____ Age
- mostly created using red or ⁴_____ pigments made from rocks
- repeated symbols may represent the earliest form of graphic ⁵_____

CRITICAL THINKING Reflecting Consider what you have learned in this unit. Do you think that studying early human migration patterns and ancient cave art is worth the time and effort? Why or why not? Note your ideas below and share with a partner.

_____

_____

VOCABULARY REVIEW

Do you remember the meanings of these words? Check (✓) the ones you know. Look back at the unit and review any words you're not sure of.

Reading A

☐ bulk*	☐ calculate	☐ descendant	☐ identical*	☐ immense
☐ rate	☐ roughly	☐ scattered	☐ trace*	☐ vanish

Reading B

☐ analogous*	☐ clue	☐ disrupt	☐ horizon	☐ intact
☐ interval*	☐ navigation	☐ phenomenon*	☐ stretch	☐ stubborn

* Academic Word List

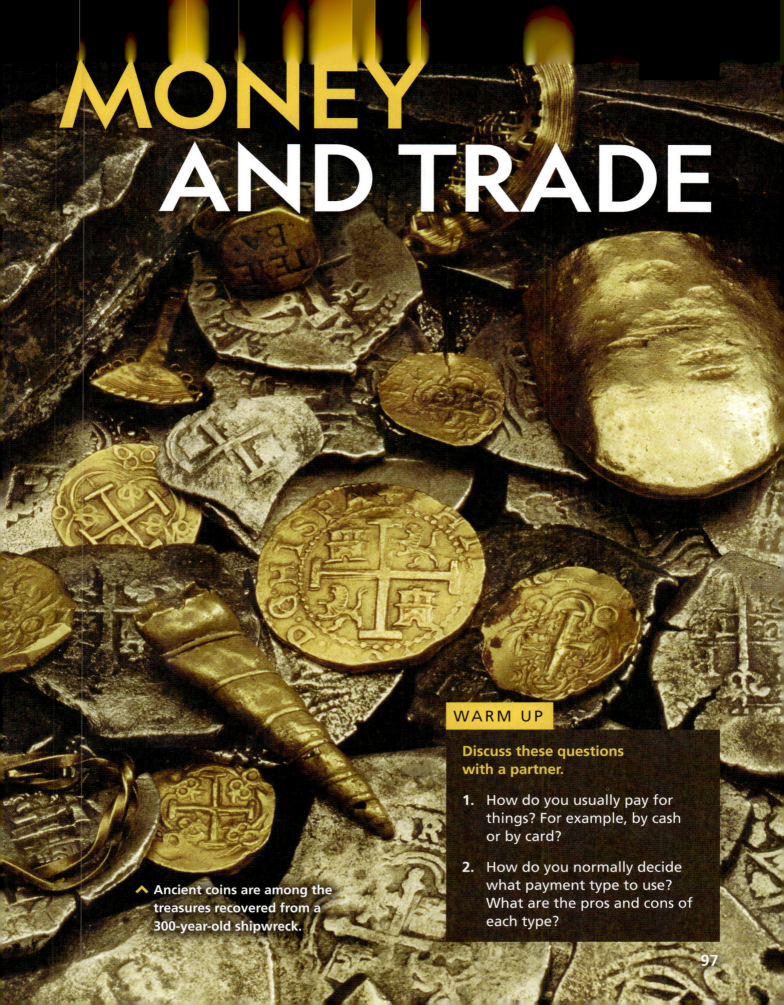

MONEY AND TRADE

Ancient coins are among the treasures recovered from a 300-year-old shipwreck.

Discuss these questions with a partner.

1. How do you usually pay for things? For example, by cash or by card?

2. How do you normally decide what payment type to use? What are the pros and cons of each type?

BEFORE YOU READ

DEFINITIONS **A.** The following money-related words appear in the reading passage. Use the words to complete the definitions (1–4).

bill	credit card	foreign exchange	inflation

1. _____ is an increase in the prices of goods and services.
2. _____ is the conversion of one country's currency into another.
3. A(n) _____ is a small piece of material, usually plastic, that can be used to pay for something.
4. A(n) _____ is a piece of paper money.

PREDICTING **B.** What methods of payment do you think people used in ancient times? Discuss with a partner. Check your ideas as you read the passage.

❤ **Workers inspect an enlarged U.S. $100 bill against counterfeit sections.**

HOW MONEY
MADE US MODERN

A About 9,500 years ago, ancient accountants in Sumer[1] invented a way to keep track of farmers' crops and livestock. They began using small pieces of baked clay, almost like the tokens used in board games today. One piece might **signify** a measure of grain, while another with a different shape might represent a farm animal or a jar of olive oil.

B Those little ceramic shapes might not seem to have much in common with today's $100 bill—or with the credit cards and online **transactions** that are rapidly taking the place of cash—but the roots of our modern methods of **payment** lie in those Sumerian tokens. Such early accounting tools evolved into a system of finance and into money itself: a symbolic representation of value that can be transferred from one person to another as payment for goods or services.

The Rise of Gold

C Since ancient times, humans have used items to represent value—from stones to animal skins, to whale teeth. In the ancient world, people often relied upon symbols that had tangible[2] value in their own right. The ancient Chinese made payments with cowrie shells,[3] which were prized for their beauty as materials for jewelry. As Glyn Davies notes in his book *A History of Money from Ancient Times to the Present Day*, cowrie shells are durable, easily cleaned and counted, and defy imitation or counterfeiting.[4]

D But eventually there arose a new, universal currency: gold. The gleaming metal could be combined with other metals at high temperatures to create alloys,[5] and was easy to melt and hammer into shapes. It became the raw material for the first coins, created in Lydia (present-day Turkey) around 2,700 years ago. Lydian coins didn't look much like today's coinage. They were irregular in shape and size and didn't have values inscribed on them; instead, they used a stamped image to indicate their weight and value.

E The result, explains financial author Kabir Sehgal, was an economic system in which "you knew the value of what you had, and what you could buy with it." Unlike modern money, ancient coins were what economists call full-bodied or **commodity** money: Their value was fixed by the metal in them.

---

1 **Sumer** was a region of ancient Mesopotamia in what is now Iraq and Kuwait.
2 If something is **tangible**, it is real or can be touched.
3 **Cowrie shells** are smooth, shiny, egg-shaped seashells.
4 **Counterfeiting** refers to creating fake money or documents.
5 An **alloy** is a metal made by mixing two metals together.

The Birth of Trade

F   Money's **convenience** made it easier for ancient merchants to develop large-scale trade networks, in which spices and grain could be bought and sold across distances of thousands of kilometers. This led to the first foreign exchanges: In the ancient Greek city-state of Corinth, banks were set up where foreign traders could exchange their own coins for Corinthian ones.

G   In the centuries that followed, trade routes forged more cultural connections between nations and regions. Besides exchanging money and goods, traders also spread religious beliefs, knowledge, and new inventions, creating connections among far-flung cultures.

H   The dangers of moving money and goods over distances—whether from storms at sea or bandits and pirates—led humans to develop increasingly complex economic organizations. In the 1600s, investors gathering in London coffeehouses began to underwrite[6] traders and colonists heading to the New World, financing their voyages in exchange for a share of the crops or goods they brought back. Investors tried to reduce their risk by buying shares of multiple ventures. It was the start of a global economy in which vast quantities of products and money began to flow across borders in search of profit.

Notes and Bills

I   By the 1700s, the global economy had grown so much that it was inconvenient to transport and store large quantities of coins. Several societies therefore shifted toward paper currency. The earliest paper bills were literally receipts that gave the bearer[7] ownership of gold or silver coins that could be collected upon demand.

J   But as Lloyd Thomas explains in his book *Money, Banking and Financial Markets*, bankers eventually realized that many people simply used their notes rather than redeeming them for gold. It meant that the bankers didn't actually need to have enough gold on hand to

---

6   If a company **underwrites** an activity, it agrees to provide money to cover any losses.

7   The **bearer** of a document is the person who owns it.

cover all the notes they issued. That revelation, Thomas says, eventually led to the concept of fiat money, which governments issue today. In contrast to commodity money, today's money has value **essentially** because a government says that it does. Its purchasing power remains relatively **stable** because the government controls the supply. That's why a U.S. $100 bill is worth $100, even though it only contains a few cents worth of raw materials.

K It's a system with an important advantage, in that human **judgment**—rather than how much gold has been dug out of the ground—determines the amount of money in circulation. On the other hand, this can become a disadvantage. If a government decides to issue too much money, it can **trigger** an inflationary spiral that raises the price of goods and services.

Toward Virtual Money

L By the 20th century, new methods of payment had begun to emerge as alternatives to cash. In the 1920s, oil companies and hotel chains began to issue credit cards: These enabled customers to make purchases and pay what they owed later. In 1950, Diners Club International issued the first universal credit card, which could be used to purchase things at a variety of places. Using plastic to make purchases eventually proved more convenient than bills, coins, or even checks.

M In 2009, yet another high-tech successor to money emerged: Bitcoin. Bitcoins are a sort of unofficial virtual Internet currency. They aren't issued or even controlled by governments, and they exist only in the cloud or on a person's computer. Parag Khanna, a financial **policy** expert, explains: "The real future is technology as money. That's what Bitcoin is about."

N From the clay tokens of Sumer to today's virtual currencies, the evolution of money has helped drive the development of civilization. Money makes it easier not only to buy and sell goods, but also to connect with the world, enabling traders to roam across continents, and investors to amass wealth. It is a type of language that we all speak. From the humblest shop clerk to the wealthiest Wall Street financier, money exerts a powerful influence upon us all.

The gold vault at the New York Federal Reserve contains 5 percent of the world's gold.

A. Choose the best answer for each question.

GIST

1. What is the best alternative title for the passage?

a. How Paper Money Changed the World
b. From Ceramic Tokens to Bitcoin: The Evolution of Money
c. Ancient Sumer and the Origins of Trading
d. A Return to Commodity Money

An ancient coin of
the Seleucid Empire

DETAIL

2. The writer says that ancient Sumerian tokens _____.

a. were all the same shape
b. were made of different materials
c. had to be heated in order to harden them
d. resembled modern board game pieces

MAIN IDEA

3. According to the writer, gatherings in London coffeehouses in the 1600s _____.

a. represented the first form of banking
b. led to the first foreign currency exchanges
c. helped bring about the global economy
d. resulted in a general move toward commodity money

DETAIL

4. A $100 bill is an example of _____ money.

a. commodity   c. fiat
b. virtual   d. universal

INFERENCE

5. Who is most likely to agree that physical money will be replaced in the near future?

a. Parag Khanna   c. Kabir Sehgal
b. Glyn Davies   d. Lloyd Thomas

CLASSIFYING

B. Do the following characteristics describe commodity money or fiat money? Complete the chart with the correct information (a–g).

a. may involve objects that are regarded as beautiful f
b. is the currency system now in use in most economies f
c. was the currency system used in ancient Lydia C
d. is valuable only because the government says it is valuable f
e. is also known as "full-bodied" money C
f. may contain precious metals such as gold C
g. is made of materials that have little actual value f

Commodity Money	Fiat Money

Understanding the Function of Sentences

As you read, try to identify the purpose, or function, of individual sentences. This can help you understand the overall organization of a text. Here are some common functions of sentences.

Defining: Sumerian tokens were an early form of money.

Classifying: There are two types of money: commodity and fiat.

Quoting: As economist Maynard Keynes said, "Ideas shape the course of history."

Reporting: According to archeologists, the first money was Sumerian tokens.

Cause-Effect: Today's money has value because a government says that it does.

Condition: If you heat gold, it melts easily, making it ideal for creating coins.

Naming: The first universal credit card was the Diners Club card.

UNDERSTANDING FUNCTION **A.** Write the function of each sentence. Use the functions in the box above.

1. But eventually there arose a new, universal currency: gold. _____

2. The result, explains financial author Kabir Sehgal, was an economic system in which "you knew the value of what you had, and what you could buy with it." _____

3. Cowrie shells are smooth, shiny, egg-shaped seashells. _____

4. But as Lloyd Thomas explains in his book *Money, Banking and Financial Markets*, bankers eventually realized that many people simply used their notes rather than redeeming them for gold. _____

5. Its purchasing power remains relatively stable because the government controls the supply. _____

6. If a government decides to issue too much money, it can trigger an inflationary spiral that raises the price of goods and services. _____

UNDERSTANDING FUNCTION **B.** Look back at paragraph M in Reading A. Underline sentences that match three of the functions in the box above. What is the function of each underlined sentence?

CRITICAL THINKING Evaluating Pros and Cons   Discuss these questions with a partner.

▶ What do you think are the pros and cons for a country to "go cashless"? Note some ideas.

Pros: _____

_____

Cons: _____

_____

▶ Which types of transactions or activities do you think are most likely to go cashless first? Give reasons for your answers.

COMPLETION **A.** Complete the paragraph with words from the box.

convenience 4   judged 5   payment 1
policy 2   transactions 3   trigger 6

Sweden will soon become a cashless society. This means that cash will no longer be accepted as ¹_____ for goods and services. Many Swedes already appreciate the ²_____ of not having to carry cash. Currently, 80 percent of all ³_____ are electronic, with most consumers using a credit card or cell phone app. The government thinks the new ⁴_____ will also cut down on tax cheats, and reduce crime. If Sweden's move is ⁵_____ a success, it could ⁶_____ a wave of other countries abandoning cash entirely.

▲ **A customer in Sweden pays for food using a phone app.**

WORDS IN CONTEXT **B.** Complete the sentences. Circle the correct words.

1. An economy with low inflation and *fairly constant / unsteady* growth is considered to be relatively **stable**.

2. Examples of **commodities** include *love and friendship / oil and natural gas*.

3. You might **signify** your agreement by *nodding your head / thinking to yourself*.

4. If something is **essentially** true, it is *basically / entirely* true.

COLLOCATIONS **C.** The words in the box are often used with the noun **policy**. Complete the sentences with the correct words from the box.

company   insurance   public   strict

1. Nearly all airlines have a very _____ no-smoking policy on flights.

2. If you purchase a car, you usually need to take out a(n) _____ policy.

3. Most businesses have their own _____ policy regarding working hours.

4. Health care and education are usually areas of _____ policy.

QUIZ **A.** Complete these sentences. Then check your answers on page 114.

1. The average lifespan of a U.S. $1 bill is six *months* / *years* / *decades*.

2. There is a total of about $1.5 *million* / *billion* / *trillion* in U.S. physical currency in circulation.

3. Physical currency makes up *11* / *33* / *80* percent of the total money supply in the U.S.

PREDICTING **B.** Read the introduction to the passage on page 107. What do you know about virtual currency? What might be some pros and cons of using it? Discuss with a partner, and check your ideas as you read the passage.

∨ A collection of coins representing Bitcoin, a type of virtual currency

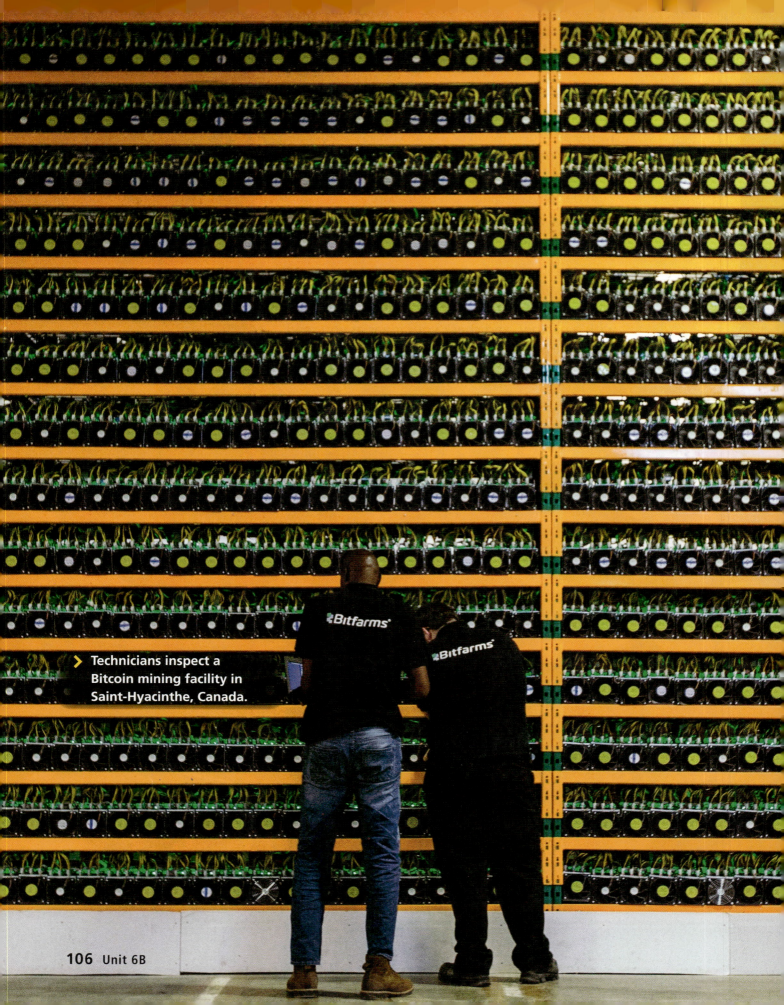

> Technicians inspect a Bitcoin mining facility in Saint-Hyacinthe, Canada.

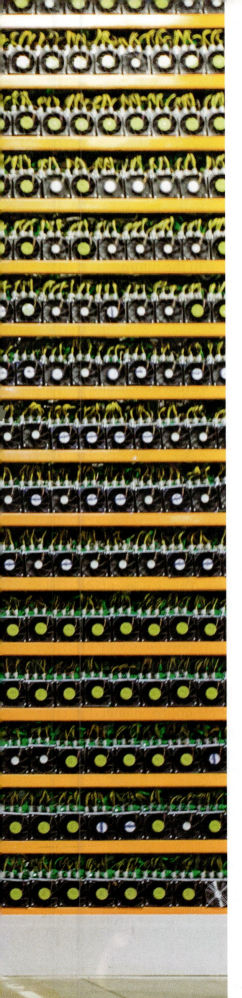

THE RISE OF VIRTUAL MONEY

It doesn't exist in any physical form, yet is increasingly used by people worldwide. Is virtual currency the money of the future?

What Is a Virtual Currency?

A According to the European Banking Authority, a virtual currency is "a digital representation of value that is neither issued by a central bank or a public authority, nor necessarily attached to a fiat currency, but is accepted [as] a means of payment and can be transferred, stored, or traded electronically." There are many types of virtual currency, but the best known is probably Bitcoin.

B In online articles, or in newspapers or magazines, you may have seen pictures of gold or silver coins marked with the Bitcoin symbol (₿). However—since Bitcoins exist only as digital constructs— these are merely representations. Bitcoin is a type of digital money known as a "cryptocurrency"; that is, it uses cryptography—secure coding—to **verify** ownership of the money. The money can be sent electronically from one user to another anywhere in the world.

C Unlike traditional currencies, Bitcoin is not controlled by a central bank or by a government agency. And unlike credit cards, the Bitcoin network is not run by a company. There is no middleman between the parties that are transferring money. It is operated by a global network of computers called a blockchain network, which records every Bitcoin transaction in the world.

How Did Bitcoin Begin?

D The first reference to Bitcoin appeared in 2008, in a paper by a writer **supposedly** named Satoshi Nakamoto. However, the name turned out to be a pseudonym[1] for a person or group who preferred to remain anonymous. A year later, Bitcoin was released as open-source software.

---

1 A **pseudonym** is a name that someone uses in place of their real name.

E Bitcoin was not the first attempt at a cryptocurrency; others had existed in one form or another for nearly 50 years, but without much success. In a short space of time, though, Bitcoin became the first cryptocurrency to be widely traded internationally. The first Bitcoins were mined in January 2009; within 200 days, one million coins had been mined. By 2019, this had risen to over 17 million Bitcoins—worth a total of U.S. $65 billion—and more than 300,000 new transactions were taking place every day.

F In its early days, Bitcoin was known for its link with illegal **drugs**, such as those bought and sold on Silk Road, an online black market set up in 2011. Silk Road connected customers and sellers on the Internet using a network that concealed a user's location and identity—and it used Bitcoin for payments. Silk Road was shut down by the FBI[2] in 2013. According to some experts, the shutdown gave Bitcoin a chance to gain some much-needed legitimacy. BitPay CEO Stephen Pair insisted that Silk Road's association would not prove fatal to Bitcoin. He said that the shutdown "shows that just because you use Bitcoin doesn't mean you can evade law enforcement."

How Does Bitcoin Work?

G Each Bitcoin can be divided out to eight decimal places. That means you can send someone a minimum of 0.00000001 Bitcoins. This smallest fraction of a Bitcoin—the penny of the Bitcoin world—is called a "Satoshi."

H Like gold or other precious metals used as money, Bitcoins are **scarce**. But their scarcity is not natural or accidental. New Bitcoins are added only by being "mined." Computer users on the blockchain network race to solve increasingly complicated mathematical problems. The first to have a verified solution receives a payment. It's like the high-tech

equivalent of a gold rush.[3] The mined Bitcoin can then be traded using special computer software.

I A useful analogy: Think of the blockchain network as an engine. Engines can be used to power all types of vehicles: cars, boats, aircraft. Bitcoin is a vehicle that uses that engine. Because it was the first major virtual currency to use blockchain, you could think of Bitcoin as an early model vehicle, like a Model T Ford.[4] More **sophisticated** uses of this engine may occur in the future.

What Are the Benefits of Using a Virtual Currency Like Bitcoin?

J In most cases, financial transactions involve exchange fees, taxes, and payment delays to guard against **fraud**. Virtual transactions, however, are speedy and cheap—and are settled immediately. And unlike a credit card exchange, where credit card numbers and security information are handed over completely for any transaction, a Bitcoin transfer is authorized only to pay a specific amount.

K Virtual currencies also make it possible to make a digital payment without needing PayPal or a credit card. This is particularly useful in many parts of Africa, Latin America, and South Asia. Immigrants to developed countries may find it a convenient way to send funds back home to their families.

L Bitcoin supporter Jonathan Mohan says, "The vast majority of [people on] the planet don't even own a bank account … Just as in Africa, [people] went directly to cell phones. In these developing nations, you're not going to see them start getting bank accounts. You're going to see them just going straight to Bitcoins."

---

3 A **gold rush** is a situation in which a lot of people move to a place where gold has been discovered to try to find gold there (e.g., the California Gold Rush of 1849).

4 A **Model T Ford** was an early model automobile, first sold in 1908.

---

2 The **FBI** (Federal Bureau of Investigation) is a government agency in the United States that investigates crimes.

Bitcoin in Perspective

The global market share for cryptocurrencies can grow a lot more

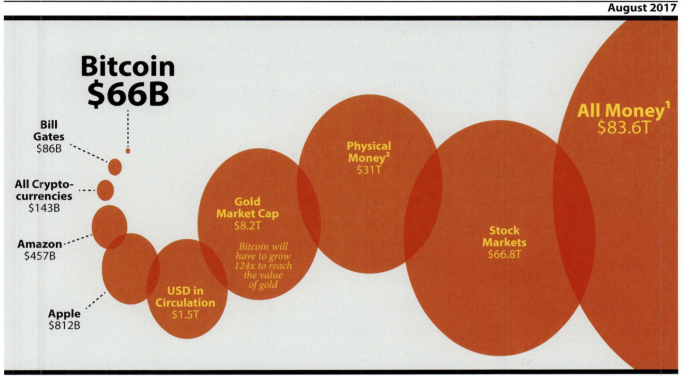

Bitcoin $66B

Bill Gates $86B

All Crypto-currencies $143B

Amazon $457B

Apple $812B

USD in Circulation $1.5T

Gold Market Cap $8.2T

Bitcoin will have to grow 124x to reach the value of gold

Physical Money[2] $31T

Stock Markets $66.8T

All Money[1] $83.6T

Sources:
https://howmuch.net/articles/worlds-money-in-perspective
https://coinmarketcap.com
https://www.forbes.com
https://www.federalreserve.gov
https://www.cia.gov

Adapted from Bitcoin IRA.

Diagram not to scale.

[1]**All Money** = money in any form including bank or other deposits, as well as notes and coins.
[2]**Physical Money** = money in forms that can be used as a medium of exchange; generally notes, coins, and certain balances held by banks.

What Are the Drawbacks of Bitcoin?

M The most obvious **drawback** is a lack of stability in the value of the currency. Bitcoin's independence makes it more stable in **principle** than traditional currencies. In reality, though, its value has fluctuated wildly over the time it has been in existence. In 2012, the price of a Bitcoin was about U.S. $12; by December 2015, it had reached U.S. $400.

Two years later, it reached a peak of almost U.S. $20,000, but then lost almost 80 percent of that value within a year. Those are some wild swings.

N So it is worth thinking twice before putting all or a substantial amount of your **assets** into a virtual currency like Bitcoin. The rule of investing in virtual currency is the same as investing in **stocks**: Never invest more than you can afford to lose.

A. Choose the best answer for each question.

MAIN IDEA

1. Which of the following statements is NOT true?

    a. Bitcoin transactions are made without middlemen.
    b. New Bitcoins are made by users in a computer network.
    c. The value of Bitcoins is controlled by a central bank.
    d. Bitcoins are created through a process known as mining.

DETAIL

2. The pictures mentioned in the first sentence of paragraph B _____.

    a. are images of old Bitcoins
    b. do not represent real objects
    c. show future versions of Bitcoins
    d. are photos of ancient gold coins

PURPOSE

3. What is the main purpose of paragraph C?

    a. to discuss different types of cryptocurrencies
    b. to trace the early history of Bitcoin
    c. to contrast Bitcoin with other methods of payment
    d. to compare traditional currencies and credit cards

DETAIL

4. According to the passage, which of the following is NOT true about Silk Road?

    a. It was in operation for about two years.
    b. Its shutdown may actually have helped Bitcoin.
    c. It continues to operate today under another name.
    d. It made use of the Internet and Bitcoin.

INFERENCE

5. According to the analogy in paragraph I, a supersonic jet plane would represent _____.

    a. an advanced form of virtual currency
    b. a new type of blockchain network
    c. one of today's cryptocurrencies
    d. a different way to mine Bitcoins

EVALUATING STATEMENTS

B. Are the following statements true or false according to the reading passage, or is the information not given? Circle T (true), F (false), or NG (not given).

1. Satoshi Nakamoto may have been more than one person.	**T** F NG
2. Before Bitcoin, earlier attempts at creating cryptocurrencies had failed due to lack of public trust.	T F **NG**
3. The value of a Satoshi is more than the value of a Bitcoin.	T **F** NG
4. Jonathan Mohan predicts that Bitcoin will be popular in Africa.	T **F** NG
5. From 2015 to 2017, the value of Bitcoin increased significantly.	**T** F NG
6. Switzerland is one of the most Bitcoin-friendly countries in the world.	T F **NG**

Summarizing (2)—Creating an Outline

As you learned in Unit 2A, a concept map is a common method of summarizing a passage; another method is to create an outline. A traditional outline uses roman numerals (I, II, III) for main ideas, capital letters (A, B, C) for subtopics, numbers (1, 2, 3) for supporting facts, and lower-case letters (a, b, c) for additional details. Alternatively, bullets can be used for the supporting facts and details. Indenting the information can also help to show the relative importance of ideas.

OUTLINING **A.** Look back at paragraphs A–F in Reading B. Then complete the outline below with words, phrases, or numbers from the reading passage.

OUTLINE: The Rise of Virtual Money

I. What is virtual money?
  A. Definition
    1. A digital representation of value
    2. Not issued by a central 1_____ or public authority
    3. Can be transferred, stored, or traded 2_____
  B. Bitcoin
    1. A type of virtual money that uses secure 3_____ to verify ownership
    2. Operated by a 4_____ network (global computer network)

II. How did Bitcoin begin?
  A. Early days
    1. First mined in January 5_____; fast growth
    2. First cryptocurrency to be widely traded internationally
  B. Early uses
    1. Known for its link with illegal 6_____
    2. Associated with an online black market called 7_____

OUTLINING **B.** Now look back at paragraphs G–N in Reading B. Highlight the most important information. Then create an outline.

CRITICAL THINKING Reflecting   Some companies have started paying their employees in Bitcoin. Would you like to be paid in Bitcoin? Why or why not? Note your answer and reasons below. Then discuss with a partner.

_____

_____

COMPLETION   **A.** Complete the information with words from the box.

drawback   principles   scarce   sophisticated   verify

Cryptocurrencies like Bitcoin seem very [1]_____, but they have some simple and ancient origins, says archeologist Scott Fitzpatrick. In fact, Bitcoin shares similarities with the famous limestone coins found on the Micronesian island of Yap.

Several hundred years ago, the Yapese used some of the same [2]_____ as Bitcoin in order to conduct business. Limestone was [3]_____ on Yap, so the islanders traveled to nearby islands to mine it—similar to how new Bitcoins are "mined" through mathematical processes. Bitcoin transactions are recorded on the public blockchain; similarly, the Yapese stored their stone money in public places where villagers could inspect and [4]_____ its quality.

∧ **A Yapese boy stands next to stone money.**

One [5]_____ of Yap's money was its large size, so the islanders pioneered a public system for "exchanging" it. The stones changed ownership without being physically moved. Bitcoin, too, changes ownership without an actual exchange of physical currency.

WORDS IN CONTEXT   **B.** Complete the sentences. Circle the correct words.

1. A **drug** is something someone might put *on their head / in their body*.
2. If something **supposedly** happened, it *definitely / may have* happened.
3. If someone commits **fraud**, they may *go to jail / get an award*.
4. Your **assets** are things that you *own / feel*.
5. When you buy **stocks**, you purchase *property / part of a company*.

WORD USAGE   **C.** The word **principle** is often confused with *principal*. A principle is a rule or law. As an adjective, principal means "the most important," and as a noun, a principal is the person in charge of a school. Circle the correct word to complete each sentence.

1. The school *principle / principal* gave a short speech on the first day of class.
2. He is a man of great *principle / principal*.
3. The *principle / principal* export of Saudi Arabia is oil.

As an experiment, a box of money is left unattended in a public place. How would most people react?

TAKE THE MONEY...
AND RUN?

$ **FREE MONEY!**

BEFORE YOU WATCH

PREVIEWING **A.** Look at the photo and caption above. Then read the extracts from the video below. Match the words and phrases in **bold** with their definitions (1–4).

"Would people's distrust keep them from taking advantage of a **no-strings-attached**, guaranteed-win situation?"

"… the money was gone **in a flash**."

"People just aren't trusting. They just assume that there's a **catch**."

"… it reflects something deep and **innate** inside of them."

1. _____ : a hidden problem or difficulty
2. _____ : very quickly
3. _____ : existing from birth; natural
4. _____ : having no special conditions or limits on an agreement or situation

MAIN IDEA **A.** Watch the video. What was the main result of the experiment? Choose the best option.

    a. Most people only took small amounts of free money.

    b. People took free money when they saw others doing so.

    c. People didn't take free money if they felt they were being watched.

COMPLETION **B.** Watch the video again and complete the chart below.

What the host did	How people reacted
• He stood in the booth and 1_____	Some people 2_____, but most people did not.
• He then went away and left the 3_____ unattended.	Most people 4_____ _____
• Finally, he placed a poster of 5_____ in the booth.	6_____ _____

CRITICAL THINKING Reflecting   Discuss these questions with a partner.

▶ How do you think you would have reacted to each stage of the experiment in the video?

▶ Would the results of the experiment change in different cultures? If so, how?

VOCABULARY REVIEW

Do you remember the meanings of these words? Check (✓) the ones you know. Look back at the unit and review any words you're not sure of.

Reading A

☐ commodity* ☐ convenience ☐ essentially ☐ judgment ☐ payment

☐ policy* ☐ signify* ☐ stable* ☐ transaction ☐ trigger*

Reading B

☐ asset ☐ drawback ☐ drug ☐ fraud ☐ principle*

☐ scarce ☐ sophisticated ☐ stocks ☐ supposedly ☐ verify

* Academic Word List

Answers to the Quiz on page 105: 1. years; **2.** trillion; **3.** 11

7

GROUP
BEHAVIOR

Participants in the
La Patum festival
in Berga, Spain

WARM UP

Discuss these questions with a partner.

1. When do you get together with people in a large group?

2. Do you think we deal with people in person differently than we do on social media? How?

A CROWD IN HARMONY

BEFORE YOU READ

DEFINITIONS **A.** Read the photo caption. Use the words in **bold** to complete these definitions (1–3).

1. _____ are people who make a journey to a holy place for religious reasons.
2. A(n) _____ place has too many things or people in it.
3. If you _____ in a sea, river, or lake, you swim or wash yourself in it.

PREDICTING **B.** What effect(s) do you think this festival has on the people who take part in it? Discuss with a partner. Then read the passage to check your ideas.

A It is before dawn on the second major bathing day of the festival, and fog shrouds the river. In a single day, tens of millions of people will bathe in the Ganges River here in Allahabad, India. In the moonlight, the crowds begin to swell on the riverbank. There are thousands here already, but the crowd is calm and united. There is no pushing or panic, only a sense of purpose as pilgrims enter the icy water to bathe and come out again. People cooperate and help one another. Afterward, they are joyful.

B As the day **progresses**, the number of people stepping into the river increases. Some splash in the water, some drop flowers into it, and others light oil lamps and set them floating on the river. There are men who splash into the water theatrically with swords in hand. There are unwilling children whose parents drag them in fully clothed. There are holy men dressed in bright orange robes with skin covered in **sacred** white ash. There are other devout men wearing the ash but little or no clothing, as their religion requires. There are people everywhere, but somehow, incredibly, no one is stepped on, no one is drowned, and no one is heard screaming for help. All is **harmony**.

C It is the Kumbh Mela, the largest and most sacred gathering of all Hindu pilgrimages. It is also considered to be the largest peaceful gathering of people anywhere in the world. Each year, as part of the Kumbh, several million Hindus bathe here in the sacred Ganges River. Every 12 years, the gathering becomes much larger, and a giant tent city is set up to house the **participants**.

D In 2013, the Kumbh lasted 55 days, and it is estimated that 120 million pilgrims participated in activities such as ritual bathing, praying, singing, feeding the poor, and religious discussion. The Kumbh tent city covered more than 25 square kilometers. It was divided into 14 areas, each with its own hospital, police station, roads, grocery store, and supplies of electricity and drinking water—an extraordinary achievement. The basic crowd-control strategy was to avoid dangerous overcrowding at "hot spots," such as bridges and train stations. "Incredibly well **organized**, incredibly clean, very efficiently run," said Rahul Mehrotra, a professor of urban design and planning at Harvard University, who observed the festival.

The Scientific Approach

E Psychologists like Stephen Reicher from the University of St. Andrews in the U.K. **suspect** that crowds have a positive impact on the health of the individuals within them. "What our research shows is that, actually, crowds are critical to **society**," he says. "They help form our sense of who we are, they help form our relations to others—they even help determine our physical well-being."

During the Kumbh Mela festival, tens of millions of Hindu pilgrims gather at the Ganges River to bathe in its waters. In spite of safety concerns and overcrowded conditions, people describe the event as a spiritual and uplifting experience.

F Reicher and his colleagues came to this, the largest Hindu festival, to test the idea that crowds are beneficial and to confirm the healthful effects of the Kumbh on its participants. Before the start of the 2011 festival, his researchers went out into the Indian countryside to question a group of **prospective** pilgrims about their mental and physical health. They also questioned people who didn't plan to attend. The researchers returned to question both groups a month after the Kumbh had ended. Those who stayed in their villages reported no real change over the period of the study. The pilgrims, on the other hand, reported a 10 percent improvement in their health, including less pain, less anxiety, and higher energy levels. What's more, the good effects lasted long afterward.

G Why should belonging to a crowd improve your health? Psychologists think a shared identity is the cause. "You think in terms of 'we' rather than 'I,'" explains Nick Hopkins from the University of Dundee in the U.K. This way of thinking alters human relationships. Members of the crowd support one another, competition becomes cooperation, and people are able to achieve their goals in a way they wouldn't be able to alone.

The Power of Crowds

H Unfortunately—in spite of the mutual support so **evident** elsewhere at the Kumbh—36 people died in a stampede[1] at the Allahabad train station on February 10, 2013. Somehow the crowd had lost its harmony. Reicher wrote that one possible cause was that the pilgrims no longer formed a psychological crowd. They no longer saw those around them as fellow pilgrims, but rather as competitors for seats on a train.

I Strangely, before this unfortunate incident, Reicher had interviewed a pilgrim who was asked to describe the feeling in the crowd at the station. "People think they are more powerful than you. They can push you around," she said. She was then asked to describe the feeling at the Kumbh: "People are concerned about you. They treat you in a polite manner." The stampede was an example of what can happen when the psychological cooperation of a crowd breaks down.

---

1 A **stampede** is a sudden rush of a large group of frightened people or animals.

Incidents such as the stampede are rare at the Kumbh, and this one is unlikely to deter pilgrims from attending the event in the future. The police will undoubtedly learn from this experience and make the station safer. But in crowds as large as those at the Kumbh, individuals must put their **faith** in the power of "psychological cooperation," as Stephen Reicher calls it. In other words, "Love thy[2] neighbor."

---

2 **Thy** is an old-fashioned word meaning *your*.

WHEN MILLIONS GATHER

While it is hard to accurately calculate the size of a crowd, below are estimates for some of the largest gatherings ever.

Number of People	Event	Location	Year
30 million*	Kumbh Mela	Allahabad, India	2013
25 million	Imam Husayn Shrine pilgrimage	Karbala, Iraq	2018
15 million	Funeral of Annadurai	Tamil Nadu, India	1969
5 million	World Youth Day	Manila, the Philippines	1995
5 million	Chicago Cubs World Series parade	Chicago, U.S.A.	2016
3.5 million	Rod Stewart concert	Rio de Janeiro, Brazil	1993
3.1 million	Hajj pilgrimage	Mecca, Saudi Arabia	2012
3 million	Coronation of Queen Elizabeth II	London, U.K.	1953

* 30 million on a single day. A total of 120 million people gathered at the Kumbh Mela over a period of 55 days.

∨ **Music fans at the 2017 Waidsee Festival in Weinheim, Germany**

A man immerses himself in the waters of the Ganges River.

A. Choose the best answer for each question.

PURPOSE

1. What is the purpose of the first two paragraphs?

   a. to explain the origins of a religious festival
   b. to describe the measures used to control a large crowd
   c. to describe the positive feeling at a religious gathering
   d. to explain how people travel to a major festival

DETAIL

2. Which of these statements does NOT describe the Kumbh Mela?

   a. It is the most sacred of all the Hindu pilgrimages.
   b. It is the largest peaceful gathering of people in the world.
   c. It is a festival that involves people bathing together in a river.
   d. It is an event that happens only once every 12 years.

PARAPHRASE

3. What is another way of saying *crowds are critical to society* (paragraph E)?

   a. It is good for crowds to criticize societies.
   b. Society determines the safety of crowds.
   c. Crowds are an important part of society.
   d. Crowds can be a disadvantage in any society.

DETAIL

4. Why did Stephen Reicher and his colleagues attend the Kumbh Mela?

   a. to test their theory that crowds are beneficial to society
   b. in the hopes of gaining a sense of peace and harmony
   c. to see how long their own positive mental attitude would last
   d. to confirm their idea that people in the countryside live happier lives

COHESION

5. The following sentence would best be placed at the end of which paragraph?
One day, it could even save your life.

   a. paragraph F   c. paragraph I
   b. paragraph H   d. paragraph J

CAUSE AND EFFECT

Review this reading skill in Unit 3A

B. Complete each sentence with two words from the reading passage.

1. Reicher and his researchers found that pilgrims reported improved health effects—effects that lasted _____ _____.

2. According to Hopkins, people who belong to a crowd tend to think more about others and less about themselves. They develop a _____ _____, which helps to improve people's health.

3. The stampede at the train station could have occurred because pilgrims were not part of a _____ _____ anymore.

4. The stampede will likely result in the police making the _____ _____.

Understanding Words from Context

A reading passage may contain words that are unfamiliar to you. You can sometimes guess the meaning of a word or phrase you don't know by looking at the words around it—the context. First, determine the word's part of speech, and then look to see if there are synonyms, antonyms, or examples that can help you determine its meaning.

In the sentence below, we may not know the words *sacred* and *pilgrims*. However, we can guess that *sacred* is an adjective that means special in some way, and that a *pilgrim* is someone who does something for religious reasons.

The water of the Ganges is **sacred** *to members of the Hindu religion, and tens of millions of* **pilgrims** *come to bathe here during the Kumbh Mela festival.*

WORDS IN CONTEXT

A. Scan the first two paragraphs in Reading A to find the words in **bold** below. Use the context to choose the best definition (a, b, or c) for each.

1. shrouds	a. lightens	b. covers	c. warms
2. swell	a. push	b. scream	c. grow
3. panic	a. extreme fear	b. extreme tiredness	c. extreme calmness
4. splash	a. move water gently	b. drink water happily	c. hit water noisily
5. drag	a. move quietly	b. push easily	c. pull with difficulty

WORDS IN CONTEXT

B. Find words or phrases in Reading A that match the definitions below (1–4). Then complete the definitions. In some cases, more than one answer is possible.

1. _____ : religious (paragraph B)

2. _____ someone _____ : to tell someone what to do in a rude way (paragraph I)

3. _____ : fails because of a problem or disagreement (paragraph I)

4. _____ : to discourage someone from doing something (paragraph J)

CRITICAL THINKING Analyzing Information   Discuss these questions with a partner.

▶ What evidence does the author provide to support the claim that being in a crowd makes people healthier? Underline the evidence in the reading passage.

▶ Do you agree that being in a crowd can make people healthier? Can you think of other possible reasons for the improved health effects? Consider the following:

- religious belief
- the effect of being in a different place
- taking time off work/school

COMPLETION **A.** Complete the information using the correct form of words from the box.

> **organized   participant   prospective   sacred**

Religious tourism is a fast-growing industry. People—whether as individuals or in larger ¹_____ tours—go on these kinds of trips for a variety of reasons. Some ²_____ go on pilgrimages, while others go as leisure travelers. Famous places to visit include the ³_____ cities of Mecca, Jerusalem, and Karbala. Other popular sites include Fátima in Portugal and Shikoku in Japan.

⌃ **A pilgrim climbs a mountain path on Shikoku island, Japan.**

Countries that receive large numbers of religious visitors expect the numbers to continue to rise. More tour companies now directly target ⁴_____ religious travelers. Rising incomes, lower travel costs, and a desire to find journeys with a purpose are fueling an increase across different religions.

WORDS IN CONTEXT **B.** Complete the sentences. Circle the correct words.
1. If an event **progresses**, it *repeats itself / moves onward / stops completely*.
2. If someone's intentions are **evident**, they are *unknown / accurate / clear*.
3. **Society** refers to a *community / family / friend* that shares common laws, traditions, and values.
4. Things that are in **harmony** *argue / connect / don't fit* with one another.
5. If you **suspect** something, you *deny / hate / believe* that it is probably true.
6. If you have **faith** in something, you have *great / little / no* confidence in it.

WORD FORMS **C.** We can add *-ant* to some verbs to form nouns (e.g., ***participate*** + *-ant* = **participant**). Use the noun form of these verbs to complete the sentences.

> **descend   occupy   participate   serve**

1. _____ in online surveys usually need to answer several personal questions.
2. The former _____ of my apartment hardly ever went out.
3. The wealthy family had _____ to cook and clean for them.
4. Many Americans are _____ of immigrants who moved to the United States in the 19th century.

BEFORE YOU READ

DISCUSSION **A.** Work with a partner to discuss these questions.

    1. Do you ever comment on other people's social media posts? What kinds of things do you comment on?

    2. Do you think the way people behave online is getting worse?

PREDICTING **B.** What do you think is the best way to deal with a negative social media post? Discuss various approaches with a partner. Then read the passage to find out what the writer thinks.

Customers at a hair salon in Hangzhou, China, check their online messages.

OUR ONLINE BEHAVIOR

Has our increased use of social media unlocked our natural cruelty? Researcher and author Agustín Fuentes examines whether the rise in social media is really to blame for our hostility online.

A In recent years, the Internet has become a particularly volatile place. **Aggression** on social media is now commonplace. In a 2017 study of 4,000 people by the Pew Research Center, four out of ten said they'd experienced **harassment** online. More than half of the victims said they did not know the identity of the perpetrator.[1] Most people agreed that the anonymity[2] of the Internet provides cover for nasty and harassing behavior.

B Does this growing aggression on social media give us a glimpse of our real human nature? Are we—at our core—belligerent[3] beasts? It's true that hate crimes are on the rise, and political **divisions** appear to be growing. The level of public bitterness—especially online—is **substantial**. But I don't believe that's because social media has unlocked our cruel human nature.

C As an evolutionary anthropologist, I have spent years researching and writing about our transformation as a species. Over the past two million years, we have evolved from groups of apelike beings armed with sticks and stones to the creators of cars, rockets, great works of art, nations, and global economic systems.

D How did we do this? Our brains got bigger, and our capacity for cooperation exploded. We are wired to **collaborate**, to create diverse social relationships, and to solve problems together. This is the inheritance[4] that everyone in the 21st century carries.

E I would argue that the rise in online aggression is a product of our evolutionary social skills, the social media boom, and the specific political and economic context in which we find ourselves. This explosive combination has opened up a space for more and more people to fan the flames[5] of aggression and **insult** online.

*   *   *

F We've all heard the expression "you are what you eat." But when it comes to our behavior, a more appropriate expression may be "you are whom you meet." How we perceive, experience, and act in the world is shaped by who and what surround us on a daily basis. This includes our families, communities, institutions, beliefs, and role models.

G These sources of influence affect our neurobiology in subtle ways. How we perceive the world is related to the patterns of people and places that we see as most connected to us. This process has deep evolutionary roots and gives humans what we call a shared reality. The connection between minds and experiences enables us to share space and work together effectively—more so than most other beings.

---

1 The **perpetrator** of a crime is the person who commits it.
2 **Anonymity** occurs when someone's name is not known.
3 A **belligerent** person is hostile or aggressive.
4 An **inheritance** is something you receive from someone after they die.
5 If you **fan the flames** of a situation, you make it more intense or extreme.

H But the "whom" in the expression "whom we meet" has been changing. We may receive more information now from online sources than from physical social experiences. We may hear more announcements from 24-hour news outlets than from conversations with other humans. The ways we socially interact, especially on social media, are increasing at a time when we are more and more divided, both socially and economically. What may be the results of this?

I Historically, we have maintained harmony by displaying compassion and friendship, and by developing connectedness when we get together. On social media, the anonymity and lack of face-to-face interaction remove a crucial part of the equation of human sociality. This opens the door to more frequent, and severe, displays of aggression. Aggressive behavior—especially to those you don't have to **confront** face-to-face—is easier than it's ever been. And for the aggressor, there are often no consequences.

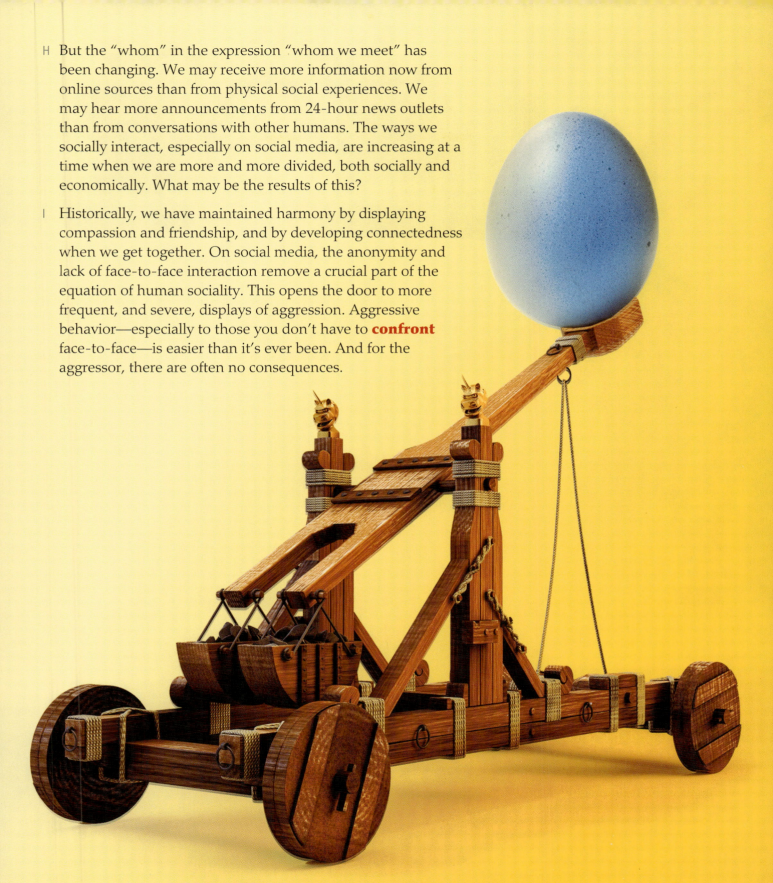

∧ How easy is it to throw insults on social media? As visualized by artist Javier Jaén, it's as easy as a catapult flinging an egg—in this case, the blue egg that was Twitter's original anonymous avatar.

Adults and children gather in Halifax, Canada, to support anti-bullying measures designed to counter online aggression.

* * *

J Humans are evolutionarily successful because our big brains have allowed us to bond and cooperate in more complex ways than any other animal. The capacity to observe how the world operates, to imagine how it might improve, and to turn that vision into reality is a key aspect of our **humanity**. And there lies the solution to the problem. We are equipped with the skill set to calm aggression, and to encourage cohesion.

K For thousands of years, people have acted collectively to punish and shame aggressive antisocial actions such as bullying[6] or abuse. On social media—where the aggressor is remote and anonymous—even the best-intentioned individual challenge may turn into a shouting match. But confronting the bully with a group action—a reasoned, communal response rather than a solo gesture—can be more effective at shutting down aggression. Look at the public **pressures** placed on media corporations to monitor hate speech and fake news online, for instance. These are examples of how humans can collaborate to encourage what's positive and discourage what's negative.

L Yes, it seems that the world is getting more aggressive, but that's not because we are more aggressive at our core. It's because we haven't been stepping up together to do the difficult social work our **contemporary** world demands. That means standing up against bullying, abuse, and aggressive harassment, and promoting pro-social attitudes and actions. In person and on social media, we must do both.

---

6 **Bullying** is aggressive behavior intended to cause hurt or harm to a person or group.

How do people respond to online aggression?

When the Pew Research Center asked people how they handled their most recent exposure to online harassment, most said they ignored it. However, 39 percent said they made some sort of response. Here are the top responses ranked by frequency:

1. Confronted the person online
2. Unfriended/blocked the person
3. Reported the person responsible to the website
4. Confronted the person face-to-face or via text/phone call
5. Discussed the problem online
6. Changed username/deleted profile

READING COMPREHENSION

A. Choose the best answer for each question.

MAIN IDEA
1. Which of the following is one of the author's main points in the article?
   a. The increase in hate crimes is caused by online aggression.
   b. The hatefulness seen online does not indicate true human nature.
   c. Online aggression has started to decline in recent years.
   d. The Internet has allowed users to understand other people's points of view.

DETAIL
2. The author of the passage is an expert on _____ .
   a. political divisions   c. human evolution
   b. Internet problems   d. brain chemistry

PARAPHRASE
3. When the author says "We are wired to collaborate" (paragraph D), he means that there is _____ basis for our ability to work together.
   a. an electronic   c. a simple
   b. a biological   d. a necessary

INFERENCE
4. The author implies in paragraph G that _____ .
   a. it is good to have competing shared realities in a society
   b. humans are rapidly becoming less and less cooperative
   c. shared reality is a modern phenomenon
   d. humans cooperate better than other species do

COHESION
5. In which position should this sentence be added to paragraph H?
   Today it may include more virtual, social media friends than physical ones.
   a. before the first sentence   c. after the second sentence
   b. after the first sentence   d. after the third sentence

COMPLETION
B. Complete these sentences about the passage using words or phrases from the box. One option is extra.

> 1 anonymity   2 cooperation   3 neurobiology
> 5 online aggression 4 online sources   shouting match

1. In a Pew Research Center study, almost all respondents said that the _____ that exists online helps account for some people's harassing behavior.

2. The author says that as humans evolved from primitive beings to modern humans, our brains grew and our talent for _____ increased.

3. Our personal environment can change even our _____ .

4. Today, we may learn more from _____ than from our real-life social experiences.

5. The author believes we have the skills to reduce _____ and at the same time promote the spirit of cooperation.

Understanding Word Roots and Affixes

Many English words consist of a **root** (which contains the basic meaning of the word) and one or more **affixes**. Affixes are prefixes or suffixes that can be added to change a word's part of speech or meaning. A word may have no affixes (e.g., *idea*), a prefix (e.g., *oversleep*), a suffix (e.g., *powerful*), or both (e.g., *multicultural*). Building your knowledge of affixes and the meanings of common word roots can greatly increase your vocabulary.

UNDERSTANDING AFFIXES

A. Work with a partner. Look at the words below from Reading B. Add them to the correct column in the chart.

apelike	argue	bitterness	expression
global	interaction	Internet	solo
successful	transformation	unfriend	unlock

Prefix only	Suffix only	Both prefix and suffix	Neither prefix nor suffix
unfriend			

UNDERSTANDING WORD ROOTS

B. Each set of words below (1–5) shares a common word root. Underline the roots and match them with their meanings (a–e).

e	**1.** nature	national	native	a. same
d	**2.** maintain	contain	retain	b. see
a	**3.** equation	equal	equivalent	c. time
b	**4.** vision	invisible	visual	d. hold
c	**5.** contemporary	tempo	attempt	e. birth; born

CRITICAL THINKING Applying Ideas   Discuss these questions with a partner.

▶ What do you think are the best ways to deal with the following problems?
- a friend who is nice to you in person but can be aggressive online
- a colleague who attacks your political views online
- a stranger who writes rude comments on your social media accounts

▶ Could each of the problems above be solved by "acting collectively," as Fuentes proposes? If so, explain how.

COMPLETION **A.** Circle the correct words to complete the information below.

Lizzie Velásquez weighs just 29 kilograms. She was born with a rare genetic condition that prevents her from gaining weight. Her condition resulted in her being bullied as a child. Later, in her teens, she came across a video of herself online. In the video, people made cruel comments and ¹**pressured** / **insulted** her appearance. She first ignored the ²**divisions** / **harassment** but later chose to ³**confront** / **collaborate** the bullies and their ⁴**aggressive** / **substantial** behavior.

The video inspired her to start an anti-bullying campaign. She has since become a successful motivational speaker, activist, YouTube star, and author of the best-selling book *Dare to be Kind*. To Velásquez, daring to be kind means seeing the ⁵**contemporary** / **humanity** in everyone, even those who hurt you.

∧ **Lizzie Velásquez speaking at a youth empowerment event in Seattle, Washington**

WORDS IN CONTEXT **B.** Complete each sentence with the correct answer (a or b).

1. Something that causes **division** _____.
   a. separates people   b. brings people together

2. _____ puts **pressure** on the environment.
   a. Using too many resources   b. Planting more trees

3. Things that are **contemporary** tend to be _____.
   a. traditional   b. modern

4. If evidence is **substantial**, there is _____ of it.
   a. very little   b. a lot

5. If you **collaborate**, you work _____.
   a. alone   b. with other people

COLLOCATIONS **C.** The words in **bold** below are often used with the word **pressure**. Circle the correct word(s) to complete each sentence.

1. Most businesses face the **financial** / **social** pressure of achieving profitability.

2. Hospital staff are **creating** / **coming under** pressure to work longer hours.

3. This resort is a good place to **apply** / **get away from** the pressure of modern life.

4. The **constant** / **blood** pressure to succeed became too much for him.

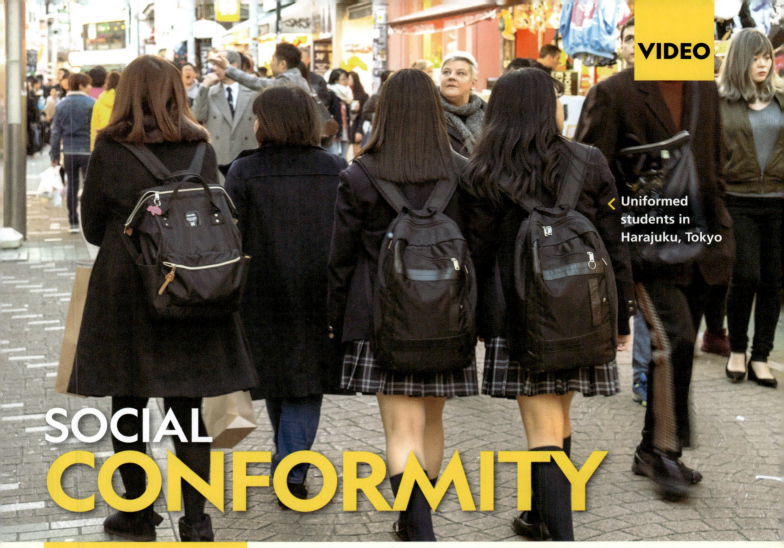

< **Uniformed students in Harajuku, Tokyo**

SOCIAL
CONFORMITY

BEFORE YOU WATCH

PREVIEWING **A.** Read the information. The words and phrases in **bold** appear in the video. Match these words and phrases with their definitions below.

Social psychologists study social conformity—the influences that change how we behave when we are in a group. We tend to conform to **peer pressure** in many social situations—even if we might think or do things differently on our own. In one experiment, **test subjects** were asked to estimate how far a dot of light in a dark room moved, even though the dot did not actually move at all. Asked individually, most people's answers varied, but when tested as part of a group, most subjects went along with the group's response. According to psychologists, the results of this experiment suggest that people are **socialized** from a young age to fit in with a social group.

1. peer pressure •   • a. a participant in a test or experiment

2. test subject •   • b. a feeling that you must do the same things as other people in your social group

3. socialized •   • c. made to behave in a way that is acceptable to a particular culture or society

DISCUSSION **B.** Can you think of some examples of social conformity in your own society or culture (e.g., at school or at work)? Discuss with a partner.

GIST **A. Watch the video. What is the main purpose of this experiment?**

    a. to observe the effect of cultural differences on social conformity

    b. to test whether people conform to the behavior of a social group

    c. to time how long it takes for people to conform to a social group

COMPLETION **B. Watch the video again. Circle the correct words to complete this summary.**

The experiment takes place in the waiting room of a(n) [1]*dentist / eye doctor*. The first test subject notices that the other people in the room [2]*stand up / drink water* each time they hear a beep. She [3]*asks / doesn't ask* why they do this. After [4]*three / five* beeps, she copies their behavior.

Next, the other people in the waiting room start to leave one by one. When the first test subject is the only patient left, she [5]*continues to conform / stops conforming* to the rules of the group.

When another unsuspecting patient arrives, the first test subject [6]*shows / doesn't show* him the actions of the previous group. As more new patients enter the room, they all eventually [7]*conform to the rules of the previous group / create a new social norm*.

CRITICAL THINKING Reflecting   Discuss these questions with a partner.

▶ How do you think you would have reacted to the experiment in the video? Would you have conformed to the group?

▶ Did anyone's behavior in the video surprise you? If so, how? Note your ideas below.

_____

_____

VOCABULARY REVIEW

Do you remember the meanings of these words? Check (✓) the ones you know. Look back at the unit and review any words you're not sure of.

Reading A

☐ evident*   ☐ faith   ☐ harmony   ☐ organized   ☐ participant*

☐ progress   ☐ prospective*   ☐ sacred   ☐ society   ☐ suspect

Reading B

☐ aggression   ☐ collaborate   ☐ confront   ☐ contemporary*   ☐ division

☐ harassment   ☐ humanity   ☐ insult   ☐ pressure   ☐ substantial

*Academic Word List

8

INVESTIGATIONS

A member of the technical and scientific police at a crime scene in Lyon, France

Discuss these questions with a partner.

1. What kinds of technology do police use to solve or prevent crimes?

2. Do you know of any mysterious deaths or unsolved crimes? What do you know about them?

WHO KILLED THE EMPEROR?

BEFORE YOU READ

DEFINITIONS **A.** Read the caption. Use the correct form of the words in **bold** to complete these definitions (1–3).

1. If something, such as a chemical or disease, is _____ in something else, it exists within it.

2. _____ is a serious disease caused by the spread of abnormal body cells.

3. A _____ is someone who has been captured by an enemy and is kept in a confined place.

PREDICTING **B.** Each heading in the passage suggests a possible reason for Napoleon's death. With a partner, discuss what kind of information might be included under each heading. Then read the passage to check your ideas.

In 1821, Napoleon Bonaparte died a **prisoner** on the island of St. Helena. The official cause of death was stomach **cancer**. However, a later analysis revealed the **presence** of arsenic—a classic poison—in Napoleon's body.

A It's a story as **compelling** as any murder mystery. It begins in 1821 on the remote British island of St. Helena in the South Atlantic Ocean. This is where Napoleon Bonaparte—one-time emperor of France—is held prisoner after losing his final battle at Waterloo in 1815. In February 1821, Napoleon's health reportedly begins to fail, and he dies three months later at the age of 51. An autopsy[1] performed the next morning reveals a stomach ulcer,[2] possibly cancerous.

B The real cause of death, however, has been in **dispute** ever since. Historians, toxicologists,[3] doctors, and other experts—as well as amateur investigators—have considered the question of how and why Napoleon died. Many are convinced that he was actually murdered. So far, though, the experts have not been able to reach an agreement.

Political Murder?

C Ben Weider, founder of the International Napoleonic Society, believes that Napoleon was **poisoned** with arsenic, a deadly chemical. Weider has **relentlessly** sought the cause of Napoleon's death for more than four decades and has put considerable resources into solving the mystery. In his view, Napoleon was poisoned by the British and by French royalists,[4] who wanted him out of the way once and for all. Weider offers as the central point of his hypothesis the hair analysis done by Pascal Kintz, a French toxicologist at the Legal Medicine Institute of Strasbourg. Kintz analyzed Napoleon's hair and confirmed that it contained arsenic. While Kintz can't say exactly how or why the arsenic was there, Weider is convinced that "the poisoning of Napoleon was planned and deliberate."

1 An **autopsy** is an examination of a dead body by a doctor to try to discover the cause of death.
2 An **ulcer** is a sore outside or inside the body that is very painful and may bleed.
3 **Toxicologists** are scientists who study poisons and their effects.
4 A **royalist** is someone who supports their country's royal family and believes that their country should have a king or queen.

Poisoned by His Wallpaper?

D David Jones, an immunologist[5] at the University of Newcastle in England, has studied the walls at Longwood House, the building on St. Helena where Napoleon lived his last years. He found that the wallpaper was painted with a substance containing arsenic. According to Jones, conditions on the hot and humid island caused the arsenic to be released into the air.

E Then again, paint may not have been the only source of arsenic on St. Helena. Some toxicologists say that it is not uncommon for people who eat large amounts of seafood to have an unusually high level of arsenic in their blood. Because St. Helena is a small island 2,000 kilometers from the nearest mainland, it is likely that a large part of Napoleon's diet consisted of seafood. Additionally, the doctors who examined Napoleon's body after his death didn't find any of the usual **symptoms** associated with arsenic poisoning, such as bleeding inside the heart.

Doctors' Mistake?

F Steven Karch, an American heart disease expert, believes that Napoleon was killed by his own doctors. They gave him large doses of dangerous chemicals commonly used as medicine at the time. According to Karch's theory, the day before Napoleon's death, he was given a massive amount of mercurous chloride—a chemical once given to patients with heart disease. That and other medications, Karch theorizes, disrupted Napoleon's heartbeat and ultimately caused his heart to **cease** beating. While Karch admits that arsenic exposure was a partial cause, he believes it was the doctors' errors that actually caused the heart attack.

Disease?

G Historian Jean Tulard believes that cancer and ulcers, as reported by doctors who examined the body, were the cause of Napoleon's death. Tulard remains unconvinced by Kintz's hair analysis. In his estimation, the hair that was tested may not even have been Napoleon's. Tulard also discounts the poisoning theory on the grounds that no one has yet found anything linking the British or the French royalists—or anyone else for that matter— to a **plot** against Napoleon's life. Still, doubts remain that cancer was one of the main causes. One cancer specialist believes that Napoleon probably didn't have advanced stomach cancer because people with that disease always lose a lot of weight. According to reports, Napoleon never lost any weight during his stay on St. Helena. In fact, he gained a fair amount.

---

5 An **immunologist** is a scientist who studies the body's immune system.

^ *Napoleon Crossing the Alps* (1802),
by French artist Jacques-Louis David

A Case of Revenge?

H "One of my ancestors did it," says François de Candé-Montholon. "I'm an aristocrat.[6] Aristocrats don't like revolution, and Napoleon made revolutions." Candé-Montholon's great-great-great-great-grandfather— the Count of Montholon—was stationed with Napoleon on St. Helena. Napoleon had a love affair with the count's wife, and there were rumors that Napoleon was in fact the father of her youngest child. The count, it is observed, had control of Napoleon's wine cellar and food. Could he, motivated by **revenge**, have poisoned the wine?

I "Everyone is right, and no one is right," says Paul Fornes of the Georges Pompidou Hospital in Paris. Fornes has reviewed the 1821 autopsy report and other historical records and concludes: "Napoleon may have died *with* cancer, but he didn't die *of* cancer." Likewise, he says that although the hair analysis indicates the presence of arsenic, no one can say if he was intentionally given the arsenic, or if it was what ultimately killed him. In Fornes's opinion, evidence for murder by poisoning is **inconclusive** and wouldn't hold up[7] in a court of law.

^ **A piece of wallpaper from Napoleon's house on St. Helena**

J Napoleon Bonaparte's body was returned to France in 1840, and it has rested in a **grand** tomb in Paris ever since. Some think it is time to open the tomb and to examine the remains using modern methods. French historian and doctor Jean-François Lemaire, however, believes that serious science and history have little to do with it anymore: "We are now in the world of entertainment," he says. It seems unlikely that new facts will settle the issue—people just enjoy the mystery too much.

---

6 An **aristocrat** is someone whose family has a high social rank, especially someone who has a title.

7 If an argument or a theory **holds up**, it seems to be true, even after close examination.

A. Choose the best answer for each question.

GIST

1. What could be another title for this reading?

    a. The Last Days of Napoleon on St. Helena
    b. A Biography of Napoleon Bonaparte
    c. Napoleon's Allies and Enemies
    d. Napoleon Death Debate Continues

DETAIL

2. Which person strongly believes that Napoleon was murdered?

    a. Ben Weider   c. Jean Tulard
    b. Pascal Kintz   d. Paul Fornes

DETAIL

3. What may have caused the wallpaper at Napoleon's house to release arsenic into the air?

    a. a doctor spilling arsenic
    b. a new paint for the ceiling
    c. the hot and humid weather
    d. the removal of old wallpaper

DETAIL

4. Which of the following do both David Jones and Steven Karch believe?

    a. Napoleon's death was due to a medical mistake.
    b. Napoleon was exposed to arsenic while living on St. Helena.
    c. Napoleon's diet contributed to his death.
    d. The reason for Napoleon's death cannot be explained.

INFERENCE

5. Why does François de Candé-Montholon seem proud that his ancestor murdered Napoleon?

    a. because he has a personal dislike of Napoleon
    b. because by murdering Napoleon, his ancestor became an aristocrat
    c. because he solved the mystery of Napoleon's death on his own
    d. because it makes his family seem more important and interesting

FACT OR SPECULATION

Review this reading skill in Unit 5B

B. Find the information below (1–7) in the passage. Is each presented as a fact or a speculation? Write **F** (fact) or **S** (speculation). Then circle the words in the passage that indicate the speculations.

1. An autopsy showed that Napoleon had a stomach ulcer when he died. _F_

2. Napoleon was poisoned by the British and by French royalists. _S_

3. The wallpaper in Napoleon's home contained arsenic. _F_

4. Napoleon ate a lot of seafood while living on St. Helena. _S_

5. The chemical mercurous chloride caused Napoleon's heart to stop beating. _S_

6. Napoleon fathered a child with another man's wife on St. Helena. _S_

7. Napoleon is now buried in Paris. _F_

Evaluating Evidence

When a text presents one or more theories on a topic, the reader needs to weigh any claims of evidence to determine how well the evidence supports the theory. Questions to ask while reading include:

- What evidence supports the theory (facts, examples, expert opinions, etc.)?
- How well does the evidence support the theory?
- How credible are the sources of information and the people making the claims?
- Could the evidence be biased to favor a particular theory?

EVALUATING EVIDENCE

A. Check (✓) the evidence the writer provides in Reading A to support each theory (1–5). In some cases, more than one answer is possible.

1. Napoleon was poisoned with arsenic as an act of political murder.
   - ☐ a. Samples of Napoleon's hair showed that it contained arsenic.
   - ☐ b. A letter was found saying the poisoning of Napoleon was deliberate.

2. Napoleon was accidentally poisoned by arsenic.
   - ☑ a. The wallpaper of the building Napoleon lived in contained arsenic.
   - ☑ b. Napoleon's diet probably consisted of large amounts of seafood.

3. Napoleon was accidentally killed by his own doctors.
   - ☑ a. Doctors gave Napoleon mercurous chloride the day before his death.
   - ☐ b. Doctors admitted that they gave Napoleon too much arsenic.

4. Napoleon's death was due to cancer and ulcers.
   - ☑ a. Doctors who examined Napoleon's body found cancer and ulcers.
   - ☐ b. Napoleon had gained some weight on St. Helena.

5. Napoleon was poisoned as an act of revenge.
   - ☑ a. An unfriendly aristocrat had control over Napoleon's wine.
   - ☑ b. Napoleon had a love affair with a count's wife.

EVALUATING EVIDENCE

B. Work with a partner. How well does the evidence presented in Reading A support each theory? Look back at the passage and choose the theory you think is best supported.

CRITICAL THINKING Interpreting / Reflecting

▶ When speaking of Napoleon's death, Jean-François Lemaire says, "We are now in the world of entertainment." What do you think he means by this? Discuss with a partner.

▶ Complete the sentence below and give your reasons. Then share with a partner.

   I *think* / *don't think* we should open Napoleon's tomb and reexamine his remains because

   _____

VOCABULARY PRACTICE

COMPLETION

A. Complete the information with words from the box. One word is extra.

2 cease	4 compelling	5 dispute
4 plot	1 poisonous	3 symptoms

Fugu, or puffer fish, is a delicacy in Japan, but it can also be ¹_____. The skin, liver, and other internal parts of the fish contain tetrodotoxin, a powerful toxin that causes nerves to ²_____ functioning properly. ³_____ of fugu poisoning include difficulty moving and breathing—eventually leading to death. You might think that this is a ⁴_____ reason to stay away from this dangerous food, but fugu is in fact quite popular.

⌃ **A plate of fugu sashimi**

The source of the fugu's poison is a subject of ⁵_____. Some believe that fugu produce their own poison, while others believe that the poison comes from the small animals that the puffer fish eat.

WORDS IN CONTEXT

B. Complete the sentences. Circle the correct words.

1. A building described as **grand** is probably *large and impressive* / *in need of repair*.
2. If a medical test is **inconclusive**, the results are *clear* / *not clear.*
3. A **plot** is a plan that is made *openly* / *in secret* by several people.
4. An attack that is **relentless** *never seems to stop* / *is easy to avoid.*
5. Someone may want **revenge** if they have been *praised* / *wronged.*

COLLOCATIONS

C. The phrases in the box contain the noun **dispute**. Complete the sentences below with the correct phrases from the box.

4 a dispute over	beyond dispute	1 bitter disputes	in dispute

1. The issue of noise pollution can lead to _____ between neighbors.
2. _____ the exact location of the border between the states of New York and Connecticut was resolved in 1731.
3. While experts disagree about the cause of Napoleon's death, the fact that he died on the island of St. Helena is not _____.
4. The vast majority of scientists agree that the existence of global warming is _____.

BEFORE YOU READ

SCANNING **A.** Scan paragraph A on the next page. Match each person (1–3) with their job description (a–c).

1. Patricia Cornwell •   • a. medical examiner
2. Alphonse Poklis •   • b. author
3. Marcella Fierro •   • c. director of toxicology

SKIMMING **B.** Read the interview questions on pages 144–145. Check (✓) the topics you think Fierro and Poklis will discuss. Then read the passage to check your answers.

☐ a. how they got their jobs
☐ b. how to perform autopsies
☐ c. technological advances in their field
☐ d. a memorable case they worked on
☐ e. their thoughts on how to prevent crime

Alphonse Poklis (left) and Marcella Fierro (right)

IN THE
CRIME LAB

A Marcella Fierro has been a professor in the Department of Legal Medicine at Virginia Commonwealth University (VCU) School of Medicine since 1973. She is also the former chief medical examiner of the Commonwealth of Virginia. She oversaw the forensic investigation of violent, **suspicious**, and unnatural deaths in Virginia, and she inspired the character Kay Scarpetta in Patricia Cornwell's best-selling crime novels. Alphonse Poklis served in the Department of Pathology at VCU for almost 30 years. As director of its toxicology laboratory, he worked with Fierro to analyze medical evidence in homicide cases, and often testified as an expert in court.

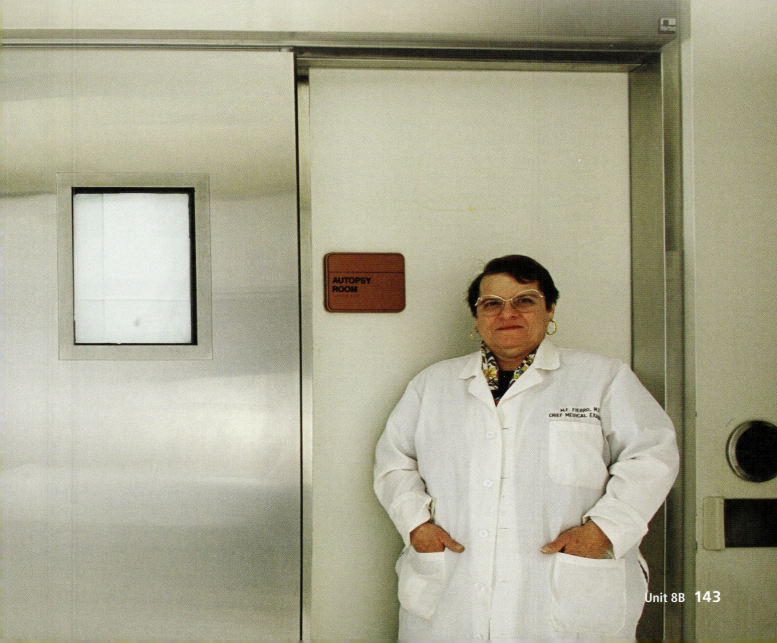

At what point do you get called in [to investigate a death]?

B   **Marcella Fierro:** We see any death that is sudden, unexpected, violent, or where there is an **allegation** of foul play. If we have the body before it's in the ground, we deal with it. But often it takes time for an allegation to be made or for someone to believe it. Perhaps a family member has a motive: There's dissension about property, inheritance, a new wife, a child not getting a fair share. Those things set a chain of events into motion. The body has to be exhumed.

Then what? How do you proceed?

C   **MF:** I take umpteen tissue samples at autopsy: heart, liver, lungs, brain, spleen, hair, nails. Blood tells you what was going on in the body at the time of death. [The tissue in] the eye is great. It's clean. No fermentation[1] or contamination from bacteria. Al and I work together. What poisons are **candidates**? What's best to collect? You have to have a strategy. We'd want to know what poison the defendant would have access to. If it's a farmer, we look for agricultural things like pesticides or herbicides. We need to have an idea of where we are going. We can easily run out of tissue and blood samples before we run out of tests to do.

So, the technology you use to detect poisons in a corpse must be pretty sophisticated?

D   **Alphonse Poklis:** Very. I call it the vanishing zero. In the 1960s, it took 25 milliliters of blood to detect morphine. Today, we can use one milliliter to do the same work. **In terms of** sensitivity, we've gone from micrograms to nanograms, which is parts per billion, to parts per trillion with mass spectrometry. You can find anything if you do the research. Of course, some substances are more apparent. You can smell cyanide the minute you open a body at autopsy. Cyanide works fast—like in movies where the captured spy bites on the capsule and dies … [E]very cell is **deprived of** oxygen. You die quickly, dramatically, violently.

---

1   Bacteria and yeast break down complex molecules through a process called **fermentation**.

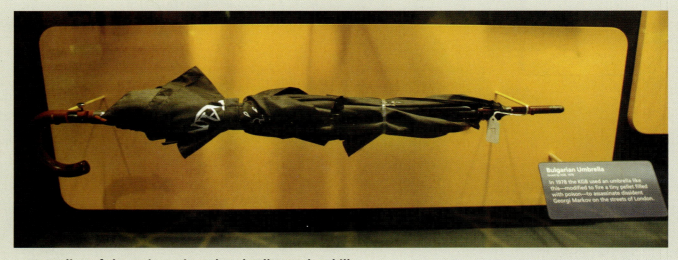

^ A replica of the poison-tipped umbrella used to kill
   Bulgarian writer Georgi Markov in 1978

Is there a personality profile specific to poisoners?

E **AP:** The poisoner tries to cover up what he or she does. Poison is the weapon of controlling, sneaky people with no conscience, no sorrow, no **remorse**. They are scary, **manipulative**; if you weren't convinced by the evidence, you wouldn't believe they could do such a thing.

A case that sticks in your mind?

F **MF:** There was this person at the University of Virginia Hospital. Kept getting admitted for **weird** [stomach] complaints. The doctors were twisting themselves inside out to figure it out. He'd get better; his wife would come in to see him in the hospital and bring him banana pudding. Someone finally ordered a [toxicity test] on him, but he was discharged before the results came back: off the charts for arsenic. By the time someone saw the labs, it was too late. We called the wife Banana Pudding Lily.

How many cases of suspected homicidal poisonings do you **evaluate** in the course of a year?

G **AP: Frankly**, relatively few … If you are going to kill someone [it's more likely] you shoot them … In [American] culture everything is solved in 30 minutes, so you aren't going to plan, go someplace to get poison, and figure out "how am I going to give it?"

You're the expert. If you had to design the perfect poison for murder, what would it be made of?

H **AP:** I could think of a few things, but I'm not going to share them.

▼ The deadly nightshade plant, or belladonna, has a long history of use as a poison.

GLOSSARY

a case: a suspected crime investigated by the police

a corpse: a dead body, usually of a human being rather than an animal (which is called a carcass)

cyanide: a poisonous white powder that smells like almonds

to exhume: to dig out (something buried, usually a dead body) from the ground

forensics: scientific tests or techniques that are used to investigate crimes

a homicide: the killing of one person by another

mass spectrometry: an instrument to measure the mass and concentration of atoms and molecules

morphine: a drug that is obtained from the opium poppy plant and used medicinally to relieve pain

a nanogram: one billionth of a gram

pathology: the study of organs, tissues, and bodily fluids to diagnose diseases

toxicity: the degree to which a substance can harm an organism

A. Choose the best answer for each question.

DETAIL

1. What is true about Marcella Fierro and Alphonse Poklis?

    ⓐ They worked together to analyze medical evidence in homicide cases.
    b. They both served as law professors at Virginia Commonwealth University.
    c. They both worked with Kay Scarpetta in the past.
    d. The author Patricia Cornwell has based characters on both of them.

CAUSE AND
EFFECT

2. According to Fierro, what might cause a body to be exhumed?

    ⓐ an autopsy performed before burial was not conducted properly
    b. new forensics techniques that didn't exist when the body was buried
    c. incorrect identification of the corpse
    ⓓ an allegation that a family member had a motive for murder

DETAIL

3. What is NOT true about cyanide?

    a. It works quickly.
    ⓑ It increases oxygen flow to the body's cells.
    c. It makes people violently ill.
    d. It has a strong smell.

INFERENCE

4. What is probably true about Banana Pudding Lily?

    a. She brought food to several patients at the hospital.
    b. Doctors quickly suspected her of trying to kill her husband.
    c. She poisoned her husband with arsenic.
    d. She wanted lab tests done on her husband.

DETAIL

5. According to Poklis, why don't more Americans use poison to kill?

    a. It's very difficult to find poison in the United States.
    b. Most Americans don't understand how poison works.
    c. Most poisons are very expensive.
    ⓓ Using a gun to kill is faster and more direct.

WORDS IN
CONTEXT

Review this
reading skill
in Unit 7A

B. Scan the reading passage to find the words and phrases in bold below (1–5). Study the context around each one and match it with its definition (a–f). One definition is extra.

  C **1. dissension** (paragraph B)   a. released

  b **2. apparent** (paragraph D)   b. clearly visible

  D **3. capsule** (paragraph D)   c. disagreement

  f **4. cover up** (paragraph E)   d. a small case or tube

  a **5. discharged** (paragraph F)   e. many

                                        f. to hide or disguise

Understanding Idiomatic Expressions

Spoken language—such as that found in interviews—often contains idiomatic expressions. As with other vocabulary, context may help you understand their meaning. To gain a richer understanding of idioms, expose yourself to them as much as possible—through reading, watching movies, and listening to podcasts. If you have no idea what an idiom means, consult a dictionary.

UNDERSTANDING
IDIOMATIC
EXPRESSIONS

A. Match the idioms in **bold** with their meanings (a–e).

__b__ **1.** You want me to quit my job? **Over my dead body**!

__c__ **2.** I know you disagree with your supervisor, but in this case it's best to **bite your tongue**.

__D__ **3.** You're new, so it will take time to **learn the ropes**.

__a__ **4.** The autopsy results can't be right. Something smells **fishy**.

__e__ **5.** This isn't the right answer. Let's **start from scratch**.

a. suspicious

b. under no circumstances

c. say nothing

d. become experienced

e. start at the beginning

UNDERSTANDING
IDIOMATIC
EXPRESSIONS

B. Find these idioms in **bold** in Reading B. Use the context around each idiom to guess its meaning. Then choose the best definition (a, b, or c) for each.

1. getting a fair share
a. receiving a reasonable amount
b. having unequal time
c. being wanted by both parents

2. umpteen
a. a messy mix of
b. a small degree of
c. a large number of

3. sticks in your mind
a. makes it worthwhile
b. causes a headache
c. is remembered clearly

4. twisting themselves inside out
a. trying extremely hard
b. arguing with one another
c. feeling unwell

5. off the charts
a. a big success
b. extremely high
c. not written down

CRITICAL THINKING Interpreting / Reflecting   Discuss these questions with a partner.

▶ Look back at how Alphonse Poklis described people who murder using poison. In your own words, what did he think of these people?

▶ Do you feel the same way Poklis did about poisoners? Give reasons for your answer.

COMPLETION   **A.** Circle the correct words to complete the information below.

⌃ **Poison was known as women's weapon of choice in medieval and early modern Europe.**

Poison is a killer. It is effective in small amounts and is often undetectable. Consider arsenic, a(n) ¹**evaluation / candidate** for the king of poisons. It is colorless, tasteless, and odorless. In fact, arsenic was the poison of choice for the Borgias, one of the most powerful families in Italy during the 15th century. The Borgias had a reputation for being immoral, violent, and ²**remorseful / manipulative**. It is ³**alleged / evaluated** that many of them resorted to blackmail, extortion, and murder by poisoning in order to increase their family's power.

Arsenic was also the preferred poison for a woman named Hieronyma Spara. A 17th-century Roman fortune teller, Spara formed a secret society that taught young wives how to poison their wealthy husbands using arsenic. This way, the deaths would not raise any ⁴**suspicions / manipulations**, and the widows would inherit the money.

DEFINITIONS   **B.** Match the words and phrases in the box with the definitions below.

deprived of   evaluate   frankly   in terms of   remorse   weird

1. _____ : to judge something's value or importance

2. _____ : very strange and unusual

3. _____ : a feeling of being sorry for doing something bad

4. _____ : lacking something that is considered necessary or important

5. _____ : honestly; in truth

6. _____ : in relation to

WORD ROOTS   **C.** The word **allegation** contains the word root *leg*, which means "law." Complete the sentences with the correct words from the box. One word is extra.

allege   legal   legislature   legitimate

1. Lawyers give their clients _____ advice.

2. Some people _____ that Napoleon Bonaparte was murdered.

3. A(n) _____ typically consists of men and women who make laws.

BEATING A LIE DETECTOR

BEFORE YOU WATCH

PREVIEWING **A.** Read the information. The words in **bold** appear in the video. Match the correct form of these words with their definitions (1–3).

You hear about lie detectors all the time in police investigations. A lie detector (also known as a polygraph) is a machine that—its supporters claim—can detect whether someone is lying by recording changes in blood pressure, breathing rate, and skin conductivity during an **interrogation**. First, the examiner asks some simple questions to establish a **baseline** for the person's physiological signals. After that, the examiner asks a series of questions related to the alleged crime. Any **spikes** in physiological activity indicate stress, which suggests the person is lying. But how accurate are these tests? Is it possible to "beat" a polygraph? To find out, scientist Jonny Phillips carried out an experiment. His findings may surprise you.

1. _____ : a starting point or level

2. _____ : the act of questioning someone (e.g., a criminal)

3. _____ : a sudden increase

PREDICTING **B.** What strategies do you think people might use to try to "beat" a lie detector? Discuss your ideas with a partner.

GIST **A.** Watch the video. Check (✓) the methods Jonny uses to try to beat the polygraph. Were any of your ideas in Before You Watch B mentioned in the video?

☐ a. lying when answering the baseline questions

☐ b. hurting himself with a pin

☐ c. using anti-perspirants beforehand

☐ d. doing math problems in his head during the test

EVALUATING STATEMENTS **B.** Watch the video again. Are the following statements true or false? Circle **T** (true) or **F** (false).

1. When people tell a lie, they usually breathe slower. **T** **F**

2. Jonny secretly pricked his toes with a pin during the baseline questions to try to increase his average stress levels. **T** **F**

3. CIA agent Aldrich Ames beat two polygraph tests in the 1980s by using the same techniques that Jonny used in his experiment. **T** **F**

4. Jonny lied to the examiner about stealing Richard's games console. **T** **F**

5. Jonny managed to beat the lie detector test. **T** **F**

CRITICAL THINKING Evaluating Reliability   Discuss these questions with a partner.

▶ On a scale of 1 to 5 (1 = not reliable at all; 5 = extremely reliable), how would you rate polygraph testing? _____

▶ Do you think polygraph test results should be allowed as evidence in a court of law? Why or why not?

VOCABULARY REVIEW

Do you remember the meanings of these words? Check (✓) the ones you know. Look back at the unit and review any words you're not sure of.

Reading A

☐ cease*   ☐ compelling   ☐ dispute   ☐ grand   ☐ inconclusive*

☐ plot   ☐ poison   ☐ relentlessly   ☐ revenge   ☐ symptom

Reading B

☐ allegation   ☐ candidate   ☐ deprived of   ☐ evaluate*   ☐ frankly

☐ in terms of   ☐ manipulative*   ☐ remorse   ☐ suspicious   ☐ weird

* Academic Word List

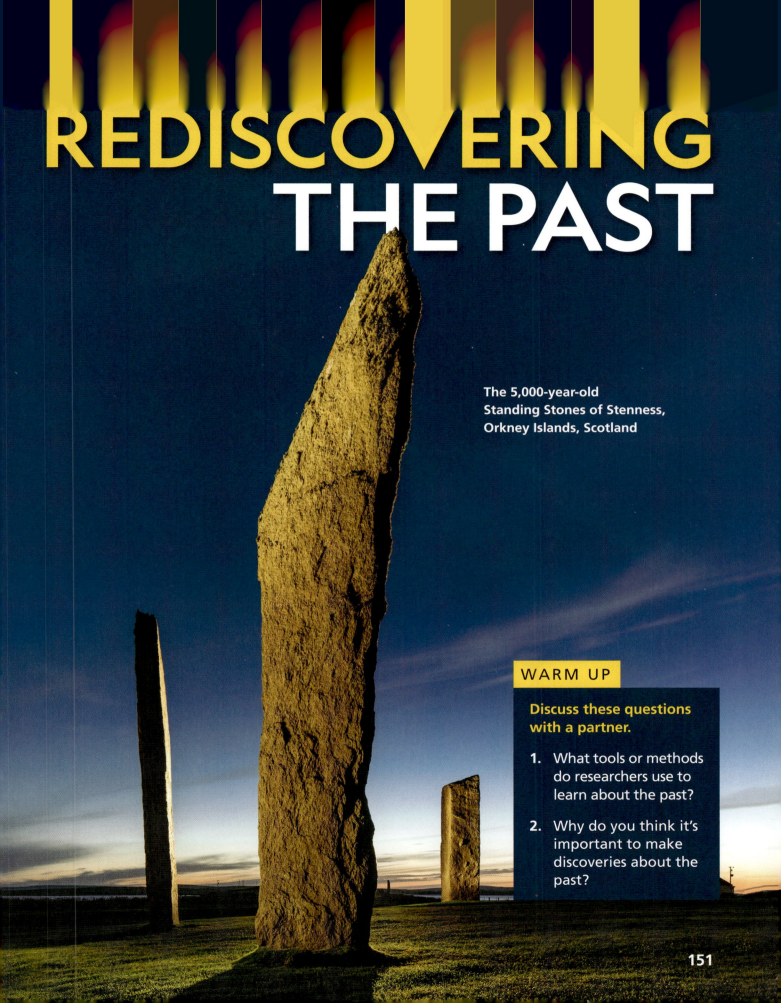

REDISCOVERING
THE PAST

The 5,000-year-old
Standing Stones of Stenness,
Orkney Islands, Scotland

WARM UP

**Discuss these questions
with a partner.**

1. What tools or methods
   do researchers use to
   learn about the past?

2. Why do you think it's
   important to make
   discoveries about the
   past?

BEFORE YOU READ

DISCUSSION **A.** Discuss these questions with a partner.

1. What structures from your country's cultural past have been preserved? Has anything been rebuilt?

2. How can technology be used to preserve the past?

PREDICTING **B.** The passage describes an architectural treasure called Rani ki Vav. Look at the photograph below and try to guess the structure's purpose. Then read the passage to check your ideas.

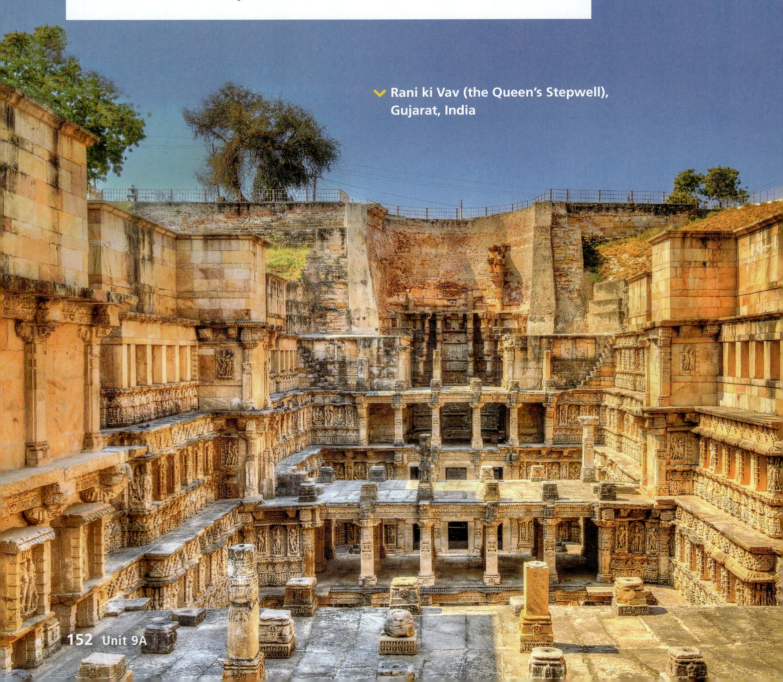

⌄ **Rani ki Vav (the Queen's Stepwell), Gujarat, India**

VIRTUALLY IMMORTAL

A After the long, dusty drive from the city, the first surprises that visitors encounter are the shade trees and the beautiful green lawn. Then they notice the birds and monkeys swooping[1] in and out of the trees. After passing through the entrance gate, a long stone pathway leads to a place where the ground begins to open up. There, on the far side of the grass, is what seems to be a magnificent temple built in a huge hole in the ground. However, it is not a temple, but a well.[2] This is Rani ki Vav—the Queen's Stepwell.

B The weather is dry most of the year in northwestern India. Then, during the summer, rain arrives suddenly and seeps[3] down through the sandy soil. Centuries ago, people dug holes to get at the water, and then built stone stairways down where the water collected. These stepwells were simple at first, but some later became architectural works of art. Rani ki Vav is among the most magnificent.

C Located near the Saraswati River in Gujarat, Rani ki Vav was built late in the 11th century by Queen Udayamati as a **memorial** to her dead king. It was rarely used, and by 1300, seasonal floods had filled it with sand. Not until the 1960s did Indian archeologists begin digging it out. Witnesses were **stunned** by what was hidden beneath all that sand.

Preserving the Past

D "We've seen photographs, but nothing compares with seeing it **firsthand**," says Lyn Wilson, an archeological scientist from Glasgow. With the latest in digital scanning technology, she and her colleagues from the Centre for Digital Documentation and Visualisation aim to reduce the chances that Rani ki Vav—or at least the data describing it—will ever be lost again.

E Of all the projects they have undertaken—from the Standing Stones of Stenness to Mount Rushmore—this is among the most difficult. By 12:30 p.m., their equipment arrives. As team members open the boxes, they meet their first challenge: two buses full of Indian schoolboys on a class trip. They crowd around Wilson as though she's a Bollywood star. A guard gently directs them to move back with a long stick.

F For the next two weeks, the team will have to fight the heat and cope with curious crowds while they aim laser beams at every surface of the stepwell in order to record the entire structure digitally. Should Rani ki Vav be lost again—through floods, war, earthquakes, or just the passage of time—there will be a precise 3-D copy available on the Internet.

---

1 When an animal **swoops**, it moves suddenly down through the air in a smooth, curving motion.
2 A **well** is a hole in the ground from which a supply of water is extracted.
3 If water **seeps** down through the earth, it moves slowly through it.

Inside the Vav

G A tour of the well reveals some of the extremely complex **carvings** the team must record. On a lower level, seven sculptures of the four-armed god Vishnu decorate the walls. Lord Kalki sits tall on a horse, one foot about to crush an enemy's head. Then there's Varaha, a god with the head of a boar.[4] A tiny goddess standing on his shoulder lovingly rubs his nose. "It reminds me of the wonderful Hollywood movie *King Kong*," remarks K. C. Nauriyal, an Indian archeologist working at the site.

H Also immortalized in stone are the Hindu gods Brahma and Shiva. Scattered among the gods slither[5] snakes and creatures called *Naga Kanya*

that are half-snake, half-woman. There are also *apsaras*—female spirits of the clouds and water—putting on lipstick or earrings, **gazing** at mirrors, or drying their hair. One of them playfully strikes a monkey as it pulls down her **garment**. Another pulls on the beard of an admiring beggar. "The spice of life," Nauriyal calls them. But one wrong blow with a hammer and their beauty would be destroyed forever.

I A stairway leads to the lowest levels, and a dark passage into the well itself. Near the bottom of the well are two statues of the god Vishnu. One is sleeping on the back of a large snake, and the other is sitting straight up. There was a belief that if there were two statues of Lord Vishnu in this form, the water would never dry up—but it did. Agricultural development and a warmer climate are two likely causes. And, like the water, the sculptures may one day disappear, surviving perhaps only as a **virtual** model online.

---

4 A **boar** is a wild pig.
5 If an animal **slithers**, it moves by twisting or sliding on the ground.

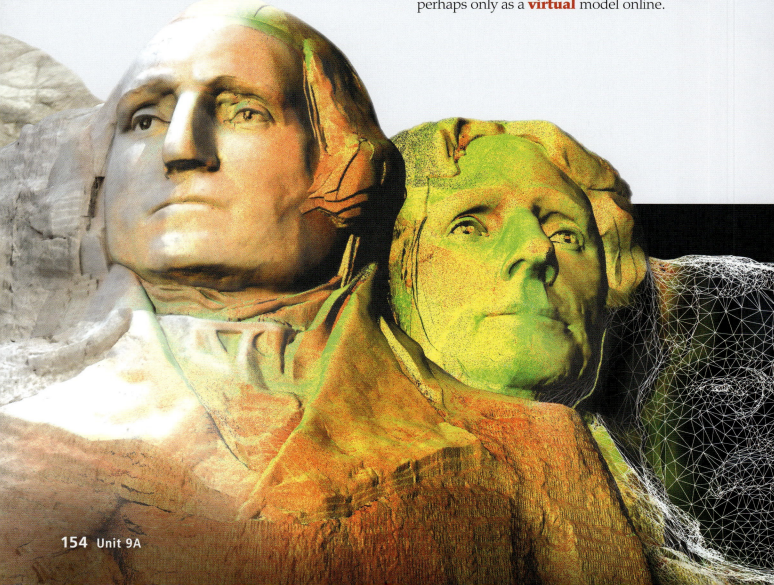

A Digital Copy

J Inside a tent at the edge of the stepwell, archeologist Justin Barton **assembles** the first pieces of the 3-D digital image of Rani ki Vav. Weirdly colored **columns** and lintels[6] appear on the screen. The colors—greenish in the brightest areas, grading to oranges and yellows—indicate reflectivity, or how readily the laser comes **bouncing back**. Barton grabs the images with the cursor, swinging them around like a child's building blocks, fitting each into the larger model of Rani ki Vav.

K Back in Glasgow, the digital copy will be completed, ultimately joining more than a hundred others already in a computer database. But that's barely the beginning. "So much heritage is being lost on a daily basis," says Barton, "through war and human aggression, environmental changes, and the wear and tear of time." Barton and his colleagues are in a race to digitally preserve for future generations as many of the world's threatened archeological treasures as they can—before they disappear forever.

---

6 A **lintel** is a piece of stone or wood over a door or window.

THE SCOTTISH TEN

The expedition to Rani ki Vav is part of the Scottish Ten—a digital preservation project, initiated by the government in Scotland, which aims to produce 3-D digital copies of 10 cultural sites. The Scottish Ten includes the following UNESCO World Heritage Sites:

- Rani ki Vav (India)
- Mount Rushmore (U.S.A.)
- Eastern Qing Tombs (China)
- Sydney Opera House (Australia)
- Nagasaki Giant Cantilever Crane (Japan)
- New Lanark, Neolithic Orkney, St. Kilda, Edinburgh, and Antonine Wall (all in Scotland)

‹ Laser beams are bounced off the surface of Mount Rushmore in the United States. Scanning the mountain in this way enables researchers to create a detailed 3-D digital model. This represents a new way of preserving our endangered architectural heritage.

A. Choose the best answer for each question.

DETAIL

1. Which of these does NOT describe Rani ki Vav?

    a. a magnificent temple

    b. a well with steps

    c. a memorial to a dead king

    d. an 11th-century structure

DETAIL

2. What happened to Rani ki Vav?

    a. It disappeared underwater.

    b. People took the stones away.

    c. It became filled with sand.

    d. Records of its existence were destroyed.

PURPOSE

3. The purpose of paragraphs G–I is to _____ .

    a. compare the upper and lower sections of Rani ki Vav

    b. describe a recent discovery made at Rani ki Vav

    c. explain how the researchers scanned Rani ki Vav

    d. allow the reader to visualize the inside of Rani ki Vav

INFERENCE

4. Which statement would Justin Barton probably agree with the most?

    a. We must act quickly to digitally preserve the world's archeological treasures.

    b. We should discourage people from visiting heritage sites until they are digitally preserved.

    c. Most of the world's important heritage sites have already been digitally preserved.

    d. We should wait until there are advances in digital copying before mapping the most valuable archeological treasures.

DETAIL

5. What is the Scottish Ten?

    a. the top 10 most visited historical sites in Scotland

    b. a project to digitally preserve cultural sites

    c. a team of 10 people working to preserve cultural sites

    d. a type of technology used to scan monuments

SCANNING

Review this reading skill in Unit 4A

B. Find the following information in the passage. Note which paragraph (A–K) each item appears in.

_____ **1.** reasons why we are losing our cultural heritage

_____ **2.** a comparison to an American movie

_____ **3.** a description of what the lowest part of the well looks like

_____ **4.** a definition of *apsaras*

_____ **5.** two examples of other projects the Scottish team has worked on

Recognizing Ellipsis

A writer may leave out, or omit, certain words from a sentence to improve the flow of the text. This is known as ellipsis. In the following examples, the omitted words (in parentheses) are not needed for the sentences to be understood.

> *You can be Sam's lab partner, and I'll be Dana's* (lab partner).
>
> *Mark can speak Arabic, and Delia* (can speak) *Hindi.*
>
> *She asked if I'd like to give a speech, and I said that I would* (like to give a speech).

Identifying what is missing is usually not a problem in short sentences, but with longer texts it can be more challenging.

RECOGNIZING ELLIPSIS

A. These sentences from Reading A contain ellipsis. Draw an arrow from the **bold** word or phrase to where it could go in each sentence.

1. However, it is not a temple, but a well. **it is** (paragraph A)

2. Then, during the summer, rain arrives suddenly and seeps down through the sandy soil. **the water** (paragraph B)

3. These stepwells were simple at first, but some later became architectural works of art. Rani ki Vav is among the most magnificent. **works of art** (paragraph B)

4. There are also *apsaras*—female spirits of the clouds and water—putting on lipstick or earrings, gazing at mirrors, or drying their hair. **putting on** (paragraph H)

5. A stairway leads to the lowest levels, and a dark passage into the well itself. **leads** (paragraph I)

RECOGNIZING ELLIPSIS

B. These famous quotes contain ellipsis. Add any missing words.

1. "Wise men speak because they have something to say; fools because they have to say something." – Plato

2. "To err is human, to forgive divine." – Alexander Pope

3. "If you don't love something, you're not going to go the extra mile, work the extra weekend, challenge the status quo as much." – Steve Jobs

CRITICAL THINKING Evaluating/Justifying

▶ Which cultural sites or artifacts do you think are most worthy of 3-D digital preservation? Consider significant buildings, sculptures, and ancient man-made sites around the world. Discuss your ideas with a partner and make a list.

_____

_____

▶ From your list above, decide on the top three sites or artifacts you think are worth preserving. Then explain to your classmates why you think these three are the most worthy.

DEFINITIONS **A.** Read the information below. Match each word in **red** with its definition (1–5).

In 1922, Howard Carter discovered the tomb of Tutankhamun, an ancient Egyptian king. When he first **gazed** upon the tomb's treasures, he was **stunned** to find they were nearly all intact. He found chests filled with ceremonial **garments** and footwear, a series of gold coffins, and the mummy of King Tut.

▲ **A coffin of solid gold held King Tut's remains.**

While it's possible to take a **virtual** tour of the tomb online, many visitors want to see it **firsthand**. But the huge numbers of tourists have damaged the tomb. So, in 2014, archeologists used laser scanners and high-definition printers to create an exact copy for tourists to see.

1. _____ : directly; from the original source
2. _____ : looked intently at something
3. _____ : extremely surprised
4. _____ : items of clothing
5. _____ : existing on computers or on the Internet

WORDS IN CONTEXT **B.** Complete the sentences. Circle the correct words.

1. Something that **bounces back** *disappears / returns to you*.

2. Someone might create a **memorial** *before a baby is born / after a friend dies*.

3. A **carving** is made by *putting together / cutting into* wood or stone.

4. If you **assemble** something, you *put the pieces together / take it apart*.

5. A stone **column** goes from *wall to wall / floor to ceiling*.

COLLOCATIONS **C.** The nouns in the box are often used with the adjective **virtual**. Complete the sentences with the correct nouns from the box. One noun is extra.

classroom	currency	reality	tour

1. It's possible to take a virtual _____ of the *Titanic*.

2. Virtual _____ is the next big thing in video gaming.

3. The students study with a teacher via a virtual _____ .

BEFORE YOU READ

DISCUSSION **A.** Do you know any stories or myths about long-lost ancient cities? What do you know about these places? Tell a partner.

PREDICTING **B.** Look at the photo below and read the caption. How do you think researchers could try to find an ancient lost city in this place? What would be the main challenges? Discuss with a partner. Check your ideas as you read the passage.

⌄ **Covering more than 50,000 square kilometers in Honduras and Nicaragua, La Mosquitia contains the largest rain forest in Central America.**

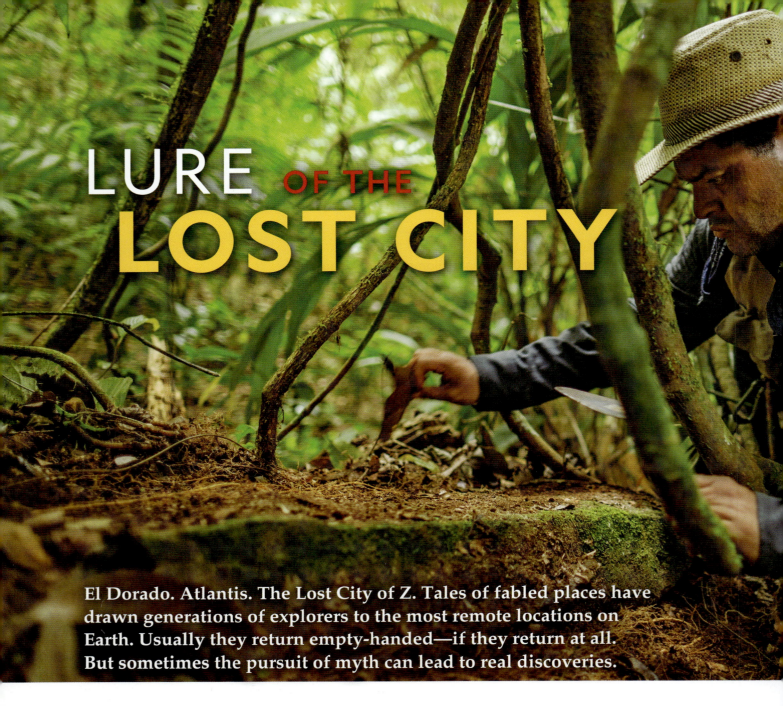

LURE OF THE
LOST CITY

El Dorado. Atlantis. The Lost City of Z. Tales of fabled places have drawn generations of explorers to the most remote locations on Earth. Usually they return empty-handed—if they return at all. But sometimes the pursuit of myth can lead to real discoveries.

A On February 18, 2015, a helicopter carrying a team of explorers headed toward the mountains of La Mosquitia, a remote area of Honduras. Below, farms gradually gave way to steep **slopes**, some covered with unbroken rain forest. The pilot headed for a V-shaped gap in a distant ridge. Beyond it lay a valley surrounded by mountains: a landscape of emerald and gold. There were no signs of human life—not a road, a **trail**, or a column of smoke. The pilot descended, aiming for a clearing along a riverbank.

B The team had come to explore a region long thought to contain "Ciudad Blanca"—a city built of white stone, known as the Lost City of the Monkey God. One of the team members was an archeologist named Chris Fisher. Fisher didn't believe in the **legend**, but he did believe that the valley—known simply as T1—contained a secret. In fact, somewhere in this valley, he believed, were the ruins of a real lost city, abandoned for at least half a millennium.[1]

---

1 A **millennium** is a period of one thousand years.

^ Archeologist Oscar Neil Cruz uncovers one of the flat stones encircling a ruined plaza in La Mosquitia.

The White City of Honduras

C The Mosquitia region of Honduras and Nicaragua contains vast areas of dense **vegetation**, swamps, and rivers. It also hides a number of dangers: deadly snakes, hungry jaguars, and insects carrying potentially deadly diseases.

D Over time, the myth of La Mosquitia's White City became part of the Honduran national consciousness. By the 1930s, it had also captured the imagination of the American public. Several expeditions were launched to find it, including three by the Museum of the American Indian in New York City. The first two came back with rumors of a lost city containing a giant statue of a monkey god.

E The museum's third expedition, a group led by a journalist named Theodore Morde, landed in Honduras in early 1940. Morde emerged from the jungle five months later with boxes of artifacts, claiming he had found evidence of an ancient walled city. He would not reveal the location for fear of looting,[2] but promised to return the following year. He never did; he died in 1954. The city—if there was one—remained unidentified.

F In the 1990s, a documentary filmmaker named Steve Elkins became **fascinated** by the legend of the White City. He spent years studying reports from explorers, archeologists, and geologists. He then studied **satellite** photographs of three valleys, which he labeled T1, T2, and T3 (T stands for "target"). The images, however, were inconclusive, and he realized he needed a better way to see through the dense jungle canopy.[3]

G Then, in 2010, Elkins learned of a new technology called lidar (light detection and ranging)—a way to explore the valleys from aircraft flying above the jungle. Lidar works by bouncing hundreds of thousands of pulses[4] of infrared laser beams off the ground below. Scanning the three valleys cost a quarter of a million dollars, but the initial results were astonishing. In an attempt to investigate the myth of the White City, Elkins had apparently **uncovered** two real ancient cities in valleys T1 and T3. To help interpret the data, he turned to Chris Fisher, a specialist on Mesoamerica.

---

2 **Looting** is when people steal from homes, businesses, or tombs.

3 A **canopy** is a layer of branches and trees that spreads out over the top of a forest.

4 A **pulse** is a single, short burst of sound, light, or electricity.

Discoveries in the Jungle

H This is how, in February 2015, Fisher and his team came to be in the dense jungle of La Mosquitia. Besides Fisher, who had **extensive** experience with lidar imagery, the team included two other archeologists, a group of scientists, and Elkins's camera crew.

I The team set out from base camp, cutting a trail through the jungle with machetes.[5] They faced plenty of challenges—snakes, insects, mud, and constant rain. Although the area was remote, they were not alone. Animals wandered around them or gathered in the trees above, seemingly unafraid. "I've never seen anything like it," one team member noted. "I don't think these animals have ever seen human beings."

J After climbing above the floodplain, they arrived at the base of a steep, jungle-covered highland— the edge of the presumed city. "Let's go to the top," Fisher said. Holding onto vines and tree roots, the explorers continued up the muddy slope. At the summit, Fisher pointed out the outline of a building. There was evidence of construction—probably an earthen **pyramid**. The team later identified one of the city's plazas, or large public spaces—an area of rain forest as level as a soccer field. Straight-edged mounds on three sides revealed the remains of walls and buildings.

K By the following afternoon, the group had mapped three more plazas and many mounds. But it appeared that the river was rising, so they prepared to leave. Suddenly, one of the cameramen called out: "Hey, there are some weird stones over here."

L At the base of the pyramid, the team found the tops of dozens of beautifully carved stone sculptures: the head of a jaguar, large jars carved with snakes, and objects that looked like seats or tables. All the artifacts were in perfect condition, apparently untouched since they had been left centuries before. There were 52 objects above ground—and probably many more below the surface.

M In the days that followed, the team recorded each object using a 3-D scanner. Nothing was touched, nothing removed. Further expeditions to the area are now being planned with the support of the Honduran government. There is still much to learn about the former **inhabitants** of La Mosquitia. Whether or not the White City is real or myth, the search for it has led to riches.

---

5 A **machete** is a large knife with a broad handle, often used to clear branches.

A scientific team inspects a construction stone found in La Mosquitia.

ARCHEOLOGY FROM ABOVE

Lidar technology is revolutionizing archeology. By measuring the distance light travels to the ground and back, researchers can detect traces of ancient settlements hidden beneath the forest canopy.

Reflected laser points are used to create a model of the forest canopy.

By identifying the laser points that reach and reflect off the ground, researchers produce topographic maps.

PLAZA

TERRACES

449 ft (137 m)

Experts then look for traces of man-made structures in the area.

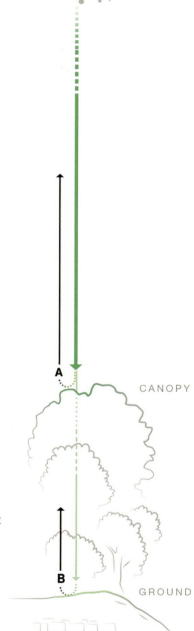

— 2,000 FT
CONSTANT ALTITUDE
ABOVE GROUND LEVEL

A

CANOPY

Lidar technology directs thousands of pulses of light toward the ground. Most beams of light reflect off the forest canopy (A); a few reach the ground and reflect back through gaps in the canopy (B).

B

GROUND

RUINS

DIAGRAM NOT TO SCALE

MANUEL CANALES, NGM STAFF; AMANDA HOBBS. ART: GREG HARLIN. DIGITAL RENDERING: STEFAN FICHTEL
SOURCES: JUAN CARLOS FERNÁNDEZ-DIAZ, NCALM/UNIVERSITY OF HOUSTON;
CHRISTOPHER T. FISHER, COLORADO STATE UNIVERSITY; ALICIA M. GONZÁLEZ; UTL PRODUCTIONS

A. Choose the best answer for each question.

MAIN IDEA

1. According to paragraph B, what were Chris Fisher's expectations as he started exploring T1?

    a. He was confident the team would find the Lost City of the Monkey God.
    b. He assumed the expedition would last a long time.
    c. He was pretty sure the team would find some ancient ruins.
    d. He thought he would meet looters in the valley.

DETAIL

2. The most conclusive evidence for the existence of a lost city came from _____.

    a. satellite photos
    b. rock samples taken by geologists
    c. aerial photos
    d. lidar images

DETAIL

3. Which of the following is NOT mentioned as one of the challenges faced by Fisher's team?

    a. wild animals
    b. unfriendly local tribes
    c. muddy ground
    d. rainy weather

SEQUENCE

4. The first sign that Fisher's team had discovered a lost city in T1 was the indication that _____ had once been there.

    a. a pyramid
    b. a plaza
    c. straight-edged mounds
    d. stone carvings

DETAIL

5. Which of the following did the team NOT observe in the T1 valley?

    a. flat areas once used as public spaces
    b. animals that were not scared of humans
    c. large buildings shaped like animals
    d. well-preserved stone sculptures

⌃ **A carved artifact uncovered in La Mosquitia**

EVALUATING STATEMENTS

B. Are the following statements true or false according to the reading passage, or is the information not given? Circle T (true), F (false), or NG (not given).

	T	F	NG
1. The Lost City of the Monkey God is also known as La Mosquitia.	T	F	NG
2. Theodore Morde's expedition to the Mosquitia region was sponsored by the Museum of the American Indian.	T	F	NG
3. The artifacts that Morde brought back included sculptures.	T	F	NG
4. It is likely there are more artifacts under the ground in T1.	T	F	NG
5. Fisher's team took the artifacts back to the U.S. for further study.	T	F	NG

Scanning for Information (3)—Summary Completion

Scanning is an important skill for taking exams, but how you approach scanning should depend on the question type. With **summary completion questions**, you are given a list of words to add to an incomplete summary. Usually, the words are synonyms or paraphrases of those from the reading passage. First, read the summary quickly and identify the likely part of speech for each missing word. Try to predict the answers and complete any you are sure of. Then scan the reading passage for the answers, remembering to look for paraphrases and synonyms of the summary's key words.

SUMMARIZING **A.** Below is a summary of paragraphs D and E from Reading B. Complete the summary with words or phrases from the box. Three options are extra.

divulge	**expedition**	**explorers**	**gold**
items	**legend**	**rain forest**	**stories**

The [1] _Legend_ of a lost city in the Amazon was well-known in the United States by the 1930s. Early [2] _explorers_ returned with stories of the city. In 1940, one man spent several months in the [3] _____ and brought back [4] _Rain forest_ he claimed were from the lost city. However, he would not [5] _divulge_ the city's whereabouts.

SUMMARIZING **B.** Below is a summary of paragraphs F and G from Reading B. Complete the summary with words from the reading passage. Use up to two words for each item.

In the 1990s, filmmaker Steve Elkins examined [1] _____ from different scientists about "Ciudad Blanca." He also looked at [2] _____ taken from space of the three valleys. The thick [3] _____ _____ meant he could not draw any conclusions, however. Years later, he used lidar technology to send pulses of infrared [4] _____ _____ into the jungle. The results were [5] _____: Elkins had uncovered evidence of two undiscovered cities in La Mosquitia.

CRITICAL THINKING Evaluating Pros and Cons   Do you think archeologists in La Mosquitia should be allowed to use invasive techniques (e.g., dig under the surface of the jungle)? Discuss with a partner. Note some reasons for and against. Consider academic, environmental, business, and technology factors.

For: _____

_____

Against: _____

_____

COMPLETION **A.** Circle the correct words to complete the information below.

The city of El Dorado has [1]**fascinated** / **uncovered** people for hundreds of years. When Spanish explorers reached South America in the 16th century, they heard about a wealthy city in what is now Colombia. The city's [2]**inhabitants** / **vegetation** owned so much gold that their chief threw gold jewels into the lake to please the gods. The Spaniards started calling this chief El Dorado; later, the name was used for the city itself.

Some researchers believe the [3]**trail** / **legend** of El Dorado may contain some truth. They hope to [4]**slope** / **uncover** the mystery using high-tech tools such as [5]**pyramid** / **satellite** technology. However, despite [6]**inhabited** / **extensive** searching, the fabled city of El Dorado, if it exists, remains hidden.

⌃ **An artist's impression of the mythical El Dorado**

WORDS IN CONTEXT **B.** Complete the sentences. Circle the correct words.

1. The **slope** of a mountain is its *side / peak / bottom.*

2. You are likely to follow a **trail** in *your house / an ocean / a forest.*

3. **Vegetation** refers to *plants, trees, and flowers / green vegetables / fruit.*

4. The sides of a **pyramid** are usually in the shape of a *square / triangle / circle.*

WORD USAGE **C.** The words *legend, myth,* and *folktale* are often confused with one another. A **legend** is a very old story that may be partly true. A myth often tells a story of creation or of a supernatural being. A folktale is a popular story passed down orally. Write the type of story next to each of these examples.

1. The German fairy tale "Hansel and Gretel" tells of a witch who kidnaps and holds two children before they eventually escape. _____

2. The Roman hero Hercules, the son of a god and a woman, is famous for his strength and unbelievable adventures. _____

3. The tales of Robin Hood describe the adventures of a man who may have lived in England's Sherwood Forest hundreds of years ago. _____

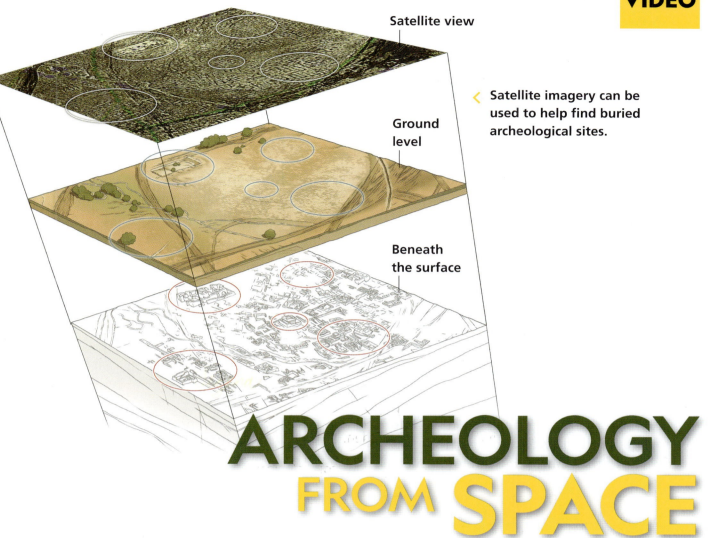

Satellite view

Ground level

Beneath the surface

< Satellite imagery can be used to help find buried archeological sites.

ARCHEOLOGY
FROM SPACE

BEFORE YOU WATCH

PREVIEWING **A.** Look at the infographic above. Then read the information below. The words and phrases in **bold** appear in the video. Match these words and phrases with their definitions (1–4).

From some 400 miles up in space, satellites are helping archeologists to uncover buried secrets. Researchers are using **state-of-the-art** satellite imagery to identify **subtle** changes in the landscape. "There is much we miss on the ground," says Sarah Parcak, a pioneer in using satellite imagery. The data can help archeologists **figure out** what lies beneath the surface, allowing them to **pinpoint** potential excavation sites.

1. _____ : to understand or solve something

2. _____ : to find or show the exact position of something

3. _____ : not immediately obvious or noticeable

4. _____ : very modern and using the latest ideas and methods

WHILE YOU WATCH

GIST **A.** Watch the video. Check (✓) the topics that are covered in the video.

☐ a. why Peru is important to archeologists

☐ b. Hiram Bingham's discovery of Machu Picchu in Peru

☐ c. how drones are being used in archeological fieldwork

☐ d. the challenges that archeologists face with using a new technology

EVALUATING STATEMENTS **B.** Watch the video again. Are the following statements true or false, or is the information not given? Circle **T** (true), **F** (false), or **NG** (not given).

1. Drones are generally more useful to archeologists than satellites in space.	T	F	NG
2. Space archeologists study satellite images by looking at different parts of the light spectrum.	T	F	NG
3. Satellites help archeologists pinpoint locations with an accuracy of within just a few centimeters.	T	F	NG
4. Space archeology has led to a reduction in looting.	T	F	NG

CRITICAL THINKING Reflecting   Discuss these questions with a partner.

▶ In 2017, Sarah Parcak launched GlobalXplorer, an online citizen science project that invites people around the world to search satellite imagery for signs of looting and archeological sites. How might this approach be helpful? Note some ideas below.

_____

_____

▶ Would you be interested in joining GlobalXplorer? Why or why not?

VOCABULARY REVIEW

Do you remember the meanings of these words? Check (✓) the ones you know. Look back at the unit and review any words you're not sure of.

Reading A

☐ assemble*   ☐ bounce back   ☐ carving   ☐ column   ☐ firsthand

☐ garment   ☐ gaze   ☐ memorial   ☐ stunned   ☐ virtual*

Reading B

☐ extensive   ☐ fascinated   ☐ inhabitant   ☐ legend   ☐ pyramid

☐ satellite   ☐ slope   ☐ trail   ☐ uncover   ☐ vegetation

* Academic Word List

10

HEALTHY LIVING

< More and more seniors are taking up sports like surfing.

WARM UP

Discuss these questions with a partner.

1. Which countries do you think have the healthiest people in the world?

2. Do you think your lifestyle is healthier or less healthy than your grandparents'? In what way(s)?

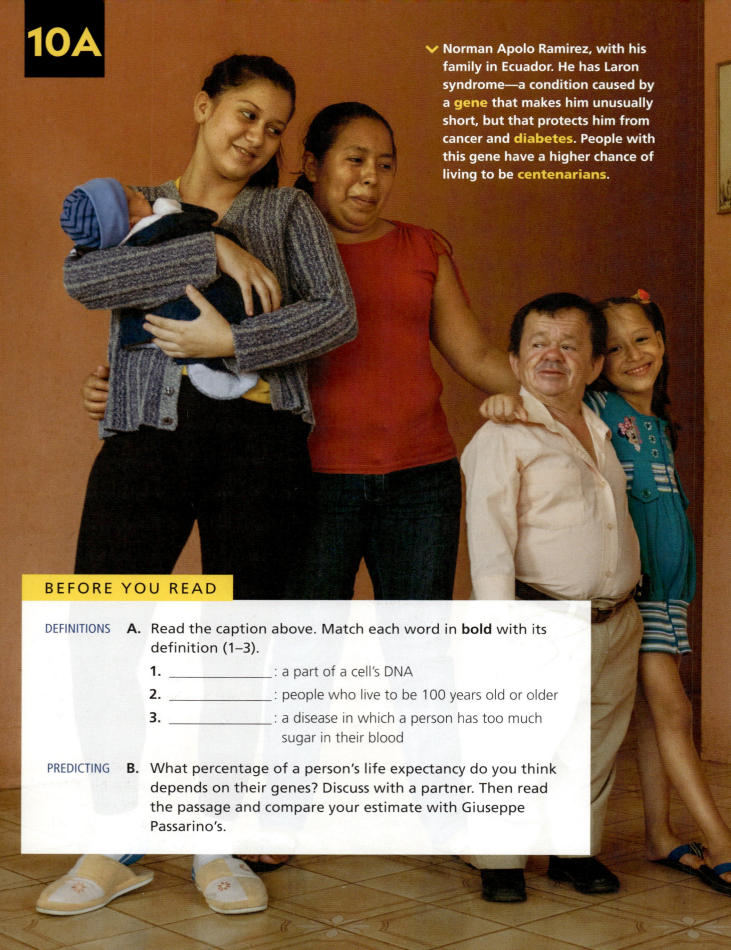

⌄ **Norman Apolo Ramirez**, with his family in Ecuador. He has Laron syndrome—a condition caused by a **gene** that makes him unusually short, but that protects him from cancer and **diabetes**. People with this gene have a higher chance of living to be **centenarians**.

BEFORE YOU READ

DEFINITIONS **A.** Read the caption above. Match each word in **bold** with its definition (1–3).

1. _____ : a part of a cell's DNA

2. _____ : people who live to be 100 years old or older

3. _____ : a disease in which a person has too much sugar in their blood

PREDICTING **B.** What percentage of a person's life expectancy do you think depends on their genes? Discuss with a partner. Then read the passage and compare your estimate with Giuseppe Passarino's.

LIVING
LONGER

A When it comes to longer **lifespans**, could genes play a more important role than diet and exercise? Scientists have begun looking at the genes of small, isolated communities to better understand the illnesses of old age and how they might be avoided. In Italy, Ecuador, and the United States, studies are revealing information related to genes that may one day help everyone reach their old age in good health.

Taste for Life

B On a cool January morning in 2013, Giuseppe Passarino drove on a mountain road through orange trees into Calabria, in the far south of Italy. Passarino, a geneticist at the University of Calabria, was headed for the small village of Molochio, a remote town with four centenarians and four 99-year-olds among its 2,000 inhabitants.

C Soon after, he found 106-year-old Salvatore Caruso in his home. Caruso told the researcher that he was in good health, and his memory seemed excellent. He recalled the death of his father in 1913, when Salvatore was a schoolboy; how his mother and brother had nearly died during the great flu **epidemic** of 1918–1919; and how he'd been dismissed from the army in 1925 after accidentally falling and breaking his leg in two places. When asked about the reasons for his long life, the centenarian smiled and said in Italian, "No drinking, no smoking, no women." He added that he'd eaten mostly figs and beans while growing up and hardly ever any red meat. Passarino heard much the same from 103-year-old Domenico Romeo, who described his diet as "a little bit, but of everything."

D Passarino is working to understand the reasons that Calabrians live such long lives. In the dim, cool hallway outside his university office stand several freezers full of blood taken from **elderly** Calabrians. The DNA from this blood has revealed that people who live into their 90s and beyond may have such long lives owing to a gene that affects their sense of taste. This gene gives people a taste for bitter foods like broccoli and field greens—vegetables that promote cellular[1] health and aid digestion.

---

1 **Cellular** means relating to the cells of animals or plants.

Size Matters

E The quest to understand more about genetic influences on aging has brought scientific attention to people like Nicolas Añazco, known as "Pajarito"—Little Bird in Spanish. Nicolas, 17, said he became aware of the reason for his nickname at age six, when he looked around at his classmates: "I realized that I was going to be smaller than them." Because of a single gene, Nicolas looks like an eight-year-old and is 115 centimeters tall. That gene causes a condition called Laron syndrome; it is due to this rare condition that he is so small.

F Nicolas is one of Ecuador's Laron people, descendants of Europeans who traveled to Ecuador in the 16th century. These travelers carried a gene that sometimes causes short stature; the same genetic mutation has been discovered in other places where these Europeans **relocated**. In Ecuador, the Laron people settled in small towns and villages scattered across the countryside. Because of a lack of roads, phones, and electricity, the area remained isolated until the 1980s. Over the centuries, the genetic mutation was **passed down** through the generations.

G In an interview, Little Bird and some friends—all with Laron syndrome—talked about their lives. Victor Rivera, now 23, was the subject of a famous photograph shown at many scientific meetings, taken when he was four. He was so small that the ear of corn he was holding was **slightly** larger than his arm. Luis Sanchez, an elder among the group, laughed along with his friends when someone asked if they knew the latest scientific reports about their condition. "We are laughing," he explained, "because we know we are **immune** to cancer and diabetes." Indeed, he is partly right.

H Researchers have found that people with Laron syndrome have a good chance of living a long life. A 2006 study revealed that no one from a group of people with Laron syndrome developed diabetes, and only one person

❮ At 106, Salvatore Caruso was still taking part in the olive harvest on his family's land in Molochio, Italy.

▼ More "wellderlies" are joining gyms as a way to keep fit.

developed cancer. In a control group of people without Laron syndrome, 5 percent developed diabetes and 20 percent died of cancer. The same gene that causes short stature may also protect people with Laron syndrome from disease.

The Gene Hunt

I Protective genes have also attracted the attention of researchers in the United States. In one study of an isolated, **homogeneous** population, University of Hawaii researchers have found a gene related to long life in Japanese-American men on the island of Oahu. In yet another study, in La Jolla, California, physician Eric Topol and colleagues are searching through the DNA of about a thousand people they call "the wellderly"— people over the age of 80 who have no **chronic** diseases such as high blood pressure, heart disease, or diabetes, and have never taken prescription drugs. "There must be modifying genes that explain why these individuals are protected from the deleterious[2] genes that affect the aging process," Topol says. "The hunt is on."

J But genes alone are unlikely to explain all the secrets of living to 100. As geneticist Passarino explains, "It's not that there are good genes and bad genes … It's certain genes at certain times. And in the end, genes are probably responsible for only 25 percent of living a long and healthy life. It's the environment, too, but that doesn't explain all of it either. And don't forget chance."

K This brought to mind Salvatore Caruso, still going strong at 106 years old. Because he broke his leg 88 years ago, it wasn't **mandatory** for him to go to Russia with the other soldiers and fight in the war. "Not a single one of them came back," he said. It's another reminder that while genes may be an important factor in living longer, a little luck doesn't hurt.

---

2 Something that is **deleterious** has a harmful effect.

A. Choose the best answer for each question.

> **Figs are among the world's healthiest foods.**

GIST

1. What is the reading mainly about?

    a. the role that genes may play in living a long life
    b. how a healthy diet can increase your lifespan
    c. a long-term study of Italian centenarians
    d. aging tips from centenarians around the world

DETAIL

2. What does the gene that Passarino discovered in older Calabrians do?

    a. It allows them to taste things more than other people.
    b. It gives them a preference for bitter foods.
    c. It lets them eat large amounts of food and still be healthy.
    d. It makes it difficult to digest certain unhealthy foods.

DETAIL

3. According to the writer, what is true for both the people of Molochio and the Laron people of Ecuador?

    a. They generally avoid red meat.
    b. The people there were all relocated.
    c. The communities are relatively small and isolated.
    d. They have the highest numbers of centenarians in the world.

DETAIL

4. What is NOT true about the Laron people?

    a. Their ancestors came from Europe.
    b. Most of them came to Ecuador in the 1980s.
    c. Because of a gene, some of them are smaller in size.
    d. They have a gene that helps protect them from certain diseases.

INFERENCE

5. Which statement would Giuseppe Passarino probably agree with the most?

    a. The answer to why centenarians live so long lies in genetics.
    b. Basically, there are two types of genes: good and bad.
    c. There will likely be fewer centenarians in Calabria in the future.
    d. Genetics, the environment, and luck all affect how long you live.

COHERENCE

B. Complete these sentences. Circle the best option for each. Then check your answers in the reading passage.

1. [P]eople who live into their 90s *beyond* may have such long lives owing to a gene that affects *their* / *our* / *your* sense of taste. (paragraph D)

2. "[W]e know we are immune to cancer and diabetes." *Before* / *But* / *Indeed*, he is partly right. (paragraph G)

3. But genes alone are unlikely to explain all the secrets of living to 100. *As* / *Indeed* / *While* geneticist Passarino explains, "It's not that there are good genes and bad genes …" (paragraph J)

Recognizing Cause and Effect Relationships (2)

As you learned previously, a writer may present one or more causes or reasons for a particular action or result (see Unit 3A Reading Skill). The reason(s) may come before or after the action, and may be connected to the action using a signal word or phrase. Words and phrases that signal reasons include *owing to (the fact that), due to (the fact that), since,* and *because (of).* In the following examples, the reason is underlined.

As / Since / Owing to the fact that <u>he never exercises,</u> he's started to put on weight.

The reason he has started to put on weight is (**that**) <u>he never exercises.</u>

He started to put on weight **because of** <u>a lack of exercise.</u>

His sudden weight gain was **due to** <u>his lack of exercise.</u>

SCANNING **A.** Scan Reading A and write short answers to the questions below.

1. According to Salvatore Caruso, what aspects of his diet as a young man helped him have a long life? (paragraph C)

_____

2. According to DNA research, why does Giuseppe Passarino think Calabrians live such long lives? (paragraph D)

_____

3. Why is Nicolas Añazco much shorter than most people his age? (paragraph E)

_____

4. Why did the area that the Laron people settled in remain isolated for so long? (paragraph F)

_____

5. Why is Luis Sanchez happy? (paragraph G)

_____

CAUSE AND EFFECT **B.** Look back at Reading A. Underline the words or phrases that signal the reasons in activity A.

CRITICAL THINKING Applying Ideas   Imagine you are a journalist writing an article about the secrets to long life. As part of your research, you are interviewing a group of centenarians. What questions would you ask them? Note five questions below and share with a partner.

_____

_____

_____

COMPLETION   **A.** Complete the paragraph with words or phrases from the box. Two options are extra.

> **chronic**   **elderly** 4   **lifespan** 3
> **passed down** 1   **relocated**   **slight** 2

Experiments on the tiny worm *Caenorhabditis elegans* may help extend human life. Researchers altered two of the worm's genes—changes that were then ¹_____ to the next generation of worms. Although each of these changes in the worm's DNA was ²_____ , together they had a significant impact on the worm's ³_____ . "Basically, these worms lived to the human equivalent of 400 to 500 years," says lead scientist Dr. Pankaj Kapahi. Scientists hope that, in combination with other therapies, this research might one day help ⁴_____ people remain healthy well into their 90s—and maybe even reach 100.

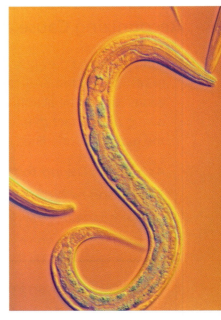

∧ *Caenorhabditis elegans*—a transparent roundworm—is about **1 mm in length.**

WORDS IN CONTEXT   **B.** Complete the sentences. Circle the correct words.
1. A flu **epidemic** would affect a *small / large* number of people.
2. If something is **mandatory**, you *have / don't have* to do it.
3. A **homogeneous** group consists of *the same kind / different kinds* of people.
4. If you are **immune** to a disease, you most likely *will / won't* get it.
5. A **chronic** disease is one that you have for a *short / long* time.
6. If someone **relocates**, they *stay in the same / move* to a new location.

WORD PARTS   **C.** The word *life* appears in a number of compound words, such as **lifespan**. Complete the sentences with the correct words from the box.

> **lifelike** 4 **lifelong** 3 **lifespan** 2 **lifestyle** 1

1. Women usually have a longer _____ than men.
2. A balanced diet and regular exercise are important for a healthy _____ .
3. Many schools offer classes to elderly students to encourage _____ learning.
4. Skilled artists can create portraits that are extremely _____ .

BEFORE YOU READ

DISCUSSION **A.** Read the caption below. What healthy habits do you think Okinawans and other long-lived people have that help them live longer? Discuss with a partner. Consider aspects like food and drink, social life, and hobbies.

SCANNING **B.** Scan the reading passage on the next four pages to find information about the healthy habits of long-lived people. Does the information match your ideas in activity A?

⟨ Kame Ogido, 89, examines pieces of seaweed—part of a low-calorie, plant-based diet that helps Okinawans live an average of 84 years.

IN SEARCH OF LONGEVITY

A   A long, healthy life is no accident. It begins with good genes inherited from your family, but it also depends on good habits. So what's the formula for success? In a study funded in part by the U.S. National Institute on Aging, scientists focused on groups living in several regions where exceptional **longevity** is the norm: Sardinia, Italy; Loma Linda, California; and the islands of Okinawa, Japan. Groups living in these three areas offer three sets of **guidelines** to follow.

Sardinians

B   Taking a break from farm work in the village of Silanus, 75-year-old Tonino Tola tickles the chin of his five-month-old grandson, Filippo, who watches from his mother's arms. "Goochi, goochi, goo," Tonino whispers. For this strong, healthy, 1.8-meter-tall man, these two things—hard work and family—form the foundation of his life. They may also help explain why Tonino and his neighbors live so long.

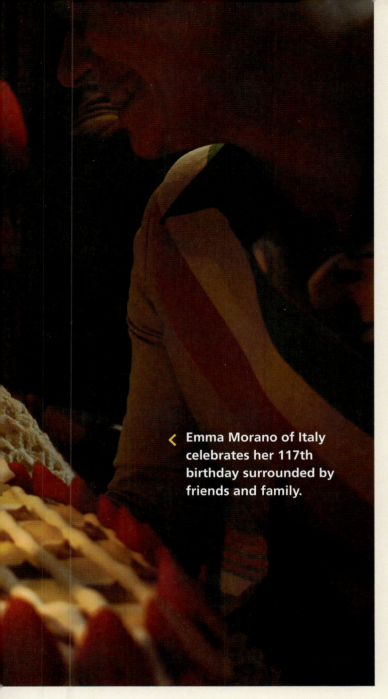

Emma Morano of Italy celebrates her 117th birthday surrounded by friends and family.

milked four cows, chopped wood, slaughtered[1] a calf, and walked over six kilometers with his sheep. Now, taking the day's first break, he gathers his grown children, grandson, and visitors around the kitchen table. Giovanna, his wife, unties a handkerchief containing a paper-thin flatbread called *carta da musica*, pours some red wine, and cuts slices of homemade pecorino cheese.

E These Sardinians also benefit from their genetic history. According to Paolo Francalacci of the University of Sassari, 80 percent of them are directly related to the first Sardinians, who arrived in the area 11,000 years ago. Genetic traits made stronger over generations may favor longevity. Nutrition, too, is a factor. The Sardinians' diet is loaded with fruits and vegetables, milk and milk products, fish, and wine. Most of these items are homegrown.

Adventists

F It's Friday morning, and Marge Jetton is speeding down the highway in her purple Cadillac.[2] She wears dark sunglasses to protect her eyes from the sun's glare, though her head is **barely** higher than the steering wheel. Marge, who turned 101 in September, is late for one of several volunteer commitments she has today. Already this morning she's eaten breakfast, walked one and a half kilometers, and lifted weights. "I don't know why God gave me the **privilege** of living so long," she says, pointing to herself. "But look what he did."

G Marge—like many other residents of Loma Linda, California—is a Seventh-Day Adventist. The Adventist Church has always practiced and been a proponent of healthy living. It **forbids** smoking, alcohol consumption, and certain foods, such as pork. The church also **discourages** the consumption of other meat, rich foods, caffeinated drinks, and most spices. Adventists also observe a sacred day of the

C A community of 2,400 people, Silanus is located on the edge of a mountainous region in central Sardinia, where dry fields rise suddenly into mountains of stone. In a group of villages in the heart of the region, 91 of the 17,865 people born between 1880 and 1900 have lived to their hundredth birthday—a rate more than twice as high as the average for Italy.

D Why do they live so long? Lifestyle is part of the answer. By 11:00 a.m. on this particular day, the **industrious** Tonino has already

---

1 To **slaughter** animals such as cows and sheep means to kill them for their meat.

2 A **Cadillac** is an American brand of car.

week on Saturday, assembling and socializing with other church members, which helps to **relieve** stress.

H A study found that the Adventists' habit of consuming beans, soymilk,[3] tomatoes, and fruit lowered their risk of developing certain cancers. It also suggested that eating whole wheat bread, drinking five glasses of water a day, and consuming four servings of nuts a week reduced their risk of heart disease. It found that not eating red meat had been helpful in avoiding both cancer and heart disease.

I In the end, the study reached a surprising conclusion, says Gary Fraser of Loma Linda University: The average Adventist's lifespan surpasses that of the average Californian by four to ten years. That compelling evidence makes the Adventists one of the most-studied cultures of longevity in the United States.

Okinawans

J The first thing you notice about Ushi Okushima is her laugh. It fills the room with pure joy. This rainy afternoon, she sits comfortably wrapped in a blue kimono. Her thick hair is combed back from her suntanned[4] face, revealing alert green eyes. Her smooth hands lie folded peacefully in her lap. At her feet sit her friends, Setsuko and Matsu Taira, cross-legged on a tatami mat[5] drinking tea.

K Ushi has recently taken a new job. She also tried to run away from home after a dispute with her daughter, Kikue. A relative caught up with her in another town 60 kilometers away and notified her daughter. Not long ago, she started wearing perfume, too. When asked about the perfume, she jokes that she has a new boyfriend. Predictable behavior for a young woman, perhaps, but Ushi is 103.

L With an average life expectancy of 81 years for men and 87 years for women, Okinawans are among the world's longest-lived people. This is undoubtedly due in part to Okinawa's warm and inviting climate and scenic beauty.

Senior citizens living in these islands tend to enjoy years free from disabilities. Okinawans have very low rates of cancer and heart disease compared to seniors in the United States. They are also less likely to develop dementia[6] in old age, says Craig Wilcox of the Okinawa Centenarian Study.

3 **Soymilk** is a drink made from soybeans.
4 If you are **suntanned**, the sun has turned your skin a darker color.
5 **Tatami mats**, made of woven straw, are the traditional material for floors in Japanese homes.
6 **Dementia** is a serious illness that affects the brain.

A robot assistant in a retirement home helps elderly people perform their daily exercises.

M A **lean** diet of food grown on the island and a philosophy of moderation—"eat until your stomach is 80 percent full"—may also be factors. **Ironically**, this healthy way of eating was born of hardship. Ushi Okushima grew up barefoot[7] and poor; her family grew sweet potatoes, which formed the core of every meal. During World War II, when the men of the island joined the army, Ushi and her friend Setsuko fled to the center of the island with their children. "We experienced terrible hunger," Setsuko recalls.

N Many older Okinawans belong to a *moai*, a mutual support network that provides financial, emotional, and social help throughout life. *Ikigai* may be another key factor. The word translates roughly to "that which makes one's life worth living," and it is something that is different for each person. "My *ikigai* is right here," says Ushi with a slow sweep of her hand that indicates her friends Setsuko and Matsu. "If they die, I will wonder why I am living."

---

7 Someone who is **barefoot** is not wearing anything on their feet.

A. Choose the best answer for each question.

PURPOSE

1. What is the main purpose of the reading?

    a. to explore the link between gender and longevity in three different cultures
    b. to compare three cultures and rank them in terms of their levels of health
    c. to investigate three cultures with high longevity and discover their habits
    d. to expose the myths about three famous cultures with high longevity

DETAIL

2. Which of the following is NOT mentioned as a factor in Sardinians' longevity?

    a. quality of medical treatment
    b. nutrition
    c. lifestyle
    d. genetic history

REFERENCE

3. In paragraph I, *that compelling evidence* refers to _____ .

    a. Adventists' reduced rates of heart disease
    b. Adventists' lifespan relative to that of other Californians
    c. Adventists' avoidance of red meat
    d. Adventists' reduced risk of certain cancers

DETAIL

4. Which of the following is NOT mentioned as a reason for the Okinawans' longevity?

    a. their social relationships   c. their religious beliefs
    b. their diet   d. their natural environment

SYNTHESIZING

5. Which statement is true about Sardinians, Adventists, and Okinawans?

    a. Climate is an important factor in their longevity.
    b. Most of their food is homegrown.
    c. They have strong friendships and family relationships.
    d. They drink red wine in moderation.

MATCHING   **B.** What lifestyle choices might help to explain people's longevity? Match each person (1–3) with the guidelines they follow (a–g) according to information from the reading passage. One guideline is extra.

1. Tonino Tola _A_ , _E_

2. Marge Jetton _D_ , _G_

3. Ushi Okushima _C_ , _F_

    a Work hard your whole life.
    b. Take a cold shower every day.
    c. Eat healthy food, but don't eat too much.
    d. Stay active by walking and lifting weights.
    e. Surround yourself with your family.
    f. Form a mutual support network with close friends.
    g. Avoid smoking, drinking alcohol, and consuming red meat.

Understanding Quantitative and Qualitative Data

Writers may include quantitative and qualitative data to support their ideas. Quantitative data is statistical information based on numbers and patterns. For example: *Eighty percent of the women said they ate mushrooms as part of their diet.* Qualitative data is nonstatistical; it relies more on observation and interpretation. Writers often use qualitative data to describe behavior or to make observations about a trend. For example: *The women got up early every morning to collect wild mushrooms for their lunch.*

COMPLETION   **A.** Complete the chart below with words or numbers from Reading B. Use one word or number for each blank.

Sardinians	Adventists	Okinawans
• hard work and 1_____ form foundation for life • 91 of 17,865 people born between 1880 and 1900 have lived to 100; this rate is more than 2_____ as high as national average • active lifestyle, e.g., milk cows, chop wood, walk • genetics—80% directly related to first Sardinians • eat mostly 3_____ food	• stay active, e.g., drive, volunteer, exercise • not allowed to smoke or drink 4_____ • to reduce risk of heart disease, study suggests drinking 5 glasses of water a day and eating 5_____ servings of nuts each week • live 4–10 years longer than the average 6_____	• stay positive—laugh! • average lifespan of 81 years (men) and 7____ years (women) • warm and inviting 8_____ • lower rates of cancer and heart disease than Americans • diet—lean foods, locally-produced • *moai*: a mutual support 9_____ • *ikigai* = "what makes life worth living"

ANALYZING   **B.** Underline the quantitative data in the chart above. Circle the qualitative data.

CRITICAL THINKING Relating to Personal Experience

▶ Which guidelines to longevity in Reading B do you already follow? Note them below. Then compare with a partner.

_____

_____

▶ Would the other guidelines mentioned in the passage be easy for you to adopt? Why or why not? Discuss with a partner.

VOCABULARY PRACTICE

DEFINITIONS
A. Read the information below. Match each word in **red** with its definition (1–5).

It seems **ironic**, but animals that **barely** eat enough to survive may actually live the longest. Some animals have shown increased **longevity** with decreased food intake. For example, mice that are fed 40 percent fewer calories than what is considered to be healthy live—on average—40 percent longer than mice fed normal diets.

Could eating less be a useful **guideline** to help slow aging in humans as well? Donald Ingram from the National Institute on Aging is investigating the effects of a **lean** diet on monkeys. It's too soon to tell if the animals will live longer—the study began in 1987, and monkeys typically live for 40 years. However, it appears that several markers of age-related disease have been reduced in the monkeys on a low-calorie diet.

1. _____ : long life
2. _____ : low in fat
3. _*barely*_ : only just; almost not
4. _*ironic*_ : a general rule or piece of advice
5. _____ : odd because it is the opposite of what one might think

▲ **Rhesus monkeys fed a lean diet seem healthier than those fed a normal diet.**

WORDS IN CONTEXT
B. Complete the sentences. Circle the correct words.

1. If someone **forbids** you from doing something, they say you *must /* (*mustn't*) do it.
2. If someone **discourages** you from doing an activity, they say you *should /* (*shouldn't*) do it.
3. Someone who is **industrious** is (*hardworking*) */ lazy*.
4. If you are given a **privilege**, you receive a *special* (*advantage*) */ punishment*.
5. If you **relieve** someone's stress, you *add to /* (*free them from*) it.

COLLOCATIONS
C. The words in the box are often used with the noun **relief**. Complete the sentences with the correct words from the box. One option is extra.

disaster	provide 3	sense of 1	sigh of 2

1. The nation felt a great _____ relief when the peace agreement was signed.
2. After the storm, the government was quick to send _____ relief.
3. This medicine should _____ relief for your headache for at least two hours.

184 Unit 10B

A typical breakfast
in rural Crete

YOU ARE WHAT
YOU EAT

BEFORE YOU WATCH

PREVIEWING **A.** Read the information. The words in **bold** appear in the video. Match these
words with their definitions below.

Historically, the people living on the Greek island of Crete have eaten only what their
land produced. Photographer Matthieu Paley went to Crete to learn more about this
quintessential Mediterranean diet. He discovered that Cretans today eat a rich variety
of foods harvested from local farms, **groves**, and the sea. "Some of the oldest food [is]
full of **omega-3**," Paley says. "It's super good for you."

1. quintessential •   • a. a small wooded area where fruit trees grow

2. grove   •   • b. a fatty acid found in some nuts, seeds, and fish

3. omega-3   •   • c. typical or representative of something

DISCUSSION **B.** Which foods do you think are a quintessential part of the Mediterranean diet?
Discuss with a partner and note some ideas below.

_____

_____

MAIN IDEA **A.** Watch the video. What is Matthieu Paley's main message in his presentation? Choose the best option.

    a. Because of their diet, many Cretans live to become centenarians.

    b. The traditional Mediterranean diet is changing due to modern lifestyles.

    c. A healthy diet is a key reason for the Cretan people's well-being.

DETAIL **B.** Watch the video again. Which of the following claims are made in the video? Check (✓) all that apply.

- ☐ a. The Mediterranean diet is the oldest diet that is still practiced today.
- ☐ b. People who follow a traditional Mediterranean diet are usually very fit.
- ☐ c. Most Cretan women know dozens of names of wild herbs and can find them easily in the fields.
- ☐ d. Crete produces more olive oil than all of the Greek islands and mainland combined.
- ☐ e. People in Crete enjoy alcoholic drinks like wine.
- ☐ f. Snails are a good source of omega-3.

CRITICAL THINKING Reflecting Look back at all the places mentioned in this unit. Would you consider living in one of these places? If so, which one? Note your answer and reasons below. Then share with a partner.

_____

_____

VOCABULARY REVIEW

Do you remember the meanings of these words? Check (✓) the ones you know. Look back at the unit and review any words you're not sure of.

Reading A

☐ chronic	☐ elderly	☐ epidemic	☐ homogeneous	☐ immune
☐ lifespan	☐ mandatory	☐ passed down	☐ relocate*	☐ slightly

Reading B

☐ barely	☐ discourage	☐ forbid	☐ guideline*	☐ industrious
☐ ironically	☐ lean	☐ longevity	☐ privilege	☐ relieve

* Academic Word List

11

GREEN
SOLUTIONS

A woman fills a watering can with rainwater from her roof.

WARM UP

Discuss these questions with a partner.

1. Do you think you use more or less water than the average person where you live?

2. What do you think the expression "waste not, want not" means?

187

BEFORE YOU READ

QUIZ **A.** How much do you know about water? Complete these sentences. Then check your answers on page 202.

1. *3 / 10 / 25* percent of the Earth's water is fresh water.

2. 70 percent of the world's fresh water is used for *drinking / farming / industry*.

3. It takes *500 / 5,000 / 50,000* liters of water to produce one kilogram of rice.

4. Compared to 100 million years ago, the world today has *less / the same amount of / more* water.

SCANNING AND PREDICTING **B.** Scan the reading to find the three regions it focuses on. What kinds of water problems do you think each region faces? Read the passage to check your ideas.

This baobab tree in Madagascar has been hollowed out and is used for storing water during droughts.

SAVING WATER

A In the Castilla-La Mancha region of Spain, Julio Escudero, a 74-year-old former fisherman, recalls an area on the Guadiana River called Los Ojos—"the eyes." Large underground springs bubbled up into the river, where Escudero and his community fished for carp and crayfish. "I would sit in my boat six or seven meters away and just watch the water coming up," Escudero says. "Now it looks like the moon." Los Ojos doesn't exist anymore—that stretch of the river dried up in 1984. Additionally, 186 square kilometers of surrounding wetlands[1] have disappeared.

B As farming in the region has increased, La Mancha has witnessed an explosion of well digging in the past 40 years that has lowered the water table[2] and **diverted** water from rivers. The number of wells has grown from 1,500 in 1960 to an official count of 21,000 today. Some experts say the real number, which includes illegal wells, could **surpass** 50,000.

A Global Problem

C La Mancha is just one of many places facing water **shortages**. This century, many countries will face the same dilemma that has confronted the people of Spain: How do you balance human needs with the requirements of natural systems that are vital for sustaining life on Earth?

D The United Nations recently outlined the **extent** of the water **crisis**. Due to water scarcity,[3] 5 billion people will face severe water shortages by 2050 if **consumption** continues at current rates. Today, lack of access to clean water means that an estimated 2.1 billion people drink water that is unsafe. More than 3 million people die each year from diseases **related to** unclean water.

E All over the world, humans are pumping water out of the ground faster than it can be replenished.[4] To address this issue, water conservationists, such as Rajendra Singh in India and Neil Macleod in South Africa, are searching for innovative ways to improve their local water situations.

---

1 A **wetland** is an area of wet, muddy land in which wild plants grow.
2 The **water table** is the layer below the Earth's surface where water is found.
3 A **scarcity** of a resource means there is not enough of it.
4 If you **replenish** something, you restore it to its former level.

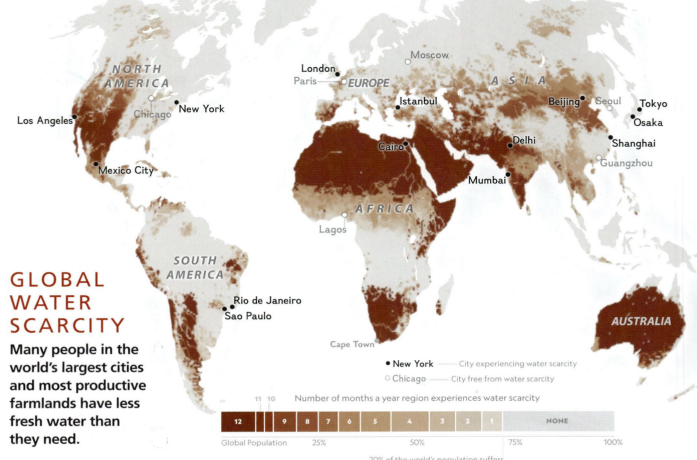

GLOBAL WATER SCARCITY

Many people in the world's largest cities and most productive farmlands have less fresh water than they need.

New York —— City experiencing water scarcity
Chicago —— City free from water scarcity

Number of months a year region experiences water scarcity

| 12 | | 11 10 | 9 | 8 | 7 | 6 | 5 | 4 | 3 | 2 | 1 | NONE |

Global Population   25%   50%   75%   100%

70% of the world's population suffers
at least one month of water scarcity a year.

A Hero in a Thirsty Land

F On arriving at the Indian village of Goratalai, Rajendra Singh was greeted by a group of about 50 people. He smiled and addressed the villagers:

"How many households do you have?"

"Eighty."

"It's been four years without much rain," said a woman. "And we don't have a proper dam[5] to catch the water."

"Do you have any spots where a dam could go?" asked Singh.

"Yes, two spots."

"I would like to help you," Singh told them, "but the work has to be done by you. You will have to provide one-third of the project through your labor, and the remaining two-thirds I will arrange."

G The villagers clapped, the women started to sing, and the group hiked to a place in the nearby rocky hills. Singh examined the area and, after a few minutes, declared it an ideal site. His organization would provide the engineering advice and materials; the villagers would supply the work. The nine-meter-high earthen dam—known as a *johad*—could be finished in three months, before the start of the rainy season. If the rains were plentiful, the dam would not only provide water for drinking and agriculture, but would also replenish dry wells. "You will not see the results immediately. But soon the dam will begin to raise the water level in your wells," Singh told the villagers.

H In recent years, Singh's johads have sprung up all over Rajasthan—an estimated 4,500 dams in about 1,000 villages, all built using local labor and native materials. His movement has caught on, he says, because it puts control over water in the hands of villagers. "If they feel a johad is their own,

---

5 A **dam** is a wall built across a river that stops the river's flow.

they will maintain it," said Singh. "This is a very sustainable, self-reliant system. I can say confidently that if we can manage rain in India in traditional ways, there will be sufficient water for our growing population."

Waste Not, Want Not

In 1992, Neil Macleod took over as head of Durban Metro Water Services in South Africa. The situation he found was a catastrophe. Durban had one million people living in the city and another 1.5 million people who lived in poverty just outside it. Macleod and his engineers found that the entire city suffered from broken water pipes, leaky toilets, and faulty plumbing, **whereby** 42 percent of the region's water was simply being wasted. "We **inherited** 700 reported leaks and bursts. The water literally just ran down the streets. Demand for water was growing 4 percent a year, and we thought we'd have to build another dam by 2000," recalls Macleod.

Macleod's crew began repairing and replacing water pipes. They put water meters on homes, replaced eight-liter toilets with four-liter models, and changed wasteful showers and faucets. To ensure that the poor would receive a basic supply of water, Macleod installed tanks in homes to provide 190 liters of water a day free to each household. Water consumption in Durban is now less than it was in 1996, even as 800,000 more people have received service. Through sensible water use, Durban's conservation measures paid for themselves within a year. Macleod says no new dams will be needed in the coming decades, despite the expected addition of about 300,000 inhabitants.

In Durban, Macleod has also turned to water recycling. At the water recycling plant, wastewater is turned into clean water in just 12 hours. According to Macleod, most people can't tell the difference between the usual drinking water and the treated wastewater. "Go to many areas of the world, and they're drinking far worse water than this," he says.

Some people still hope that new technology, such as the desalination[6] of seawater, will solve the world's water problems. "But the fact is, water conservation is where the big gains are to be made," says Sandra Postel, a leading authority on freshwater issues and director of the Global Water Policy Project. The **dedication** and resourcefulness of people like Rajendra Singh and Neil Macleod offer inspiration for implementing timely and lasting solutions to the world's water concerns.

---

6 **Desalination** is the process of removing salt from seawater.

> **A Rajasthani woman draws water from a well in the Thar Desert, India.**

A. Choose the best answer for each question.

GIST

1. What could be another title for this reading?
    a. Water for the Rich, Not for the Poor
    b. Why We Waste Water: Two Points of View
    c. Water Shortages and Problem Solvers
    d. Politics and Water: Fighting for a Drink

DETAIL

2. Which of these statements about Castilla-La Mancha is NOT true?
    a. Its situation is common to many places around the world.
    b. Overfishing has caused a great deal of environmental damage.
    c. Illegal well digging is a significant problem.
    d. The Los Ojos area has been dry for over 30 years.

MAIN IDEA

3. What is Rajendra Singh's solution to water shortages in India?
    a. build more dams   c. fix leaky pipes
    b. pump more groundwater   d. desalinate seawater

PARAPHRASE

4. In paragraph J, what does the phrase *[the] measures paid for themselves* mean?
    a. The solutions were inexpensive.   c. The costs were less than expected.
    b. The benefits outweighed the costs.   d. The government paid for the service.

INFERENCE

5. What did Sandra Postel mean by "water conservation is where the big gains are to be made" (paragraph L)?
    a. Water conservation is an opportunity for large profits for businesses.
    b. Water conservation is the most effective method to address water shortages.
    c. Water conservation technology is still in need of many improvements.
    d. Water conservation is required by law in order to ensure large gains.

CAUSE AND
EFFECT

B. Complete this information with words from the reading passage. Use one word for each blank.

Review this
reading skill
in Unit 3A

Due to a rise in ¹_____ in one part of Spain, people began to dig more ²_____, lowering the ³_____ table. Over time, this caused a large area of wetlands to disappear.

In the drought-stricken Indian village of Goratalai, residents asked an expert to help them build a ⁴_____ to catch water. This will ⁵_____ water levels in the village's wells.

The South African city of Durban used to have serious problems with its plumbing system—nearly half of the city's water was being ⁶_____. Major repairs were made, which led to a reduction in water ⁷_____ in the city. Using less water means the city won't have to build new ⁸_____ for many years to come.

Identifying Sources of Information

Writers often include material from a variety of sources to support their ideas. For example, a writer might include scientific data on global warming to support an argument about climate change. As you read a text, identify the sources the writer has used and assess how credible they are. Are the sources from experts in the field? Are they from academic journals? In some cases, a writer may not provide a source. Ask yourself why. The information may be obvious and not need a source, but it may also be because the source is less credible or even unknown.

IDENTIFYING
SOURCES

A. Look back at Reading A. Write the names of these sources.

1. a resident of Castilla-La Mancha: _Julio Escudero_

2. the head of Durban Metro Water Services: _Neil Mcleod_

3. the director of Global Water Policy Project: _Sandra Postel_

IDENTIFYING
SOURCES

B. The statements below (1–5) relate to Reading A. Choose the correct source (a, b, or c) for each statement. In some cases, no source is given.

1. There may be 50,000 or more wells in La Mancha. (paragraph B)

   a. an official count   (b.) some experts   c. no source given

2. La Mancha is just one of many places facing water shortages. (paragraph C)

   a. a health organization   b. a politician   (c.) no source given

3. If consumption continues at current rates, 5 billion people will face severe water shortages by 2050. (paragraph D)

   a. a health organization   (b.) the United Nations   c. no source given

4. There hasn't been much rain in Goratalai in four years. (paragraph F)

   a. a firsthand account   b. a scientific journal   (c.) no source given

5. Water conservation holds the most promise for solving the world's water problems. (paragraph L)

   a. a website   (b.) a leading authority   c. no source given

CRITICAL THINKING Evaluating Sources   Imagine you are writing an article about water use in farms in your country. What would be the pros and cons of each of these sources of information? Discuss with a partner.

- a firsthand account from a farmer

- research from a scientific journal

- statistics from a government department

- a report from an environmental organization

COMPLETION **A.** Complete the information with words or phrases from the box. Four options are extra.

consumption	**crisis** 3	**dedication**	**diverted**	**extent** 4
inherit 5	**related to**	**shortages** 2	**surpass** 1	**whereby**

By 2025, the number of people in the world will ¹_____ 8 billion; roughly 3 billion of these could face severe water ²_____ . Water scarcity is therefore a global ³_____ that needs to be addressed.

Water conservation efforts will depend on people becoming more aware of the ⁴_____ of the problem. Unfortunately, when water is cheap, people don't see the need to conserve it.

△ **A dry riverbed with an old dam in southern Namibia**

Raising the cost of using water could reduce people's ⁵_____ levels. When Chile raised the price of water, for example, the amount of fresh water that farmers ⁶_____ into their fields decreased by a quarter.

DEFINITIONS **B.** Match the words or phrases in **red** in activity A with these definitions (1–4).
1. _whereby_ : by which way or method ~related to~
2. _whereby_ : connected to; associated with ←
3. _inherit_ : to receive something (e.g., money, a problem) from someone who has left or died
4. _dedication_ : the willingness to give a lot of time and energy to something because it is important

COLLOCATIONS **C.** The verbs in **bold** below are often used with the noun **extent**. Circle the correct verb to complete each sentence.
1. A report **understood / (revealed)** the extent of the water shortage in parts of Spain.
2. Water conservationists say it's important to **(acknowledge) / ignore** the extent of the water scarcity problem before it's too late.
3. Doctors often don't **exaggerate / (know)** the full extent of an injury until they have done tests such as X-rays.

BEFORE YOU READ

DISCUSSION **A.** Discuss these questions with a partner.

1. When you get a new phone or other electronic device, what do you do with the old one?

2. What do you think happens to old phones, TVs, or computers when they are thrown away?

SKIMMING AND PREDICTING **B.** Read just the first sentence of paragraphs C–G on the next two pages. What problems do you think e-waste causes? Discuss with a partner. Check your ideas as you read the whole passage.

▼ **Electronic waste at a junkyard in Hamburg, Germany**

TECHNOLOGY AS TRASH

A   As the sun heats the humid air in Accra—the capital city of Ghana—a terrible-smelling black smoke begins to rise above the Agbogbloshie Market. Past the vegetable merchants is a scrap[1] market filled with **piles** of old and broken electronics waste. This waste—consisting of broken TVs, computers, and monitors—is known as "e-waste." Further beyond the scrap market are many small fires. Fueled by old car tires, they are burning away the plastic covering from valuable wire in the e-waste. People walk through the poisonous smoke with their arms full of brightly colored computer wire. Many of them are children.

B   Israel Mensah, 20, explains how he makes his living here. Each day, scrap sellers bring loads of old electronics. Mensah's friends and family buy a few computers or TVs. They break them apart to remove valuable metals and wires, as well as any parts that can be resold. Then they burn the plastic covering off the wire and sell it. The key to making money is speed, not safety. "The gas goes to your nose, and you feel something in your head," Mensah says as he knocks his fist against his head. "Then you get sick in your head and your chest." Broken computer and monitor cases are unwanted, and are thrown in a nearby lagoon.[2] The next day, the rain will wash them into the ocean.

The Problem of E-waste

C   E-waste is being produced on a scale never seen before. Computers, cell phones, and other electronic equipment become **obsolete** in just a few years, leaving consumers with little choice but to buy newer ones to keep up. Each person in the world **discards**, on average, over six kilograms of e-waste every year. That's enough e-waste to fill 1.2 million trucks lined up from New York to Bangkok—and back again.

D   Sadly, in most of the world, the bulk of all this waste ends up in landfills.[3] There it poisons the environment; e-waste contains a variety of **substances** that are **toxic**, such as lead, mercury, and arsenic. Recycling is, in many ways, the ideal solution to the problem: E-waste contains significant amounts of valuable metals such as silver, gold, and copper. In theory, recycling gold from old computers is far more efficient—and less environmentally destructive—than digging it from the earth. The problem is that a large percentage of e-waste dropped off for recycling in wealthy countries is diverted to the developing world—to countries like Ghana. As the quantity of e-waste increases worldwide, it poses an increasing threat to the health of people living in the developing world.

E   In 1989, 170 nations signed the Basel Convention to address the problem of the international trade in e-waste. The agreement required developed nations to **notify** developing nations of **hazardous** waste shipments coming into the country. Six years later, after pressure from environmental groups and developing nations, the Basel Convention was modified to ban hazardous waste shipments to poor countries completely. In the European Union—where recycling **infrastructure** is well developed—one law holds manufacturers responsible for the safe disposal of the electronics they produce.

---

1 **Scrap** is material from old, damaged cars or machines.
2 A **lagoon** is an area of water that is separated from the ocean by a line of rock or sand.
3 A **landfill** is a large, deep hole where garbage is buried.

F If e-waste continues to be shipped overseas, it may ultimately come back to harm the developed world. Jeffrey Weidenhamer, a chemist at Ashland University in Ohio, bought some jewelry made in a developing country for his class to analyze. It was **distressing** that the jewelry contained high amounts of lead, but not a great surprise, as jewelry with lead has turned up before in U.S. stores. More revealing were the quantities of metals such as copper and tin mixed in with the lead. Weidenhamer argued in a scientific paper that the proportions of these metals suggest that the jewelry was made from recycled computer parts.

G Since the developed world is sending large quantities of materials containing lead to developing nations, it's to be expected that those countries will make use of them in their manufacturing processes. "It's not at all surprising things are coming full circle and now we're getting contaminated products back," says Weidenhamer. In a global economy, it's no longer possible to get rid of something by sending it to other countries. As the old saying goes, "What goes around comes around."

A Small Solution?

H There is hope, however, that more countries will **transition** to a "circular economy"— one that focuses on reusing materials and minimizing waste in the first place. An example is Australia, which has recently opened what has been called the world's first e-waste microfactory. The microfactory—which is only 50 square meters in size—includes several small machines that recycle e-waste. A machine first breaks down the discarded e-waste. A robot then identifies and separates the parts, which are heated and transformed into valuable materials that can be reused and repurposed. The process is clean, relatively inexpensive, and—if repeated—could help reduce the huge amount of e-waste that currently ends up in Australian landfills.

I Because of their small size, microfactories could significantly alter the way e-waste is handled and processed. This is true especially in remote locations where transporting and recycling e-waste is very expensive. Professor Veena Sahajwalla of the University of New South Wales says e-waste microfactories have the potential to tackle e-waste problems locally and provide business opportunities— a win-win for the environment and business. It also provides a model that could be picked up in other countries that currently send their e-waste overseas. Innovations such as e-waste microfactories, says Sahajwalla, "offer a cost-effective solution to one of the greatest environmental challenges of our age."

At Australia's first e-waste microfactory, machines turn discarded smartphones and laptops into reusable materials.

A. Choose the best answer for each question.

MAIN IDEA **1.** What is the main idea of the reading?

    a. E-waste provides significant business opportunities.
    b. E-waste is enriching parts of the developing world.
    c. The world is facing a serious e-waste problem.
    d. Developed countries are largely to blame for the e-waste crisis.

DETAIL **2.** What causes the fires at the Agbogbloshie Market?

    a. the burning of unwanted computer and monitor cases
    b. the burning of the covering from metal wires
    c. the burning of old newspapers and magazines
    d. the burning of discarded cell phones and batteries

VOCABULARY **3.** In paragraph C, what does *keep up* mean?

    a. to keep the computer they already have
    b. to learn more about computers currently sold
    c. to have a positive attitude toward computers
    d. to obtain the latest, best-performing computers

PARAPHRASE **4.** In paragraph G, what does the saying "What goes around comes around" mean?

    a. Your actions have consequences that will eventually affect you.
    b. Whether or not your actions are correct, bad things will happen to you.
    c. No matter how unfairly you are treated, continue to treat others fairly.
    d. Don't worry about the actions of others, because you can't control them.

DETAIL **5.** Which of these is NOT mentioned as a possible benefit of microfactories?

    a. They are small in size.   c. They are not very expensive.
    b. They can be operated by anyone.   d. They can help create jobs.

IDENTIFYING PURPOSE **B.** Match each paragraph with its purpose (a–g). One purpose is extra.

    1. Paragraph A _____
    2. Paragraph B _____
    3. Paragraph C _____
    4. Paragraph E _____
    5. Paragraph F _____
    6. Paragraph H _____

    a. to explain how a series of machines recycles e-waste
    b. to present arguments for and against the recycling of e-waste
    c. to describe efforts to ban hazardous waste shipments to poor countries
    d. to profile how one person makes money from e-waste
    e. to describe a scrap market full of e-waste
    f. to explain why there is so much e-waste in the world
    g. to give an example of how shipping e-waste overseas can impact the developed world

Understanding a Writer's Attitude

Writers use adjectives, adverbs, and other phrases to express their attitude about a topic. Recognizing how a writer feels can help you better understand their position or argument. As you read, look for these kinds of words and phrases that indicate a writer's feeling.

Adjectives: *worthy, impressive* (+); *shameful, overrated* (−)

Adverbs: *luckily, pleasingly* (+); *unfortunately, regrettably* (−)

Transitions to introduce a contrast: *but, however, nevertheless, on the other hand*

In some cases, a writer's feelings may not be indicated explicitly, and must be inferred.

CLASSIFYING **A.** Do these words in the box indicate a positive, neutral, or negative attitude? Add them to the correct column in the chart.

arrogantly	attractive	fortunately	ideal	sadly
secretly	selfish	typical	ultimately	valuable

Positive	Neutral	Negative

UNDERSTANDING ATTITUDE **A.** Find each of the paraphrased statements below (1–4) in Reading B. Note if the writer feels positively (+) or negatively (−) about each statement. Underline any words in the passage that helped you decide.

_____ **1.** In most of the world, the bulk of e-waste ends up in landfills. (paragraph D)

_____ **2.** Recycling is, in many ways, the solution to the problem. (paragraph D)

_____ **3.** A large percentage of e-waste that is dropped off for recycling in wealthy countries is diverted to the developing world. (paragraph D)

_____ **4.** Jewelry sold back to the United States contained high amounts of lead. (paragraph F)

CRITICAL THINKING Inferring Attitude   Look back at Reading B. Do you think the writer is critical of the people in Ghana who make their living from e-waste? If not, do you think the writer blames anyone? What clues in the passage help you decide? Discuss with a partner.

COMPLETION   **A.** Circle the correct words to complete the information below.

Many companies send used electronics to developing nations. They claim to be recycling, and also helping the developing world so it can modernize its economy and [1]**substances / infrastructure**. However, the reality may be quite different.

It has been reported that three-quarters of the supposedly reusable electronics shipped to Nigeria are, in fact, broken. Consequently, large [2]**piles / transitions** of e-waste end up being [3]**notified / discarded**. Often, it's picked apart by poor people, who come into contact with [4]**substances / notifications** that are highly [5]**toxic / distressing**, such as lead. Lead is known to be especially [6]**obsolete / hazardous** to the health of growing children.

⌃ **A boy carries copper wires at a market in Ghana.**

WORDS IN CONTEXT   **B.** Complete the sentences. Circle the correct words.

1. The word **distressing** is commonly used to describe *gifts / people / problems*.

2. If a country **transitions** from one state or stage to another, it *changes gradually / avoids changing / relocates* from one to the other.

3. If you are **notified** about something, you are *unsure / angry / told* about it.

4. Technology that is **obsolete** is *very new / no longer useful / very popular*.

COLLOCATIONS   **C.** The words in the box are often used with the noun **substance**. Complete the sentences with the correct words from the box. One word is extra.

banned	natural	toxic	unknown

1. Lead is a very _____ substance. High lead exposure can even cause death.

2. Calcium is a(n) _____ substance in food that is important for bone growth.

3. Performance-enhancing substances, such as steroids, are _____ in most professional sports.

YOUR WATER FOOTPRINT

Cotton mill workers in Madhya Pradesh, India. Cotton products have a big impact on the environment.

BEFORE YOU WATCH

DISCUSSION   **A.** Read the definition below. Then answer the questions (1–3) with a partner.

cotton (*n*.): a soft, white, fibrous substance that surrounds the seeds of the cotton plant; it is commonly used to make a fabric also known as *cotton*.

1. What are you wearing now that is made from cotton?

2. What advantages does cotton have over other fabrics?

3. Besides clothing, what else can cotton be used for?

PREDICTING   **B.** In what ways do you think wearing cotton might affect the environment? Discuss with a partner and note some ideas. Consider aspects like clothing production and maintenance, and the resources used.

_____

_____

GIST **A.** Watch the video. Were any of your predictions in Before You Watch B mentioned in the video? What other impacts are mentioned? Note them below.

_____

_____

COMPLETION **B.** Complete the paragraph below using numbers from the box. One option is extra. Then watch the video again and check your answers.

1/3	5	40	70	900	2,700

What's the cost of a T-shirt? Well, making one cotton T-shirt requires [1]_____ liters of water—enough for one person to drink for [2]_____ days. One load of drying uses [3]_____ times more energy than washing. One load of washing uses [4]_____ gallons of water. So, you can help by not drying and ironing your freshly washed T-shirt—this could save [5]_____ of your T-shirt's carbon footprint.

CRITICAL THINKING Evaluating Solutions Imagine your city or country is facing a severe water shortage. What are some actions that can be taken by (a) the government, and (b) individuals to help solve the problem? Discuss with a partner and note some ideas.

_____

_____

VOCABULARY REVIEW

Do you remember the meanings of these words? Check (✓) the ones you know. Look back at the unit and review any words you're not sure of.

Reading A

☐ consumption*   ☐ crisis   ☐ dedication   ☐ divert   ☐ extent

☐ inherit   ☐ related to   ☐ shortage   ☐ surpass   ☐ whereby*

Reading B

☐ discard   ☐ distressing   ☐ hazardous   ☐ infrastructure*   ☐ notify

☐ obsolete   ☐ pile   ☐ substance   ☐ toxic   ☐ transition*

*Academic Word List

Answers to the Quiz on page 188: 1. 3; **2.** farming; **3.** 5,000; **4.** the same amount of

12

EARTH
AND BEYOND

A view of the moon and Earth's
atmosphere as seen from the
International Space Station

WARM UP

**Discuss these questions
with a partner.**

1. What can we learn about
    Earth from studying our
    solar system?

2. Can you think of any
    recent, interesting news
    stories about space
    exploration?

DISCUSSION **A.** Read the caption below. Why might astronomers be interested in finding exoplanets like CT Cha b? Discuss with a partner.

SKIMMING **B.** Look at the reading title and headings on the next three pages, and quickly skim the passage and infographic. Check (✓) the topics you think will be covered in the passage. Then check your answers as you read.

- [ ] a. how astronomers locate other Earth-like planets
- [ ] b. the search for life on other Earth-like planets
- [ ] c. establishing human colonies on other Earth-like planets

⌄ **Jupiter and Saturn may be large relative to our home planet, but they're small compared to CT Cha b, one of the 3,900-plus exoplanets—planets circling stars outside our own solar system—that astronomers have so far discovered.**

EARTH

SATURN
95 EARTHS

JUPITER
318 EARTHS

CT CHA b
5,403 EARTHS
MORE THAN 500 LIGHT-YEARS AWAY

PLANET HUNTERS

A It took humans thousands of years to explore our own planet, and centuries to comprehend our neighboring planets. Nowadays, though, new worlds are being discovered every week.

B **To date**, astronomers have identified more than 3,900 "exoplanets"—worlds orbiting[1] stars other than the sun. There's a "hot Saturn" 260 light-years from Earth that orbits its parent star so rapidly that a year there lasts less than three days. Circling another star 150 light-years out is a "hot Jupiter," whose upper **atmosphere** is being blown away by the star's solar winds. Astronomers have also found five planets orbiting a pulsar—the remains of a once mighty star shrunk into an **atomic** city-size nucleus[2] that **spins**. Some worlds have fallen into their suns. Others have been thrown out of their systems to become "floaters" that wander in eternal darkness.

C Among all these, astronomers are eager to find a hint of the familiar: planets that **resemble** Earth. That is, they are looking for planets that orbit their stars at just the right distance— neither too hot nor too cold—to support life. However, we have not yet found planets that are quite like our own. To see a planet as small and dim as ours amid the glare of its star is like trying to see a firefly in a fireworks display. Yet by pushing technology to the limits, astronomers are rapidly approaching the day when they can find another Earth.

In Search of Other Earths

D The most direct approach to finding a planet is to take a picture of it with a telescope. Astronomers have detected more than half of the confirmed exoplanets this way. All of them are big and bright and conveniently far away from their stars.

E A more effective way to detect an exoplanet, though, is to use a method known as the Doppler technique. This involves analyzing starlight for evidence that the star's movement is affected by the gravitational pull of a planet. In recent years, astronomers have refined the technique. They can now tell when a planet is pulling its star by only one meter a second— about human walking speed. That's enough to detect a giant planet in a big orbit, or a small planet if it's close to its star.

F Another approach is to watch a star for a slight dip in its brightness. This occurs when an orbiting planet passes in front of the star and blocks part of its light. At most, a tenth of all planetary systems are oriented so that these mini-eclipses[3]—called transits—are visible from Earth. So, astronomers have to monitor a lot of stars to capture just a few transits.

---

1 If a planet **orbits** a star, it circles or goes around it.

2 The **nucleus** is the central part of an atom or cell.

3 An **eclipse** occurs when the light from an object in the sky cannot be seen because another object has come between it and the observer.

HUNTING FOR NEW WORLDS

Of the 3,900-plus exoplanets discovered so far, very few are in a zone that supports life as we know it. To find more planets within this zone, NASA launched the Transiting Exoplanet Survey Satellite in 2018. Its mission? To monitor 500,000 nearby stars for possible Earth-sized exoplanets.

STAR
HOT ORBITAL ZONE
WARM ORBITAL ZONE
COLD ORBITAL ZONE

TOO HOT

Planets here orbit close to their suns, so any surface water evaporates into space.

JUST RIGHT

Water present on planets in this zone could remain in liquid form.

TOO COLD

Here, planets orbit far from their suns, so any surface water stays frozen.

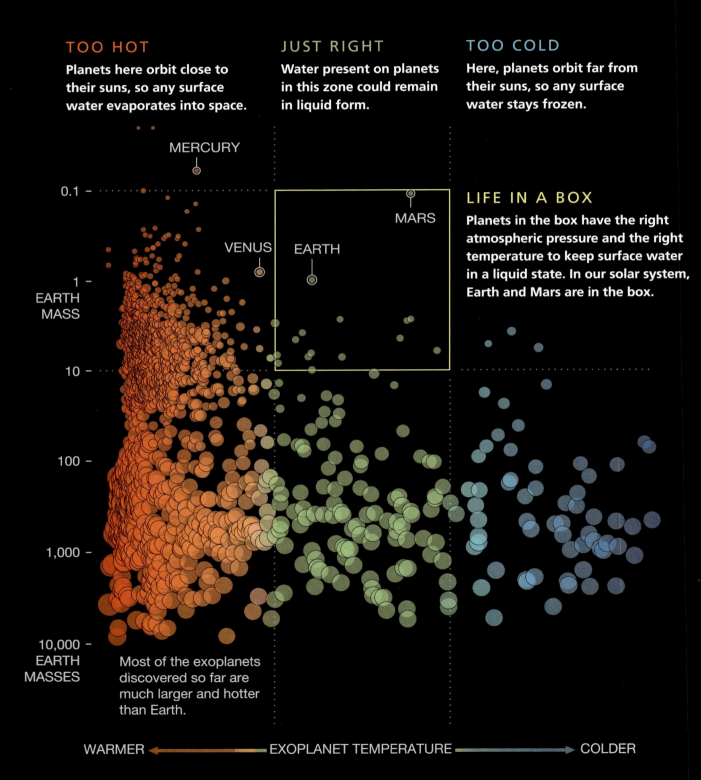

LIFE IN A BOX

Planets in the box have the right atmospheric pressure and the right temperature to keep surface water in a liquid state. In our solar system, Earth and Mars are in the box.

Most of the exoplanets discovered so far are much larger and hotter than Earth.

MERCURY

0.1

VENUS   EARTH   MARS

1
EARTH
MASS

10

100

1,000

10,000
EARTH
MASSES

WARMER ⟵————— EXOPLANET TEMPERATURE —————⟶ COLDER

G The dream of astronomers is to discover a rocky planet roughly the size of Earth orbiting in a habitable zone—that is, not so close to a star that the planet's water has boiled away, but not so far out that it has frozen into ice. If they succeed, they will have found what biologists believe could be a promising abode[4] for life.

H The best places to look may be dwarf stars, which are smaller than the sun. Dwarf stars are plentiful; seven of the ten stars nearest to Earth are dwarf stars. They also provide a steady supply of sunlight to any life-bearing planets within their habitable zone.

I Additionally, dwarf stars are dim, so the habitable zone lies closer in. If the planet is closer to the star, it's easier for astronomers to detect a transit observation. A close-in planet also has a stronger pull on its star. That makes it easier to detect with the Doppler method. Indeed, one of the most promising planets yet found—the "super Earth" Gliese 581 d—orbits in the habitable zone of a red dwarf star only one-third the mass of the sun.

Life—But Not as We Know It?

J If an Earth-like planet is found within a star's habitable zone, a space telescope could be used to look for signs of life. Most likely, scientists will examine the light coming from the planet for possible indications of past or present life, such as atmospheric methane and oxygen. They might also look for the "red edge" produced when chlorophyll[5]-containing plants reflect red light.

K Directly detecting and analyzing the planet's own light will not be easy. Its light might be just one ten-billionth the light of the star's. But when a planet transits, starlight shining through the atmosphere could reveal clues to its **composition** that a space telescope might be able to detect.

L The challenge facing scientists is not just having to perform a chemical analysis of planets they cannot see. They must also keep in mind that life there may be very different from life here at home. The lack of the red edge from an exoplanet, for instance, does not **exclude** the possibility of life. Life **thrived** on Earth for billions of years before land plants appeared and populated the continents.

M The problem is that biological evolution is very unpredictable. It is possible that life originated on an Earth-like planet at the same time it did here. But life on that planet today would almost certainly be very different. As the biologist Jacques Monod once commented, life evolves not only through necessity, but also through chance—the unpredictable intervention of countless accidents.

N Chance has played a role many times in our own planet's history. The most dramatic examples are the mass extinctions that wiped out millions of species and created room for new life forms to evolve. Some of these accidents appear to have been caused by asteroids[6] or comets[7] colliding with Earth. An impact 66 million years ago, for instance, helped kill off the dinosaurs and opened up opportunities for the distant ancestors of human beings. **Hence**, scientists look not just for exoplanets identical to modern Earth, but for planets resembling the Earth as it used to be, or that it might have been.

O It was not easy for earlier pioneers to undertake explorations of the ocean floors, map the far side of the moon, or find evidence of oceans beneath the frozen surfaces of Jupiter's moons. Neither will it be easy to find life on the planets of other stars. But we now have reason to believe that billions of such planets exist. They hold the promise of expanding not only the **scope** of human knowledge, but also the richness of the human imagination.

---

4 An **abode** is another word for *home*.

5 **Chlorophyll** is the green substance in plants that enables them to convert sunlight into energy.

6 An **asteroid** is a large rock moving through outer space.

7 A **comet** is a bright, icy object that travels around the sun and has a long "tail" of gas.

A. Choose the best answer for each question.

GIST

1. What could be another title for this reading?

    a. How Exoplanets Were First Discovered

    b. Is There Intelligent Life on Other Planets?

    c. The Search for Earth-like Planets Around Other Stars

    d. The Story of "Hot Saturn," "Hot Jupiter," and "Super Earth"

DETAIL

2. When this article was written, how many exoplanets had been discovered?

    a. 260   c. nearly 4,000

    b. about 390   d. billions

UNDERSTANDING INFOGRAPHICS

3. Look at the infographic on page 206. Which of these statements is true?

    a. Mercury orbits at a great distance from its sun.

    b. Mercury is larger than Earth.

    c. Any water found on Venus would be frozen.

    d. Venus and Earth are similar in size.

INFERENCE

4. The author indicates in paragraph K that observing and analyzing light from an exoplanet _____ .

    a. will probably show signs of life

    b. will be difficult but not impossible

    c. has been accomplished several times

    d. will require technology not presently available

INFERENCE

5. The author implies that on some exoplanets, _____ .

    a. life may have evolved without chlorophyll-bearing plants

    b. chlorophyll-bearing plants would not produce a "red edge"

    c. atmospheric methane and oxygen may produce a "red edge"

    d. life will be similar to that on Earth if it originated at the same time

FACT OR SPECULATION

Review this reading skill in Unit 5B

B. Are the statements below (1–6) presented as fact or speculation in the reading passage? Write **F** (fact) or **S** (speculation) next to each statement. Then circle the words in the passage that indicate the speculations.

1. A year on "hot Saturn" lasts less than three days. (paragraph B) _____

2. Some planets have fallen into their suns. (paragraph B) _____

3. Astronomers have used telescopes to detect more than half of the confirmed exoplanets. (paragraph D) _____

4. The best place to look for Earth-like planets is around dwarf stars. (paragraph H) _____

5. Life thrived on Earth for billions of years before land plants appeared. (paragraph L) _____

6. Any form of life on an Earth-like planet will be very different from that on Earth. (paragraph M) _____

Recognizing Cause and Effect Relationships (3)

As you learned in Units 3A and 10A, signal words such as *because (of), due to*, and *thus* indicate cause and effect relationships. Often, though, the author may not state these relationships directly—you have to infer them from the context. Take a look at the cause (underlined) and the effect (circled) in this example from the reading passage:

> There's a "hot Saturn" 260 light-years from Earth <u>that orbits its parent star so rapidly</u> that *a year there lasts less than three days.*

In this example, the effect of the "hot Saturn" exoplanet traveling so quickly around its star is that a year there is very short.

CAUSE AND EFFECT

A. Match these effects (1–6) with their causes (a–g) according to information from Reading A. One cause is extra.

_____ **1.** To observe transits, astronomers will have to observe many stars.

_____ **2.** Scientists have been able to detect these exoplanets using a telescope.

_____ **3.** When searching for signs of life on an exoplanet, scientists look for a "red edge."

_____ **4.** These exoplanets become "floaters" that wander in eternal darkness.

_____ **5.** The upper atmosphere of this exoplanet is being blasted off by the star's solar winds.

_____ **6.** Mass extinctions of plants and animals took place.

    a. Only about 10 percent of transits, or "mini-eclipses," can be seen from our planet.

    b. Some exoplanets are thrown out of their original orbits.

    c. Chlorophyll-bearing plants reflect a red light.

    d. In the distant past, the Earth was struck by asteroids and comets.

    e. The "hot Jupiter" exoplanet orbits relatively close to its parent star.

    f. Life existed on Earth for a very long time before land plants appeared.

    g. More than half of the known exoplanets are big, bright, and far away from their stars.

CRITICAL THINKING Justifying an Opinion   Space exploration requires a great deal of money, time, and effort. Which of the following statements do you agree with the most? Why? Check (✓) the option that best reflects your opinion. Then discuss your reasons with a partner.

☐ I think space exploration is very important and is worth all the resources we invest in it.

☐ I think space exploration is a waste of resources that could be better used on Earth.

☐ I think space exploration is important, but we should limit it to just within our own solar system.

COMPLETION **A.** Circle the correct words to complete the information below.

[1]**Hence / To date**, scientists hoping to make contact with aliens have focused on sending radio waves through our [2]**atmosphere / exclusion** and out into space. But a new study suggests sending physical material—a sort of message in a bottle—may be preferable. A physical message can hold more information and journey farther than radio waves.

▲ **NASA's Kepler Space Telescope discovered over 2,600 exoplanets during its lifetime.**

The problem, though, is that this method is slow. As astronomer Seth Shostak says, "It's like the difference between sea post and airmail." Some astronomers feel we should forget about trying to communicate within the [3]**exclusion / scope** of our own lifetimes. It would take thousands of years for a physical message to reach and return from an exoplanet. A two-way conversation is [4]**spun / hence** out of the question.

WORDS IN CONTEXT **B.** Complete the sentences. Circle the correct words.

1. **Atomic** energy is another term for *solar / nuclear / electrical* energy.
2. If something **spins**, it goes *in and out / up and down / around and around* quickly.
3. If you **resemble** someone, you are *similar to / different from / identical to* them.
4. If you **thrive** in a new job, you are *really / moderately / not very* good at it.
5. If you **exclude** someone from a group, they are *part / occasionally part / not part* of it.
6. The **composition** of an object refers to *its total cost / the parts it is made of / its various colors*.

WORD PARTS **C.** The prefix *com-* in **composition** means "together" or "with." Complete the sentences using the words in the box. One word is extra.

combine	compared	compile	composed

1. Mars's atmosphere is mostly _____ of carbon dioxide, argon, and nitrogen.
2. Hydrogen and oxygen atoms _____ to make water molecules.
3. The exoplanet Kepler-452b's star is apparently older than the Earth's sun—6 billion years, _____ to 4.5 billion years.

BEFORE YOU READ

DEFINITIONS **A.** Read the caption below. Match each word in **bold** with its definition (1–3).

1. _____ : a large hole in the ground made by something hitting it or by an explosion

2. _____ : a piece of rock or metal that has fallen to the ground from outer space

3. _____ : the width of a circle when measured through the center

SCANNING **B.** Scan the reading on the next four pages. Match each person (1–4) with their description (a–d).

1. David Tholen •   • a. is developing a spaceship to deflect asteroids heading for Earth.

2. Ann Hodges •   • b. noticed an object heading for Earth.

3. Ed Lu •   • c. thinks a bomb could be the solution.

4. Vadim Simonenko •   • d. was hit by a meteorite.

Meteor Crater is a **meteorite** impact site located in Arizona, U.S.A. The **crater** is approximately 1,200 meters in **diameter**.

SUDBURY
248 kilometers (155 miles) wide
1.9 billion years ago

METEOR CRATER
1.17 kilometers (0.73 miles) wide
50,000 years ago

CHESAPEAKE BAY
85 kilometers (53 miles) wide
35 million years ago

CHICXULUB
170 kilometers (106 miles) wide
65 million years ago

The colored dots in these images of Earth are places where meteorites have struck our planet and left craters as evidence.

THE THREAT FROM SPACE

A It was just after 9 p.m. on June 18, 2004, at an observatory[1] in Arizona, in the United States. Astronomer David Tholen was scanning the sky for asteroids when he noticed an object headed toward Earth. He and his colleagues hoped to take a closer look later that week but, unfortunately, were prevented by rain. By the time the team finally got another look at it, they realized they had a problem. The object was a large asteroid, which they named Apophis, after the Egyptian god of evil. Bigger than a sports arena, it comes frighteningly close to our planet every few years. By December, Tholen had calculated that the chance that Apophis would **smash** into Earth on April 13, 2029, was one in 40.

B Alarm about the threat started to spread. Then, on December 26, 2004, a real **catastrophe** struck: the Indian Ocean tsunami, which claimed hundreds of thousands of lives. The public forgot about Apophis. Meanwhile, astronomers had found earlier images of the asteroid. The extra data enabled them to calculate its orbit, and they discovered that it would actually fly safely by Earth in 2029. However, this alarming **scenario** started a race among scientists to find solutions to the threat of large objects striking Earth.

---

1 An **observatory** is a building with a large telescope from which you can study the stars and planets.

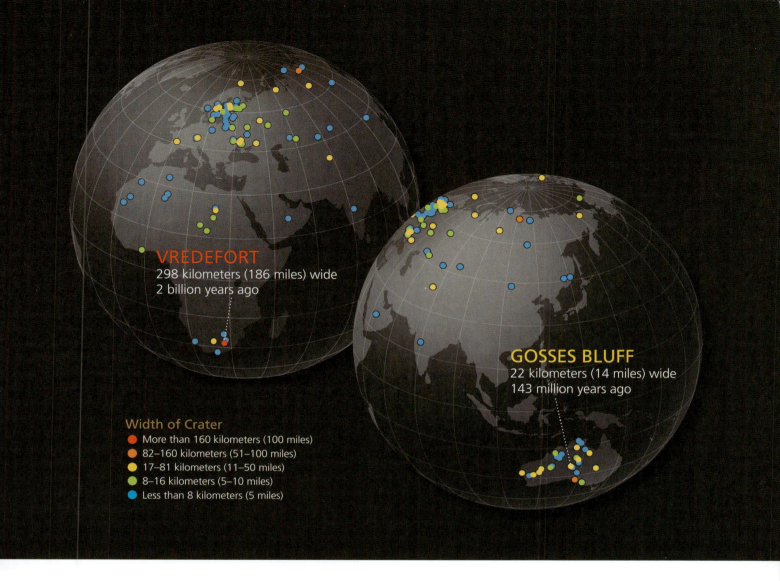

VREDEFORT
298 kilometers (186 miles) wide
2 billion years ago

GOSSES BLUFF
22 kilometers (14 miles) wide
143 million years ago

Width of Crater
- More than 160 kilometers (100 miles)
- 82–160 kilometers (51–100 miles)
- 17–81 kilometers (11–50 miles)
- 8–16 kilometers (5–10 miles)
- Less than 8 kilometers (5 miles)

Near Misses

C Every day, tons of dust[2] from comets and pieces of asteroids the size of grains of
sand burn up in the Earth's upper atmosphere. Most days, a piece or two of rock or
metal—the size of an apple or bigger—actually makes contact with Earth. Yet it's
unlikely you'll ever be struck by a meteorite. Very few meteorites are ever known to
have hit a person. In 1954, a grapefruit-sized rock bounced off Ann Hodges's radio
and hit her as she lay on her sofa near Sylacauga, Alabama, in the United States. She
escaped with only a bruised hip and wrist.

D Since then, there have been some spectacular near misses. On August 10, 1972,
an object the length of a car and weighing 150 tons traveled through the upper
atmosphere. Hundreds of people saw its bright trail that sunny afternoon as it
crossed the sky from Utah, in the United States, to Alberta, Canada, before flying
back out into space. On March 22, 1989, a rock measuring 300 meters across came
within several hundred thousand kilometers of Earth, which—in astronomical
terms—is uncomfortably close.

---

2 **Dust** particles are extremely small pieces of dirt or sand.

Smash Hits

E There is evidence that, in the past, massive comets or asteroids have struck Earth's surface. Thirty-five million years ago, a 3-kilometer-wide rock smashed into the ocean floor, 160 kilometers from what is now Washington, D.C., leaving an 85-kilometer-wide crater buried beneath Chesapeake Bay. Another giant rock called Titan—10 kilometers in diameter—smashed into the Gulf of Mexico around 66 million years ago, unleashing thousands of times more energy than all the **nuclear** weapons on the planet combined. "The whole Earth burned that day," says Ed Lu, a physicist and former astronaut. Three-quarters of all life forms, including the dinosaurs, went extinct.

F Astronomers have identified **numerous** asteroids big enough to cause a catastrophe for the entire planet. None is on course to do so in our lifetimes, but there are many smaller asteroids that could strike—with devastating effects—in the near future. On June 30, 1908, an object as big as a 15-story building fell in Tunguska, a remote part of Siberia. The object—an asteroid or a small comet—exploded several kilometers before impact, burning and blowing down trees across 2,000 square kilometers. Clouds of tiny particles of dust and ice filled the sky. The particles reflected the sun's light onto the Earth, and for days people in Europe could read newspapers outdoors at night. More recently, in 2013, a 20-meter meteor exploded over Chelyabinsk Oblast, Russia, injuring dozens of people on the ground. It was the largest object to enter the Earth's atmosphere since Tunguska.

G The next time a large object falls out of the sky, we may be taken by surprise—though an early-warning system for near-Earth objects has recently been put into place. Sky surveys—like the one done by Tholen—are also helping to fill the gap. "Every couple of weeks," says Lu, "we're going to be finding another asteroid with, like, a one-in-a-thousand chance of hitting the Earth."

What Can Be Done?

H Within decades, the world's leaders may be faced with a **dilemma**: what to do about an incoming space object. Few experts are giving this much thought, according to NASA astronomer David Morrison. "The number would roughly staff a couple of shifts[3] at McDonald's," he says.

I Ed Lu—one of these few experts—is working on a plan that employs a spaceship to **deflect** asteroids. "We were originally thinking about how you would land on an asteroid and push it," he says. "But that doesn't work well." If the surface isn't solid, you have trouble landing or

---

3 A **shift** is a group of workers who work together for a set time before being replaced by another group.

keeping anything on it. Moreover, asteroids are always **rotating**.

J Pulling the asteroid along would be much easier. "Rather than having a physical line between you and the thing you're towing,[4] you're just using the force of gravity between them," Lu says. A nearby spacecraft would pull the asteroid off course very slowly but steadily, using only gravity. Just a slight change in course could mean missing Earth by tens of thousands of kilometers.

An Asteroid Bomb?

K The drawback to Lu's plan is that it would work only for asteroids up to a few hundred meters across that could be **engaged** far from

---

4 If a vehicle **tows** something, it pulls it along behind it.

Earth. Russian scientist Vadim Simonenko and his colleagues concluded that the best way to deflect a larger asteroid up to 1.5 kilometers wide would be to explode a nuclear bomb nearby. The explosion would destroy smaller rocks. For larger ones, the explosion would burn a layer of rock off the asteroid's surface. The expanding gas would act as a rocket **motor**, pushing the asteroid onto a new course.

L As Apophis swings past Earth in 2029, there is a small chance that Earth's gravity will deflect the asteroid just enough to put it on a certain collision course with our planet on the next pass, in 2036. The odds are currently estimated at one in 45,000, so a strike is extremely unlikely. Meanwhile, astronomers will continue to track Apophis to learn if it will merely taunt us again, or actually strike.

A. Choose the best answer for each question.

PURPOSE

1. What is the purpose of this reading?

    a. to explain the problem of objects hitting Earth and to explore solutions

    b. to give reasons why an impact from space is very unlikely

    c. to convince the reader that Apophis will probably strike Earth

    d. to encourage the reader to get involved in saving our planet

CAUSE AND EFFECT

2. Why did the public forget about Apophis in 2004?

    a. Some experts doubted its existence.

    b. No one ever saw the asteroid again.

    c. The Indian Ocean tsunami struck.

    d. A nuclear bomb went off.

SEQUENCE

3. Which of the following impacts is the oldest?

    a. Chesapeake Bay

    b. Gulf of Mexico

    c. Tunguska

    d. Sylacauga

VOCABULARY

4. In paragraph G, *fill the gap* means _____.

    a. cover the space between Earth and the sun

    b. add to our knowledge about objects that could strike Earth

    c. measure the gap between the ground and a falling object

    d. complete our understanding of why objects explode above Earth

DETAIL

5. Which method of deflection would not work well on a rotating asteroid?

    a. exploding a nuclear bomb nearby

    b. hitting it with a spacecraft

    c. pulling it using gravity

    d. landing on it and pushing it

SHORT ANSWER

Review this reading skill in Unit 1B

B. Write short answers for these questions. Use information from the reading passage.

1. What is the asteroid Apophis named after? _____

2. What injuries did Ann Hodges have after being hit by a meteorite?

    _____

3. How large was the crater left after a meteorite hit the ocean floor 35 million years ago? _____

4. What unusual nighttime activity could people in Europe do after an object exploded over Siberia in 1908? _____

5. According to current estimates, what are the odds that Apophis will collide with Earth in 2036? _____

Interpreting Analogies

Writers sometimes use analogies to present a clearer picture of the comparative size of an object. They often do this because an actual number is not important or meaningful. For example, in the sentence below, it's easier for most people to visualize an elephant than a weight of around 5,400 kilograms.

The meteorite weighed as much as an average-sized elephant.

Sometimes writers use analogies to give readers a better sense of their opinion about the comparison. In the example below, the use of *incredibly* suggests the author is amazed at how long the rocket was.

Incredibly, the Saturn V rocket was longer than a football field.

INTERPRETING **A.** Choose the description (a or b) that is closer to each underlined analogy.

1. Incredibly, Sputnik, the first satellite in space, only weighed <u>about the same as a refrigerator</u>.

   a. surprisingly heavy   b. surprisingly light

2. The number of people in space right now <u>can be counted on one hand</u>.

   a. is very few   b. is exactly five

3. There are millions of meteorites—many <u>the size of grains of sand</u>.

   a. that are tiny   b. that are huge

4. Instead of taking two long days, astronauts can now happily fly to the International Space Station in <u>the time it takes to watch three movies</u>.

   a. not much time at all   b. still an uncomfortably long time

INTERPRETING **B.** The phrases below are analogies from Reading B. Rank them from 1 (smallest comparison) to 6 (largest comparison). Then find the phrases in the passage. Discuss with a partner why you think the writer used these analogies.

_____ bigger than a sports arena   _____ grapefruit-sized

_____ the length of a car   _____ the size of an apple

_____ the size of grains of sand   _____ as big as a 15-story building

CRITICAL THINKING Evaluating Pros and Cons   Imagine an asteroid is heading toward your part of the world. Do you think your government should (a) warn the public about it, or (b) consult experts while keeping it a secret? What are the pros and cons of each approach? Discuss with a partner and note your ideas.

_____

_____

_____

COMPLETION **A.** Complete the paragraph with words from the box. One word is extra.

> catastrophic   deflected   dilemma
> numerous   scenario   smashed

How did our moon form? ¹_____ theories have been proposed over the years. Today, the most widely accepted one is that the moon was created when another object ²_____ into Earth. In this ³_____, a huge object—perhaps as large as Mars—struck the Earth billions of years ago. This ⁴_____ impact caused pieces of rocky material to be ⁵_____ into space, where they eventually formed our moon.

∧ **A rare "supermoon" rises over Hull, England.**

COMPLETION **B.** Complete the sentences using the correct form of words from the box.

> dilemma   engage   motor   nuclear   rotate

1. Our Earth _____ once every 24 hours.

2. The conference provides an opportunity for members of the public to _____ with engineers from NASA and other space agencies.

3. Governments today face a(n) _____: Should they spend money on a space program or use the money to improve people's lives on Earth?

4. To help vehicles navigate the surface of Mars, each wheel has its own _____.

5. In 2015, NASA announced that it was considering using _____ energy to fuel future missions to Mars.

WORD PARTS **C.** The prefix *di-* in **dilemma** means "two." Complete the sentences using the words in the box. One word is extra.

> dialog   dilemma   divided   divorce

1. The International Space Station (ISS) is _____ into two sections: the Russian part and the American part.

2. _____ between Russian and American astronauts is crucial if the ISS is to be successful.

3. With limited financial resources, NASA faces the _____ of whether to continue funding the ISS or finance explorations into deep space.

A meteor shower as seen from
Pike National Forest, Colorado

SHOOTING
STARS

DISCUSSION **A.** Look at the photo above. What do you know about meteors or meteor showers? What adjectives would you use to describe a meteor shower? Discuss with a partner.

PREVIEWING **B.** Read this information. The words in **bold** appear in the video. Match these words with their definitions below.

Among the most stunning sights of the night sky are meteor showers. These appear to us as **streaks** of light, and are commonly called "shooting stars." Legend has it that if you wish upon a shooting star, your wish will come true. This tradition is thought to date back to the time of the Greek astronomer Ptolemy (around A.D. 127–151). We now know that shooting stars are not stars at all—they are just bits of rock! There is a huge amount of rocky **debris** in outer space. As these pieces of rock crash through Earth's atmosphere, they sometimes create spectacular meteor shower events. Meteor showers are a reminder of our place in a dynamic, **mystical** solar system.

1. streak • • a. inspiring a sense of awe and fascination

2. debris • • b. a long, thin line or mark that is easily noticed

3. mystical • • c. fragments or remnants of something

GIST **A.** Watch the video. Check (✓) the topics that are covered in the video.

☐ a. superstitious beliefs about meteors

☐ b. the science behind meteor showers

☐ c. times of the year when most meteor showers occur

☐ d. the difference between meteors and meteorites

☐ e. the names of some meteorites from Mars

EVALUATING STATEMENTS **B.** Watch the video again. Are the following statements true or false, or is the information not given? Circle **T** (true), **F** (false), or **NG** (not given).

1. Meteoroids are smaller than asteroids.	**T F NG**
2. When a meteoroid enters Earth's atmosphere, it cools down.	**T F NG**
3. There are about 21 meteor showers every year worldwide.	**T F NG**
4. Meteor showers are named after the constellation from which the meteors appear to originate.	**T F NG**
5. The largest meteorite ever found was discovered in Namibia.	**T F NG**
6. Space debris is a threat to active satellites and spaceships.	**T F NG**

CRITICAL THINKING Ranking Projects **Which of these projects from this unit do you think is most important for scientists to focus on? Rank them 1–3 (1 = most important; 3 = least important). Then compare answers with a partner and give reasons.**

_____ Searching for Earth-like exoplanets

_____ Attempting to make contact with other life forms

_____ Researching ways to reduce damage from asteroids and meteorites

VOCABULARY REVIEW

Do you remember the meanings of these words? Check (✓) the ones you know. Look back at the unit and review any words you're not sure of.

Reading A

☐ atmosphere	☐ atomic	☐ composition	☐ exclude*	☐ hence*
☐ resemble	☐ scope*	☐ spin	☐ thrive	☐ to date

Reading B

☐ catastrophe	☐ deflect	☐ dilemma	☐ engage	☐ motor
☐ nuclear*	☐ numerous	☐ rotate	☐ scenario*	☐ smash

* Academic Word List

Photo and Illustration Credits

Cover © Kelvin Yuen, **3** © Kelvin Yuen, **4–5** Simon Hofmann/Redferns/Getty Images, **7** © Jobit George, **8–9** CB2/ZOB/WENN/Sydney/New South Wales/Australia/Newscom, **10–11** © Annapurna Mellor, **15** Linda Marakov/NGIC, **16–17** © Annie Griffiths, **18–19** © Annie Griffiths, **22** Tino Soriano/NGIC, **23** © Annie Griffiths, **25** John Cancalosi/Photolibrary/Getty Images, **26–27** David Liittschwager/NGIC, **29** (tl) (tr) (cl1) (cl2) (cr1) (cr2) (bl) (br) David Liittschwager/NGIC, **30** Eleanor Lutz/NGIC, **32** © Jamie Dunning, University of Nottingham, **33** David Liittschwager/NGIC, **34–35** Tim Laman/NGIC, **36–37** NGM Art/NGIC, **40** Tim Laman/NGIC, **41** Elitsa Deykova/iStock/Getty Images, **43** Luca Locatelli/NGIC, **44–45** Luca Locatelli/NGIC, **46–47** Ted Horowitz/Corbis/Getty Images Plus/Getty Images, **50** Audi Santoso/EyeEm/Getty Images, **51** Pallava Bagla/Corbis Historical/Getty Images, **52–53** Jim Richardson/NGIC, **54–55** © Barbara Murphy/National Academy of Sciences, **56** Dorling Kindersley/Getty Images, **58** Photo Researchers/Science Source, **59** John Coletti/Photolibrary/Getty Images, **61** Renaud Visage/Photographer's Choice/Getty Images, **62–63** Robert Clark/NGIC, **64** Scott Camazine/Alamy Stock Photo, **65** Wanted Collection/Shotshop GmbH/Alamy Stock Photo, **66** (tr) Ingo Arndt/Minden Pictures, (br) David Hancock/AFP/Getty Images, **67** Andy Rouse/The Image Bank/Getty Images, **68** blickwinkel/Alamy Stock Photo, **69** Tom Cockrem/Lonely Planet Images/Getty Images, **70** dpa picture alliance/Alamy Stock Photo, **71** Valentyn Volkov/Alamy Stock Photo, **72–73** Ole Spata/picture alliance/Getty Images, **76** Guy Corbishley/Alamy Stock Photo, **77** David Gruber/NGIC, **79** David Lyons/Alamy Stock Photo, **80–81** Cecilie_Arcurs/E+/Getty Images, **82** NG Maps/NGIC, **86** Robin Hammond/NGIC, **87** Herbert Kane/NGIC, **88–89** David Hiser/NGIC, **90–91** John T. Burgoyne/NGIC, **91** (br) Stephen Alvarez/NGIC, **94** Kenneth Garrett/NGIC, **95** Javier Trueba/MSF/Science Source, **97** Bill Curtsinger/NGIC, **98–99** Tony Law/Redux, **100** David Evans/National Geographic Stock/NGIC, **101** Randy Olson/NGIC, **102** Christophel Fine Art/Universal Images Group/Getty Images, **104** Idealink Photography/Alamy Stock Photo, **105** incamerastock/Alamy Stock Photo, **106–107** Lars Hagberg/AFP/Getty Images, **109** Adapted from Bitcoin IRA/Cengage, **112** Design Pics Inc/NGIC, **113** NGIC, **115** Brooke Whatnall/NGIC, **116–117** Ritesh Shukla/NurPhoto/Getty Images, **118–119** Simon Hofmann/Redferns/Getty Images, **120** Fredrik Renander/Alamy Stock Photo, **122** Taro Karibe/Getty Images News/Getty Images, **123** John Stanmeyer/NGIC, **125** Javier Jaén/NGIC, **126–127** Brian Shumway/Redux, **130** Mat Hayward/Getty Images Entertainment/Getty Images, **131** Kaedeenari/Alamy Stock Photo, **133** Xavier Rossi/Gamma-Rapho/Getty Images, **134–135** akg-images/Erich Lessing, **136–137** Active Museum/Alamy Stock Photo, **138** Cary Wolinsky/NGIC, **141** kuri2341/iStock/Getty Images, **142–143** Cary Wolinsky/NGIC, **144** Mark Wilson/Getty Images News/Getty Images, **145** Naturfoto Honal/Corbis Documentary/Getty Images, **148** The Love Potion, 1903 (oil on canvas)/Morgan, Evelyn De (1855–1919)/De Morgan Foundation/De Morgan Collection, courtesy of the De Morgan Foundation/Bridgeman Images, **149** Thomas Pflaum/Visum/The Image Works, **151** Jim Richardson/NGIC, **152–153** Leonid Andronov/iStock/Getty Images, **154–155** NGM Staff/NGIC, **158** Kenneth Garrett/NGIC, **159** Dave Yoder/NGIC, **160–161** Dave Yoder/NGIC, **162** Dave Yoder/NGIC, **163** Gregory A. Harlin/NGIC, **164** Dave Yoder/NGIC, **166** Mark Stevenson/UIG/Collection Mix: Subjects/Getty Images, **167** © 5W Infographics, **169** Joe McBride/The Image Bank/Getty Images, **170–171** Fritz Hoffmann/NGIC, **172** Fritz Hoffmann/NGIC, **173** Stephen Simpson/DigitalVision/Getty Images, **174** New Africa/Shutterstock.com, **176** Sinclair Stammers/Science Photo Library/Getty Images, **177** David McLain/Cavan Images, **178–179** Xinhua News Agency/Getty Images, **180–181** Philippe Lopez/AFP/Getty Images, **184** Oleg Senkov/Shutterstock.com, **185** Matthieu Paley/NGIC, **187** Pete McBride/NGIC, **188–189** Pascal Maitre/Panos Pictures, **190** NGIC, **191** hadynyah/E+/Getty Images, **194** wallix/iStock/Getty Images, **195** Thomas Trutschel/Photothek/Getty Images, **197** Quentin Jones/UNSW, **200** Peter Essick/NGIC, **201** Atlantide Phototravel/Corbis Documentary/Getty Images, **203** NASA, **204–205** Sean McNaughton/NGIC, **206–207** John Tomanio/NGIC, **210** NASA Image Collection/Alamy Stock Photo, **211** turtix/Shutterstock.com, **212** Sean McNaughton/NGIC, **213** (tl) (tr) Sean McNaughton/NGIC, **214–215** Andrzej Wojcicki/Science Photo Library/Getty Images, **218** Danny Lawson - PA Images/Getty Images, **219** Danita Delimont/Alamy Stock Photo

NGIC = National Geographic Image Collection

Text Credits

9–11 Adapted from "The Visual Village," by James Estrin: NGM, Oct 2013, **16–19** Adapted from "A Camera, Two Kids, and a Camel," by Annie Griffiths: National Geographic Books, 2008, **27–30** Adapted from "Luminous Life," by Olivia Judson: NGM, Mar 2015, **35–37** Adapted from "Feathers of Seduction," by Jennifer S. Holland: NGM, Jul 2007, and based on information from "'Moonwalking' Birds and Other Crazy Courtship Rituals," by Amelia Stymacks: news.nationalgeographic.com, **45–47** Adapted from "Food: How Safe?" by Jennifer Ackerman: NGM, May 2002, **52–55** Adapted from "Food: How Altered?" by Jennifer Ackerman: NGM, May 2002, and "Scientists Say GMO Foods Are Safe, Public Skepticism Remains," by Tamar Haspel: www.nationalgeographic.com, **63–66** Adapted from "Designs from Nature: Biomimetics," by Tom Mueller: NGM, Apr 2008, and based on information from "5 Natural Air-Conditioning Designs Inspired by Nature," by Brian Clark Howard: news.nationalgeographic.com, **71–73** Adapted from "Dreamweavers," by Cathy Newman: NGM, Jan 2003, and based on information from "Twisting Everyday Fibers Could Make 'Smart Clothes' a Reality," by Jane J. Lee: news.nationalgeographic.com, **81–83** Adapted from "Human Journey," by James Shreeve: NGM, Mar 2006, **88–91** Adapted from "Pioneers of the Pacific," by Roff Smith: NGM, Mar 2008, **99–101** Adapted from "The Journey of Humankind: How Money Made Us Modern," by Patrick J. Kiger: news.nationalgeographic.com, **107–109** Adapted from "Money 3.0: How Bitcoins May Change the Global Economy," by Timothy Carmody: news.nationalgeographic.com, **117–119** Adapted from "Karma of the Crowd," by Laura Spinney: NGM, Feb 2014, **124–127** Adapted from "Are We as Awful as We Act Online?" by Agustín Fuentes: NGM, Aug 2018, **135–138, 143–145** Adapted from "Pick Your Poison—12 Toxic Tales," by Cathy Newman: NGM, May 2005, **153–155** Adapted from "Laser Archeology," by George Johnson: NGM, Dec 2013, **160–163** Adapted from "Lure of the Lost City," by Douglas Preston: NGM, Oct 2015, **171–173** Adapted from "Longevity," by Stephen S. Hall: NGM, May 2013, **178–181** Adapted from "New Wrinkles on Aging," by Dan Buettner: NGM, Nov 2005,

189–191 Adapted from "Water Pressure," by Fen Montaigne: NGM, Sep 2002, **196–197** Adapted from "High-Tech Trash," by Chris Carroll: NGM, Jan 2008, **205–207** Adapted from "Worlds Apart: Seeking New Earths," by Timothy Ferris: NGM, Dec 2009, **212–215** Adapted from "Target Earth," by Richard Stone: NGM, Aug 2008

NGM = National Geographic Magazine

Acknowledgments

The Authors and Publisher would like to thank the following teaching professionals for their valuable feedback during the development of the series.

Akiko Hagiwara, Tokyo University of Pharmacy and Life Sciences; **Albert Lehner**, University of Fukui; **Alexander Cameron**, Kyushu Sangyo University; **Amira Traish**, University of Sharjah; **Andrés López**, Colégio José Max León; **Andrew Gallacher**, Kyushu Sangyo University; **Angelica Hernandez**, Liceo San Agustin; **Angus Painter**, Fukuoka University; **Anouchka Rachelson**, Miami Dade College; **Ari Hayakawa**, Aoyama Gakuin University; **Atsuko Otsuki**, Senshu University; **Ayako Hisatsune**, Kanazawa Institute of Technology; **Bogdan Pavliy**, Toyama University of International Studies; **Braden Chase**, The Braden Chase Company; **Brian J. Damm**, Kanda Institute of Foreign Languages; **Carol Friend**, Mercer County Community College; **Catherine Yu**, CNC Language School; **Chad Godfrey**, Saitama Medical University; **Chen, I-Ching**, Wenzao Ursuline University of Languages; **Cheng-hao Weng**, SMIC Private School; **Chisako Nakamura**, Ryukoku University; **Chiyo Myojin**, Kochi University of Technology; **Chris Valvona**, Okinawa Christian College; **Claire DeFord**, Olympic College; **Davi Sukses**, Sutomo 1; **David Farnell**, Fukuoka University; **David Johnson**, Kyushu Sangyo University; **Debbie Sou**, Kwong Tai Middle School; **Devin Ferreira**, University of Central Florida; **Eden Kaiser**, Framingham State University; **Ellie Park**, CNC Language School; **Elvis Bartra García**, Corporación Educativa Continental; **Emiko Yamada**, Westgate Corporation; **Eri Tamura**, Ishikawa Prefectural University; **Fadwa Sleiman**, University of Sharjah; **Frank Gutsche**, Tohoku University; **Frank Lin**, Guangzhou Tufu Culture; **Gavin Young**, Iwate University; **Gerry Landers**, GA Tech Language Institute; **Ghada Ahmed**, University of Bahrain; **Grace Choi**, Grace English School; **Greg Bevan**, Fukuoka University; **Gregg McNabb**, Shizuoka Institute of Science and Technology; **Helen Roland**, Miami Dade College; **Hersong Tang**, Shih Chien University; **Hiroshi Ohashi**, Kyushu University; **Hiroyo Yoshida**, Toyo University; **Hojin Song**, GloLink Education; **HuangFu Yen-Fang**, Tainan University of Technology; **Huey-Jye You**, NTUST; **Jackie Bae**, Plato Language School; **Jade Wong**, Belilios Public School; **James McCarron**, Chiba University; **Jane Kirsch**, INTO George Mason University; **Jenay Seymore**, Hong Ik University; **Joanne Reid**, Shin Min Senior High School; **John Appleby**, Kanda Institute of Foreign Languages; **John Nevara**, Kagoshima University; **Jonathan Bronson**, Approach International Student Center; **Joseph Zhou**, UUabc; **Josh Brunotte**, Aichi Prefectural University; **Junjun Zhou**, Menaul School; **Kaori Yamamoto**, **Katarina Zorkic**, Rosemead College; **Keiko Miyagawa**, Meiji University; **Kevin Tang**, Ritsumeikan Asia Pacific University; **Kieran Julian**, Kanda Institute of Foreign Languages; **Kim Kawashima**, Olympic College; **Kyle Kumataka**, Ritsumeikan Asia Pacific University; **Kyosuke Shimamura**, Kurume University; **Lance Stilp**, Ritsumeikan Asia Pacific University; **Li Zhaoli**, Weifang No.7 Middle School; **Lichu Lin**, NCCU; **Liza Armstrong**, University of Missouri; **Lucas Pignolet**, Ritsumeikan Asia Pacific University; **Luke Harrington**, Chiba University; **M. Lee**, KCC; **Maiko Berger**, Ritsumeikan Asia Pacific University; **Mandy Kan**, CNEC Christian College; **Mari Nakamura**, English Square; **Masako Kikukawa**, Doshisha University; **Matthew Fraser**, Westgate Corporation; **Mayuko Matsunuma**, Seijo University; **Mei-ho Chiu**, Soochow University; **Melissa Potts**, ELS Berkeley; **Michiko Imai**, Aichi University; **Monica Espinoza**, Torrance Adult School; **Ms. Manassara Riensumetharadol**, Kasetsart University; **My Uyen Tran**, Ho Chi Minh City University of Foreign Languages and Information Technology; **Nae-Dong Yang**, NTU; **Narahiko Inoue**, Kyushu University; **Neil Witkin**, Kyushu Sangyo University; **Noriko Tomioka**, Kwansei University; **Olesya Shatunova**, Kanagawa University; **Patricia Fiene**, Midwestern Career College; **Patricia Nation**, Miami Dade College; **Patrick John Johnston**, Ritsumeikan Asia Pacific University; **Paul Hansen**, Hokkaido University; **Paula Snyder**, University of Missouri-Columbia; **Ping Zhang**, Beijing Royal School; **Reiko Kachi**, Aichi University / Chukyo University; **Robert Dykes**, Jin-ai University; **Rosanna Bird**, Approach International Student Center; **Ryo Takahira**, Kurume Fusetsu High School; **Sadie Wang**, Feng Chia University; **Samuel Taylor**, Kyushu Sangyo University; **Sandra Stein**, American University of Kuwait; **Sanooch Nathalang**, Thammasat University; **Sara Sulko**, University of Missouri; **Serena Lo**, Wong Shiu Chi Secondary School; **Shih-Sheng Kuo**, NPUST; **Shin Okada**, Osaka University; **Silvana Carlini**, Colégio Agostiniano Mendel; **Silvia Yafai**, ADVETI: Applied Tech High School; **Stella Millikan**, Fukuoka Women's University; **Summer Webb**, University of Colorado Boulder; **Susumu Hiramatsu**, Okayama University; **Suzanne Littlewood**, Zayed University; **Takako Kuwayama**, Kansai University; **Takashi Urabe**, Aoyama-Gakuin University; **Teo Kim**, OROMedu; **Tim Chambers**, **Toshiya Tanaka**, Kyushu University; **Trevor Holster**, Fukuoka University; **Wakako Takinami**, Tottori University; **Wayne Malcolm**, Fukui University of Technology; **Wendy Wish**, Valencia College; **Xiaoying Zhan**, Beijing Royal Foreign Language School; **Xingwu Chen**, Xueersi-TAL; **Yin Wang**, TAL Education Group; **Yohei Murayama**, Kagoshima University; **Yoko Sakurai**, Aichi University; **Yoko Sato**, Tokyo University of Agriculture and Technology; **Yoon-Ji Ahn**, Daks Education; **Yu-Lim Im**, Daks Education; **Yuriko Ueda**, Ryukoku University; **Yvonne Hodnett**, Australian College of Kuwait; **Yvonne Johnson**, UWCSEA Dover; **Zhang Lianzhong**, Beijing Foreign Studies University

These words are used in *Reading Explorer* to describe various reading and critical thinking skills.

Analyze to study a text in detail, e.g., to identify key points, similarities, and differences

Apply to think about how an idea might be useful in other ways, e.g., solutions to a problem

Classify to arrange things in groups or categories, based on their characteristics

Evaluate to examine different sides of an issue, e.g., reasons for and against something

Infer to "read between the lines"—information the writer expresses indirectly

Interpret to think about what a writer means by a certain phrase or expression

Justify to give reasons for a personal opinion, belief, or decision

Rank to put things in order based on criteria, e.g., size or importance

Reflect to think deeply about what a writer is saying and how it compares with your own views

Relate to consider how ideas in a text connect with your own personal experience

Scan to look through a text to find particular words or information

Skim to look at a text quickly to get an overall understanding of its main idea

Summarize to give a brief statement of the main points of a text

Synthesize to use information from more than one source to make a judgment or comparison

INDEX OF EXAM QUESTION TYPES

The activities in *Reading Explorer, Third Edition* provide comprehensive practice of several question types that feature in standardized tests such as TOEFL® and IELTS.

Common Question Types	IELTS	TOEFL®	Pages
Multiple choice (gist, main idea, detail, reference, inference, vocabulary, paraphrasing)	✓	✓	12, 20, 31, 38, 48, 56, 67, 74, 84, 92, 102, 110, 120, 128, 139, 146, 156, 164, 174, 182, 192, 198, 208, 216
Completion (notes, diagram, chart)	✓		32, 42, 57, 60, 96, 111, 114, 183
Completion (sentence, summary)	✓	✓	120, 128, 132, 165, 192, 202
Short answer	✓		21, 175, 216
Matching headings / information	✓		12, 68, 74, 156, 198
Categorizing (matching features)	✓	✓	56, 67, 102, 182
True / False / Not Given	✓		31, 48, 78, 92, 110, 150, 164, 168, 220
Rhetorical purpose		✓	20, 56, 74, 110, 120, 156, 182, 216

The following tips will help you become a more successful reader.

1 Preview the text

Before you start reading a text, it's important to have some idea of the overall topic. Look at the title, photos, captions, and any maps or infographics. Skim the text quickly, and scan for any key words before reading in detail.

2 Use vocabulary strategies

Here are some strategies to use if you find a word or phrase you're not sure of:

- **Look for definitions** of new words within the reading passage itself.
- **Identify the part of speech and use context** to guess the meaning of homonyms and new words or idioms (see pages 13, 121, and 147).
- **Identify the word roots and affixes** (if any) of new words (see page 129).
- **Use a dictionary** if you need, but be careful to identify the correct definition.

3 Take notes

Note-taking helps you identify the main ideas and details within a text. It also helps you stay focused while reading. Try different ways of organizing your notes, and decide on a method that best suits you.

4 Infer information

Not everything is stated directly within a text. Use your own knowledge, and clues in the text, to make your own inferences and "read between the lines" (see page 199).

5 Make connections

As you read, look for words that help you understand how different ideas connect. For example:

- words that signal **cause and effect** (see pages 49 and 175)
- words that indicate **sequence**
- words that indicate a **speculation or theory** (see page 93)

6 Read critically

Ask yourself questions as you read a text. For example, if the author presents a point of view, are enough supporting reasons or examples provided? Is the evidence reliable? Does the author give a balanced argument? (see pages 57, 140, and 193)

7 Create a summary

Creating a summary is a great way to check your understanding of a text. It also makes it easier to remember the main points. You can summarize in different ways based on the type of text. For example:

- **timelines or flow charts**
- **T-charts** (see pages 57 and 102)
- **concept maps** (see page 32)
- **outline summaries** (see page 111)